~RIDING~ THE LIMITEDS' LOCOMOTIVES

THE BROADWAY LIMITED (left) and THE TWENTIETH CENTURY LIMITED leaving Engle-wood, Illinois, eastbound

Pennsylvania Rail Road Photo

RIDING THE LIMITEDS' LOCOMOTIVES

By
Colonel
Howard G. Hill,
USAR (Ret.)

First Steam Locomotive Built in U.S. for Overseas Service in World War II

Designed by Major Howard G. Hill, CE – USA, 1941

SUPERIOR PUBLISHING COMPANY-SEATTLE

FIRST EDITION

DEDICATION

TO THE MEMORY OF MY FATHER, EVERETT
LEFOREST HILL, SR., (1859-1900), OF BOSTON,
WHOSE GREAT LOVE FOR THE STEAM LOCOMO-
TIVE WAS INHERITED BY ME,

AND

TO MY WIFE, ETHEL, WHOSE ENCOURAGE-
MENT, PATIENCE AND HELP MADE THIS BOOK
POSSIBLE,

I DEDICATE THIS BOOK.

FOREWORD

THOSE of us who recall the fascination and excitement of the steam locomotive can't help but envy the author of this book. Colonel Hill has literally spent years in the engine cab, not as an engineman on the same run day after day, but as a troubleshooter and lubrication expert on different locomotives all over the world. The major portion of this book is devoted to an account of a truly remarkable experience, a pair of continuous trips in the cabs of the steam locomotives of America's two finest passenger trains, all the way from New York to Chicago.

In those days, almost forty years ago, the New York Central and the Pennsylvania were spirited competitors in every sense of the word. There were no thoughts of merger or diversification to keep the two roads healthy, and it was not yet stylish for railroad managements to view the passenger train with contempt. Every single day the Twentieth Century Limited and the Broadway Limited set forth in a dramatic duel to defend the honor of two giant enterprises. The attention paid to every detail of operating these two trains was out of all proportion to the actual revenue they generated. Their locomotives, of course, were nursed with particular care, for their performance was crucial. To be a firsthand observer of their skillful operation must have been a rare privilege indeed.

In truth, all the author learned during these two trips could have been acquired piecemeal in a much more leisurely manner. For some individuals, it would be enough to endure the jolts and roar and cinders and choking smoke in an engine cab for just one division. But Colonel Hill had to go the whole distance, not once but twice! Only one conclusion can be drawn about this man; he loved his locomotives like a sailor loves his ships. He got that way by starting out in the Texas & New Orleans shops in Houston as an apprentice machinist in 1914, and working his way up to a mechanical engineer. After serving with the Army in World War I, he gained his commission in the reserve in 1923. His work with railway supply firms took him all over the country during the years when the steam locomotive was in its prime.

As World War II approached, Colonel Hill was called to active duty in Washington, serving the Army Corps of Engineers in the railroad branch. Here he was responsible for preparing detailed specifications for two famous groups of Army locomotives, the 200 Mikados for Middle East service, as well as the more numerous six-wheel tank switchers which appeared all over Europe. Later he served in Sicily, earning the Legion of Merit and a citation from General Patton for his work as General Manager of a U. S. military railway. Still later he distinguished himself as a consultant on railway missions to Mexico and Japan.

In other words, this book is written by a man who knows his subject, and perhaps more important, thoroughly enjoys and respects the steam locomotive.

William D. Edson
Senior Engineer
Federal Railroad Administration.
Potomac, Maryland, September 1970

PREFACE

BREATHES there a man with soul so dead that he does not thrill at the sight of a modern steam locomotive at work? Somewhere in the breast of every normal homo sapiens there stretches a cord that vibrates only to the sight and sound of a fine steam locomotive. Even now, with airplanes and motors to bid against it in its own fields of romantic interest, the steam locomotive retains its fascination. There are probably a number of reasons for this. I can think of at least two — its unusually demonstrative nature, and its extraordinary beauty.

Man has devised no other machine that expresses its feelings so frankly and unmistakably. A locomotive sighs, it pants, it coughs, it barks; it emits impassioned shrieks and mournful toots; it puts forth powerful staccato protests at hauling a heavy load or climbing a steep grade; it purrs ecstatically as it romps along the rails at a mile a minute; it can hiss and throb and snort and tinkle. And, in addition to all these auditory forms of expression, it has its visual signs: its plumes of steam, spelling surplus energy; its belching of black smoke, denoting determination; and its sparks at night, registering passion.

As for its beauty, I confess to a certain reluctance in directing attention to it. "I hope", wrote Elie Faure, the French critic, "that the American engineer will never take note of the beauty of the utilitarian structures that he builds. It could prove his undoing. For when the conception of the beautiful qualifies the conception of the useful, utility misses its mark, and beauty is done for." He is speaking of buildings, but his words apply equally as well to locomotives. The reason they have succeeded in becoming so beautiful is because their designers never thought of them as such. I repeat, the steam locomotive, especially in its latest phases, was beautiful, with a beauty of dignity and power and dash that made an unmistakable appeal.

New York Tribune, 1927.

ACKNOWLEDGEMENTS

THE preparation of this book has obviously involved a great deal of painstaking study and research, and many people. A list of sources of dates, technical data, and other pertinent information is given under REFERENCES.

Nevertheless, the accounts of my two trips in the locomotive cabs of THE BROADWAY LIMITED and THE TWENTIETH CENTURY LIMITED are my own work, and are based on brief notes which I made during the trips, on brief reports submitted immediately after the trips, and, to a great extent, on my keen recollections of the details of those trips. Even at this late date, 40 years later, the events of those two trips are vividly impressed on my memory.

To Miss Joan Boehm, Secretary, and Mr. Joseph Parillo, Jr., Assistant, to the Hon. Daniel E. Button, M. C., for their very efficient help in securing certain material for this book, I am sincerely grateful.

I am especially indebted to Mr. William D. Edson, formerly Chief Mechanical Engineer, New York Central Lines, for his constructive criticism of the manuscript, and for furnishing a number of photographs. He also very kindly wrote the foreword for this book.

Mr. Bert B. Brooks, Mechanical Engineer, is due my sincere thanks for many valuable suggestions, and for proof-reading the manuscript. His comments on the work have been most encouraging.

Others to whom I am very grateful for assistance, photographs, and other data are: Pennsylvania Rail Road, George M. Hart, Frederick Westing, Harold C. Zieber, C. B. Cheney, Lt. Col. T. Martin Flattley, Jr., H. L. Broadbelt, Harry Beichert, Clarence L. Weaver, Richard J. Dent, Miss Ann Kuss, Lt. Col. John W. Haubennestel, Charles M. Smith, Arnold Haas, Clement R. Brown, Sr., Dr. Richard R. Randall, Loyal Phillips, Mason Peters, Edward L. May, Thomas Norrell, American Locomotive Co., Baldwin-Lima-Hamilton Corporation, Smithsonian Institution, New York Central Lines, Penn Central Transportation Co., The American Society of Mechanical Engineers, Engineering Societies Library, University of Maryland Engineering Library, Rand McNally & Co., W. B. Knight, BALDWIN LOCOMOTIVES, RAILWAY AGE, RAILWAY GAZETTE, AMERICAN Magazine, ARGOSY Magazine, and THE LOCOMOTIVE. To each and every one of those who have helped me, I say a sincere "Thank You!"

And last, but not least, I owe my sincere thanks and appreciation to my beloved wife for the many things she did to help me in this project, such as checking the manuscript against the original draft, and painstakingly proof-reading the final manuscript. She patiently bore almost complete neglect many times while I was deep in research, or was laboriously typing the manuscript. I am very grateful to her for her patience and very valuable assistance.

HOWARD G. HILL
Colonel, USAR (Ret.)

Bladensburg, Md.
September 4, 1971

REFERENCES

James Dredge—The Pennsylvania Rail Road, 1879.

Thomas M. Cooley and Others—The American Railway, 1889.

Baldwin Locomotive Works—Motive Power Development on the Pennsylvania Rail Road System, 1831-1924. By Paul T. Warner, 1924. Records of Recent Construction. BALDWIN LOCOMOTIVES.

Pennsylvania Rail Road — Altoona Locomotive Test Plant Bulletins, 1914, etc. The Pennsylvania News, 1931.

The New York Tribune, 1927.

Edward Hungerford—The Run of The Twentieth Century, 1930. Men and Iron, 1938.

New York Central Lines—Classification and Diagrams of Locomotives, 1941.

G. T. Wilson—The Development and Performance of the Hudson Type Locomotive, 1930.

E. P. Alexander—The Pennsylvania Rail Road, 1947.

Alvin F. Staufer—New York Central Steam Power, 1961. Pennsy Power, 1962. Steam and Electric Locomotive Diagrams, Pennsylvania Rail Road, 1965. New York Central's Early Steam Power, 1967.

Lucius Beebe—20th Century, 1962.

Frederick Westing—Apex of the Atlantics, 1963.

William D. Edson and Edward L. May—Locomotives of the New York Central Lines, 1966.

Railway Age.

Railroad Magazine.

Kalmbach Publishing Company.

Samuel Smiles—The Life of George Stephenson and of his son Robert Stephenson, 9th Edition, 1868.

J. G. H. Warren—A Century of Locomotive Building by Robert Stephenson & Co., 1923.

Ralph Johnson—The Steam Locomotive, 2nd Edition, 1945.

Joseph Lingford & Son, Ltd.—Weardale Railway Centenary, 1847-1947.

Alfred W. Bruce—The Steam Locomotive in America, 1952.

Henry V. Poor—Manual of Railroads, 1888.

Railway Gazette, London.

TABLE OF CONTENTS

Page

Dedication 5

Foreword 6

Preface 7

Acknowledgements 8

References 9

Table of Contents 10,11

Illustrations ....

Chapter 1. Some Recorded Trips on Locomotives.................................14

Chapter 2. The Influence of the Locomotive Upon the Unity of Our Country 19

Chapter 3. The Development of Steam Passenger Motive Power on the
Pennsylvania Rail Road 24

Chapter 4. Riding the BROADWAY LIMITED'S K4s Pacifics 48

Chapter 5. The Development of Steam Passenger Motive Power on the
New York Central Lines 77

Chapter 6. Riding the J-1 Locomotives on the CENTURY 96

Epilogue — Farewell to The CENTURY 117

Appendix: 119

    Item from The Pennsylvania News, February 15, 1931 119

    Table 1. THE EXPOSITION FLYER 120

    Table 2. Pacific Type Locomotives of the Pennsylvania Rail Road 121

    Table 3. Pennsylvania Rail Road Class K4s Pacific (4-6-2) Type Locomotives 122

    Table 4. THE BROADWAY LIMITED—Locomotive Runs...................123

    Table 5. THE BROADWAY LIMITED—Log of Performance 124

    Table 6. THE TWENTIETH CENTURY LIMITED—Locomotive Runs 125

    Table 7. THE TWENTIETH CENTURY LIMITED—Log of Performance.........126

    Table 8. Summary of Performance.................................127

    Table 9. New York Central Lines Class J Hudson (4-6-4) Type Locomotives.........128

    Locomotive Specifications 128

ILLUSTRATIONS

The Eastbound LIMITEDS Leaving Englewood, Illinois   Frontispiece

Fig. No.	Eng. No.	Railroad	Class	Type	Page
A	23	"Medford," B&M RR.		4-4-0	15
B		An Early Mine Locomotive, 1822.		0-4-0	12
C		"Rocket," Liverpool & Manchester RR.		0-2-2	13
D		"Stourbridge Lion," D&H Canal Co.		0-4-0	18
E	91	AT&SF Ry.		4-4-0	22
1	274*	Pennsylvania R. R.	C(D3)	4-4-0	27
2	10	Pennsylvania R. R.	K(D6)	4-4-0	27
3	568	Pennsylvania R. R.	O(D10a)	4-4-0	27
4	1639	Pennsylvania R. R.	P(D13c)	4-4-0	28
5	1659	Pennsylvania R. R.	P(D14)	4-4-0	28
6	88	Pennsylvania R. R.	P(D16a)	4-4-0	28
7	296	Pennsylvania R. R.	D16a	4-4-0	29
8	101	Pennsylvania R. R.	L(D16a)	4-4-0	29
9	1395	Pennsylvania R. R.	D16a	4-4-0	30
10	955	Pennsylvania R. R.	D16a	4-4-0	30
11	7002	Pennsylvania R. R.	E7sa	4-4-2	31
12	1968	Pennsylvania R. R.	E2	4-4-2	32
13	2024	Pennsylvania R. ,R.	E3a	4-4-2	32
14	7374	Pennsylvania R. R.	E2b	4-4-2	33
15		West Philadelphia Engine Terminal			33
16	7067	Pennsylvania R. R.	K28	4-6-2	34
17	3337	Pennsylvania R. R.	K2	4-6-2	35
18	3379	Pennsylvania R. R.	K2	4-6-2	35
19	7049	Pennsylvania R. R.	K2a	4-6-2	36
20	8704	Pennsylvania R. R.	K21s	4-6-2	37
21	3375	Pennsylvania R. R.	K2sb	4-6-2	37
22	150	Pennsylvania R. R.	K2s	4-6-2	38
23	9999	Pennsylvania R. R.	K2s	4-6-2	39
24	8661	Pennsylvania R. R.	K3s	4-6-2	39
25	8662	Pennsylvania R. R.	K3s	4-6-2	40
26	3395	Pennsylvania R. R.	K29s	4-6-2	41
27	1737	Pennsylvania R. R.	K4s	4-6-2	42
28	1737	Pennsylvania R. R.	K4s	4-6-2	43
29	5453	Pennsylvania R. R.	K4s	4-6-2	43
30	5698	Pennsylvania R. R.	K5	4-6-2	44
31	5699	Pennsylvania R. R.	K5	4-6-2	45
32	4700	Pennsylvania R. R.	M1	4-8-2	45
33	6703	Pennsylvania R. R.	M1a	4-8-2	46
34	5533	Pennsylvania R. R.	T1	4-4-4-4	47
35	900	U. S. Railroad Administration	Y-3	2-8-8-2	57
36	2056	Norfolk and Western Railway	Y-3a	2-8-8-2	57
37	132	Norfolk and Western Railway	K2a	4-8-2	58
38	201	Norfolk and Western Railway	K-3	4-8-2	58
39	2063	Norfolk and Western Railway	Y-3a	2-8-8-2	59
40		The Late Frederick W. Hankins			60
41	5400	Pennsylvania R. R.	K4s	4-6-2	60
42	3768	Pennsylvania R. R.	K4s	4-6-2	61
43	5400	A Typical Heavy, Modern, High-Speed Passenger Locomotive	K4s	4-6-2	62
44		Penn Station, New York City			63
45		Main Concourse, Penn Station, New York City			64
46	3930	Pennsylvania R. R.	L5pdw	2-4-4-2	65
47	5439	Pennsylvania R. R.	K4s	4-6-2	66
48	5439	Pennsylvania R. R.	K4s	4-6-2	67
49	5417	Pennsylvania R. R.	K4s	4-6-2	68

*(See Appendix for Specifications of Locomotives Illustrated.)

Fig. No.	Eng. No.	Railroad	Class	Type	Page
50		Profile of Middle Division, P. R. R.			69
51	5075	Pennsylvania R. R.	E6	4-4-2	70
52	7116	Pennsylvania R. R.	K4s	4-6-2	71
53		The Horseshoe Curve, P. R. R., 1870			72
54		The Horseshoe Curve, P. R. R., 1924			72
55	1361	Pennsylvania R. R.	K4s	4-6-2	73
56	5373	Pennsylvania R. R.	K4s	4-6-2	74
57	3878	Pennsylvania R. R.	K4s	4-6-2	75
58		Profile, Lines West, Fort Wayne-Chicago, PRR.			76
59	567	New York Central & Hudson River RR.	C-9	4-4-0	81
60	317	Lake Shore & Michigan Southern Ry.		4-4-0	82
61	160	Lake Shore & Michigan Southern Ry.	Q(C-53)	4-4-0	83
62	862	New York Central & Hudson River RR.	I	4-4-0	84
63	871	New York Central & Hudson River RR.	I	4-4-0	84
64		Train Shed, Grand Central Depot, New York City			85
65	2960	New York Central & Hudson River RR.	I	4-4-2	86
66	107	Lake Shore & Michigan Southern Ry.	F	4-6-0	86
67	660	Lake Shore & Michigan Southern Ry.	J-40b	2-6-2	87
68	4670	Lake Shore & Michigan Southern Ry.	J-40c	2-6-2	87
69	613	Lake Shore & Michigan Southern Ry.	I-1	4-6-0	88
70	604	Lake Shore & Michigan Southern Ry.	I	4-6-0	88
71	2701	New York Central & Hudson River RR.	K-1	4-6-2	89
72	8452	Michigan Central RR.	K-80b	4-6-2	89
73	3565	New York Central & Hudson River RR.	K-2e	4-6-2	90
74		Five Sections of Train No. 26 at Chicago, 1927.			90
75	3426	New York Central & Hudson River RR.	K-3a	4-6-2	91
76	4723	New York Central Lines	K-41a	4-6-2	91
77	3406	New York Central & Hudson River RR.	K-3c	4-6-2	92
78	3359	New York Central & Hudson River RR.	K-3g	4-6-2	92
79	6510	Cleveland, Cincinnati, Chicago & St. Louis RR.	K-5b	4-6-2	93
80	5241	New York Central Lines	J-1b	4-6-4	93
81	5442	New York Central Lines	J-3a	4-6-4	94
82	5445	New York Central Lines	J-3a	4-6-4	94
83	6001	New York Central Lines	S-1b	4-8-4	95
84		Main Concourse, Grand Central Terminal, New York City			102
85		Gate 27, Grand Central Terminal			103
86		A CENTURY Departure Quay, Grand Central Terminal			104
87	1174	New York Central Lines	T-3a	B-B+B-B	105
88	1153	New York Central Lines	T-1b	B-B+B-B	104
89	1166	New York Central Lines	T-2b	B-B+B-B	105
90	5302	New York Central Lines	J-1d	4-6-4	106
91		Bob Butterfield, Locomotive Engineer, New York Central Lines			107
92		Bob Butterfield, Locomotive Engineer, New York Central Lines			108
93		Bob Butterfield, Locomotive Engineer, New York Central Lines			109
94	5215	New York Central Lines	J-1d	4-6-4	109
95		Two CENTURIES at Harmon			110
96	5271	New York Central Lines	J-1c	4-6-4	111
97		Controls in the Cab of a Hudson Type Locomotive			112
98	5240	New York Central Lines	J-1b	4-6-4	111
99	5214	New York Central Lines	J-1b	4-6-4	113
100	5271	New York Central Lines	J-1c	4-6-4	114
101	1050	Cleveland Union Terminals	P-1a	2-C-C-2	114
102	5246	New York Central Lines	J-1b	4-6-4	115
103		Map of the Pennsylvania System, 1947			116
104		Map of the New York Central Lines, 1926.			116

11

Fig. B. An Early Mine Locomotive built in 1822 by George Stephenson and Nicholas Wood for Service at the Hetton Colliery in England.

Howard G. Hill Collection.

Fig. C. Replica of the "Rocket" constructed by Robert Stephenson & Co. Ltd.

THE LOCOMOTIVE, London, June 15, 1929
Howard G. Hill Collection.

13

CHAPTER 1
SOME RECORDED TRIPS
ON LOCOMOTIVES

GEORGE STEPHENSON established the superiority of the steam locomotive, crude though it was, over horses and winding engines as motive power on the primitive English tramways and railways early in the 19th Century. He had built and placed in service several locomotives by 1820 to move coal from the collieries to the wharves on nearby rivers.

Mr. William James, of West Bromwich, a land-surveyor and coal-owner, had built a number of tramways, using horses as motive power. He became interested in the proposed plans for a tram-road between Liverpool and Manchester, and was employed in 1821 to make a preliminary survey of the proposed route.

In order to study the work of existing steam locomotives, he proceeded to Killingworth to observe several of Stephenson's locomotives in action. He was greatly impressed by their performance, and predicted that the steam locomotive would revolutionize transportation and society.

Shortly afterward, Mr. James, accompanied by his two sons, made a second trip to Killingworth, at which time George Stephenson invited his three visitors to "jump up" for a ride on one of his locomotives. Since cabs were unknown in those days, they had to stand on a rather small "footplate," behind the boiler, or on a narrow running board alongside the boiler. This appears to be the first recorded instance of any person other than the engineer being allowed to ride on the locomotive.

Construction of the Liverpool and Manchester Railway proceeded, and Stephenson's locomotive "Rocket," winner of the 1829 locomotive competition at Rainhill, pulled the first experimental train of passengers on January 1, 1830, over Chat Moss, a very difficult piece of construction which had been successfully completed by George Stephenson. The first trip over the entire line from Liverpool to Manchester was performed on June 14, 1830, with the new locomotive "Arrow," built by George Stephenson, who was at the throttle on that memorable occasion. Beside him on the footplate was Captain Scoresby, the circumpolar navigator, who timed the speed of the train. On the return trip, the "Arrow" crossed Chat Moss at a speed of nearly 27 miles per hour.

During the ensuing weeks, George Stephenson made several trips over the line, testing the eight new locomotives built at his Newcastle Works. On one trip, on August 25, 1830, he invited a distinguished young lady to ride on the locomotive with him. She was Miss Frances Ann ("Fanny") Kemble, (1809-1893), a very talented young actress, whose first appearance on the stage at Covent Garden on October 5, 1829, was an overwhelming success and the beginning of a notable career. She later came to the United States, married a Mr. Butler, and lived on a plantation in Georgia for a number of years.

In a letter written on the day after her trip on the locomotive, Miss Kemble gave a most interesting description of her trip with George Stephenson. She said he explained the construction and working of the locomotive to her in a very clear manner, and said he made the statement that he could soon make her a famous engineer! She described the engine as consisting of a boiler, a stove, a platform, a bench, and, behind the bench, a barrel containing enough water "to prevent her being thirsty for fifteen miles." She described the piston rods, connecting rods and driving wheels, and even referred to the water glass which indicated the level of the water in the boiler.

She referred to their initial speed as 10 miles per hour as they rolled through Olive Mount Cutting, just east of Liverpool, where they had cut a right-of-way for two tracks through solid rock, with vertical walls over 100 feet high and over two miles long.

After making a water stop a few miles out, she stated that they soon reached a speed of 35 miles per hour, and she described her feelings as a sensation of flying, yet she had a feeling of perfect security, with not the slightest sense of fear. What an unusual privilege she had—the experience of riding on a locomotive with the great George Stephenson!

———————————

My first ride in a steam locomotive cab occurred when I was a little over four years old. I remember that experience as clearly as I remember things which happened this morning, as it made an indelible impression on my young mind.

My father was keenly interested in steam loco-

Fig. A. No. 23. "Medford." Boston & Lowell R. R. (B&M). Built by Lowell Machine Shops, Lowell, Mass., 1855. Probably the locomotive on which I had my first ride in a Steam Locomotive cab about September, 1899.

Thomas Norrell Collection.

motives, and he rode in their cabs frequently on the Boston & Maine Rail Road during the last quarter of the 19th Century. Since he was well acquainted with many of the enginemen, he was frequently permitted to fire or run the locomotives. As a young man, he wanted to become a locomotive engineer, but his parents vetoed the idea— they were afraid he would get his hands dirty!

One day in the late summer of 1899, during a visit with an aunt in Somersworth, N. H., my father decided to visit a cousin in Dover, about six miles south-east of Somersworth by 'the steam cars.' He knew the engineer who was running that day, so he took me into the cab with him. We sat on the left seatbox — I was on the front edge, while my father sat behind me, making sure that I did not fall off as we bounced along on branch line rails which could hardly be considered to be expertly lined and surfaced.

To this day I can clearly see the engineer on the right seatbox as he adjusted the throttle and reverse lever, although I did not know at that time what it was all about. I can still see the fireman as he stood unsteadily on the heaving deck, bailing the "real estate" into the firebox. The locomotive on which we were riding was quite likely the old "Medford," Boston & Lowell Rail Road No. 23, which ran on the Somersworth branch for many years. She was the second engine to carry that name, and was built in 1855 at Lowell Machine Shops, Lowell, Mass., a 4-4-0 type with 15-inch by 22-inch outside cylinders, a diamond stack, and a 4-wheeled tender.

At Rollinsford Junction, 3 miles east of Somersworth, we passed through a right-hand curve and entered the westward track of the double-track main line of the Boston-Portland Division. Our trip in the engine cab ended 3 miles down the main line at Dover. As I recall that trip 71 years later, I have no recollection of even the slightest feeling of nervousness or fear as we dashed along at the tremendous speed of about 20 miles per hour, bouncing and pitching along over the high centers and low joints, with the stack roaring. I seemed to feel perfectly at ease, and was all eyes, watching everything which was taking place. It was an experience I have never forgotten.

Eleven years passed before I began to develop an interest in steam locomotives. While I was in High School in Houston, Texas, in 1910, I suddenly "went off the deep end" and developed an intense interest in the locomotives then being operated in the Houston area, "where 17 railroads meet the sea." I spent every possible hour at the local roundhouses, yards, and stations, watching the locomotives in action, and I began a serious study of them, devouring every book I could find on the subject of locomotives and railroads. (Since then, I have accumulated a library

of over 700 books on locomotives and railroads, many early and rare editions, several of which are over 100 years old.)

Finally, in August 1914, Mr. George Mccormick, Assistant General Manager —Motive Power and Equipment, Southern Pacific Lines, Texas and Louisiana, gave me a letter to Mr. J. A. Power, Superintendent Shops at the T&NO Shops in Houston, who promptly put me to work as an apprentice machinist at 10 cents per hour, 9 hours per day, 6 days per week, but, because I had been studying mechanical drawing for about a year, he assigned me to the Drafting Office as blue-print boy under Alfred A. Meister, Chief Draftsman.

That opened up a whole new world for me, and I missed no opportunity to learn all I could about locomotives, shop operations, and railroading in general. In addition to making thousands of blue-prints for the various shops on the system, I was soon assigned to work on the drawing board, and also performed sketching and inspection work in the shops and roundhouse. After serving as Instructor of Apprentices for about 9 months, I was assigned to inspection work on locomotives which required me to travel over the entire system in Texas and Louisiana, visiting every shop and enginehouse, as well as remote branch lines where locomotives were permanently assigned.

While traveling over the road, I invariably rode in the locomotive cabs, which gave me a wonderful opportunity to study locomotive operation and train control. I watched the engineers intently as they operated all classes of power over the prairies and mountain divisions. I soon became an expert oil-burner fireman, and fired all classes of power on the main lines and on many branch lines. To make the picture perfect, I was, on numerous occasions, permitted to run the locomotive myself, and that, at the time, seemed to me to be about the ultimate achievement! It all gave me much wonderful experience.

Later, my work carried me all over the United States, into Mexico and into Canada, and I continued my studies of locomotive design and operation under widely varying conditions. I rode in the cabs of many of the finest modern locomotives, some of them hauling some of the crack Limited trains. I resolved that one day I would ride in the cabs of the locomotives hauling THE BROADWAY LIMITED and THE TWENTIETH CENTURY LIMITED, the two Queens of the fleets of luxury limited trains then being operated by our American Railroads. How I achieved that ambition is told in this book so that others may share my experiences.

Through all of my experiences, I became more and more convinced that the Steam Locomotive was a pretty wonderful machine, and that it had played a vital part in the building of our country from a vast wilderness to the great nation which it is today. I do not think there was ever another machine like it, and I do not think there will ever be another one like it. It will always occupy its own place in history, and in the hearts of all who loved it, as I did. Nothing can take away from the Steam Locomotive the fact that IT BUILT AMERICA!

I think the finest tribute to the Steam Locomotive I have ever seen was a paper written in 1925 by Mr. Clement R. Brown, Sr., while he was a student at Catholic University, Washington, D. C. His paper appeared in the December 1925 issue of Mechanical Engineering, the Journal of The American Society of Mechanical Engineers, New York City. Mr. Brown and the Society have very kindly granted me permission to reprint the paper as Chapter 2 in this book.

The first recorded continuous trip in the locomotive cabs of a fast train from New York to Chicago was described in a story written by Cy Warman, formerly a locomotive engineer on the Denver & Rio Grande Railway in 1883, and later a writer of some prominence during the latter part of the 19th Century. His story described a trip he made on September 26-27, 1893, in the cabs of eight locomotives hauling THE EXPOSITION FLYER from New York to Chicago via the NYC&HR-LS&MS joint operation. It was published in McClure's Magazine in January 1894.*

In 1928, Christopher Morley, the American novelist, wrote a brief story about his trip in the cab of an electric locomotive hauling THE TWENTIETH CENTURY LIMITED from Grand Central Terminal, New York City, to Harmon, where he climbed into the cab of Class J-1b Hudson (4-6-4) type locomotive No. 5217 to continue his trip to Albany. His description of the trip was colorful but was strictly a layman's impression.

*(See Appendix for details of the performance of this train).

He rode in the steam locomotive cab from Harmon to Albany only. His story was published in a small pamphlet distributed by the New York Central Lines.

In 1930, the New York Central Lines published a very interesting and detailed study entitled, "The Run of The Twentieth Century," by Edward Hungerford, who described his ride in the cab of Class T-3a electric locomotive No 1174 from Grand Central Terminal to Harmon. At the latter point he climbed into the cab of Class J-1c Hudson (4-6-4) type locomotive No. 5273 for the run to Albany. His detailed description of that run was most interesting, and showed the hand of a real railroad writer. He referred to the engineer as "Bob Bentfield" as a composite of the group of highly qualified men who ran regularly on the difficult Hudson River Division, but I am sure he was referring to Bob Butterfield, with whom I made the same run about a year later. As in Morley's case, Hungerford's cab trip ended at Albany.

Pennsylvania Rail Road officials stated that they had no record of anyone having ridden in the locomotive cabs of THE BROADWAY LIMITED the entire distance from New York to Chicago prior to my trip on February 5-6, 1931, as reported in Chapter 4.* I have been unable to find any evidence that anyone, other than myself, ever rode the locomotives of THE TWENTIETH CENTURY LIMITED westbound the entire distance from New York to Chicago. Therefore, I think I can safely claim that I am the only person ever to ride in the locomotive cabs of both THE BROADWAY LIMITED and THE TWENTIETH CENTURY LIMITED for the entire westbound trips from New York to Chicago.

The accounts of my BROADWAY and CENTURY trips were copyrighted by me in 1965. They were combined and published in greatly condensed form in TRAINS Magazine in October 1968. They have been given by me as illustrated lectures on several occasions before railroad historical groups.

Fig. D. On August 8, 1829, Horatio Allen operated the "Stourbridge Lion" on the Delaware & Hudson Canal Company's railroad. This was the first time a Steam Locomotive had ever been operated on a railroad in America. Allen was 25 years of age when he went to England early in 1828 to contract for the construction of the "Stourbridge Lion" by Foster, Rastrick & Co., of Stourbridge, England. The "Lion" arrived in Gotham in May 1829, and in July was moved by water to the gravity line at Honesdale, Pa.

ARGOSY Magazine.
Howard G. Hill Collection.

CHAPTER 2
THE INFLUENCE OF THE LOCOMOTIVE UPON THE UNITY OF OUR COUNTRY

By Clement R. Brown
The Charles T. Main 1925 Prize Award Paper*

> There are three things which make a nation great and prosperous: a fertile soil, busy workshops, and easy conveyance of men and commodities from place to place. — LORD BACON

Ever since the day of the Stourbridge Lion, the first locomotive to run in America, the locomotive has been one of the greatest factors in establishing unity in the United States. It is not necessary to recount here the quite familiar, yet very interesting, story of the invention and development of the locomotive. As to its introduction into America, however, it is well to remember the date, 1829, and the fact that the first locomotives built in America were not dominated by English ideas, as is often supposed. They were purely original developments of characteristic American ingenuity, and it was these locomotives that blazed the trail of civilization across the continent.

A study of the influence of the locomotive upon the unity of America can be conveniently divided according to three principal types of national unity. First, the locomotive has had a tremendous effect upon the history, political thought, and government of the United States. Second, its influence upon the industrial, commercial, and financial life of the nation is very great. Third, the social relations and ideas of the people and their language have been affected to a large extent by the locomotive. This paper will therefore be developed under the three types of unity, namely, political, economic, and social, all of which together constitute the unity of our country.

The influence of the locomotive in our national development can best be understood after a short outline of the development of the railroad system in America has been presented. The principal periods in American railroad history are:

1. *Experimental Period* (1830-1850). Railroads short and disconnected. Served principally as connections between waterways with no apparent objective.
2. *Trunk-Line Period* (a) From 1850 to Civil War. Trunk Lines created, connecting Chicago and Mississippi with Atlantic. Much construction in old Northwest Territory and consequent network effect. (b) From Civil War to 1890. Transcontinental lines built, uniting East and West. Improvement of old lines.
3. *Period of Combination* (1890-   ). Great combinations formed. Government regulation. Great development. Better cooperation and organization.

In this manner the "railroad system" of the United States has been formed and unity has been developed in the railroad itself.

THE WESTWARD PROGRESS OF THE RAILROAD

Buffalo from Albany 1842
Cincinnati from Lake Erie 1851
Chicago 1854
Mississippi River 1859
Missouri River 1859
Pacific Ocean 1869

POLITICAL UNITY

The political unity of a nation is best measured by its transportation facilities. Its expansion, development, and its organization into a united nation depend to a large extent upon the ease of communication within its borders. Especially has this been true in America, for the locomotive has been the greatest single factor in shaping the history of this great nation. It first developed the settled seaboard and Middle West, then pushed the frontier westward to open up new territory and to add new states to the Union which it had preserved in its hour of need. The locomotive has influenced the shaping of national political thought and the formation of a strong national government, while it has been continuing its work so that now every community is united to every other community with ever-increasing bonds.

At the close of the first quarter of the nineteenth century there was no country in the world where the opportunity for benefits from transportation were so great as in America. The growing commercial cities of New England and the Atlantic States needed better transportation facilities. New

*Published in MECHANICAL ENGINEERING, December 1925, Vol. 47, No. 12.

states had been formed west of the mountains which demanded communication with the East. Beyond them stretched the vast Louisiana Territory of untold resources. The south, too, was expanding, and wanted inland connections with New England and the West. There was much enthusiasm for the building of canals and turnpikes, but withal, transportation facilities were very poor. Indeed, the East, South, and West threatened to be developed individually as separate national states. Such was the situation when the locomotive suddenly appeared on the horizon to solve the problem.

The first function of the locomotive in America was to provide easy and cheap transportation in territory already well settled. It united inland cities and towns with the seaports and brought the products of the fertile Ohio Valley across the mountains to the East, bringing manufactured goods in return. In performing this work the locomotive has further developed and organized the country. Especially was this true in the "Old Northwest" where the opportunity was greatest. Development of this nature was but little shared by the South until after 1880. With the formation of new states in the West this function has continued to be performed admirably by the railroads in developing national unity.

GAIN IN POPULATION, EAST AND WEST
FROM 1815 TO 1860

	1815	1860
East	5,800,000	15,806,000
West	1,500,000	15,484,000

RAILROAD MILEAGE BY 1860,
EAST AND SOUTH, AND NORTHWEST

East and South 19,506
"Old Northwest" 9,413

Note: Mileage in the South increased from 20,600 in 1880 to over 50,000 in 1900.

A more important function of the locomotive, however, and one which is peculiar to America, is that of advancing the frontier and developing new territory into new states. This has been the chief task of the locomotive beyond the Mississippi. Here it is noticeable that the locomotive preceded the pioneer, as the pioneer preceded the immigrant. Lines of travel were "destined to be along parallels of latitude," and under the influence of the locomotive the frontier moved rapidly westward until, with the completion of the last transcontinental railroad in 1884, it suddenly disappeared forever. The tremendous resources of the Great Plains and the Far West had been opened up to the world, but the task of the locomotive was not finished. It now transformed this vast territory from a wilderness into a thriving land of cities, towns, and farms within less than a century. Its objective in this work has been the formation of new states. Probably the formation of none of the states east of the Mississippi can be accredited to the locomotive since most of them

had been formed prior to its importance; but certainly many of the states west of the river owe their present existence directly to the locomotive.

RAILROAD MILEAGE BY SECTIONS
OF THE COUNTRY, 1860-1890

Section	1860	1870	1880	1890
New England	3660	4494	5977	6832
Middle Atlantic	6353	10577	15147	20038
Central Northern	9583	14701	25109	36926
South Atlantic	5463	6481	8474	17301
Gulf and Mississippi States	3727	5106	6995	13343
Southwest	1162	4625	14085	32888
Northwest	655	5004	12347	27294
Pacific	23	1934	5128	12031

The influence of the locomotive upon the Civil War cannot be overlooked. It is no exaggeration to say that the locomotive preserved the Union. There was twice as much mileage of better-organized and better-equipped railroads in the North than in the South, which was of importance in the moving of troops, ammunition and food. The factor of most importance, however, was completed before the war. During the decade preceding the struggle the locomotive had united the people of the Ohio Valley with those along the Great Lakes, and these in turn with those of the East, an accomplishment destined to be the deciding factor in the coming crisis. Thus the locomotive was of great aid in winning the war and in preserving that Union to which it has since added many states.

Not only has the locomotive created a large and populous nation, but it has united the people of that nation with ever-increasing bonds. It is eradicating sectionalism in political thought and is making Americans of all. It has been very influential in making our government national in character. In fact, it makes representative government successful because it permits extensive personal political campaigns and easy communication between the representative and his constituents.

POPULATION AND RAILWAY MILEAGE
IN 1860

	Population	Mileage
North	20,310,000	20,274
South	11,133,000	10,352

The locomotive has had a tremendous influence upon the political unity of America. It has been seen how the locomotive has developed America into a united nation, an accomplishment which would have required centuries without its influence, and which never could have been accomplished so thoroughly. The test of its work came with the World War, which found America united and ready, and with its railroads able to play an important part when acting as a single unit. The locomotive was unquestionably proven, but its work was not finished, for it is still continuing to establish further unity in our country.

ECONOMIC UNITY

The locomotive has brought economic unity to the United States. The nation is not made up of many isolated areas, with no economic connections between them. Instead, under the influence of the locomotive, America's great natural resources have been developed and her products have been distributed over the entire land, so that a well-organized economic system now exists.

The presence of remarkable natural resources in America is well known and transportation facilities have formed the basis of their development. "This is preeminently and primarily an agricultural country." In the development of its agricultural resources the locomotive has played an important part, especially in the opening up of the grain lands of the Ohio and the Mississippi and the grazing lands of the Great Plains and the Southwest. America has rich mineral deposits, but it is the locomotive that makes their extraction profitable. The enormous production of the ores of Lake Superior and the Rockies, the coal of the Alleghenies, and the oil of Oklahoma is due in a large measure to cheap transportation. Timber is another important resource of the United States, and the locomotive has been a vital factor in developing the lumber industry of both the Old Northwest and the New Northwest, as well as that of the South. These are but a few of the many natural resources of America, all of which owe much of their development to the locomotive.

It is in the field of transportation that the locomotive has had its greatest influence upon the economic unity of our country. Easy and cheap transportation has increased the area of production of every commodity so that it can now be produced profitably at a great distance from the market as well as nearby. It facilitates the gathering together of the raw materials from all parts of the country to the centers of distribution and manufacture. Modern transportation permits the localization of industry near the source of supply or at points best suited for the manufacture of a particular article. The locomotive has widened the market of every commodity produced in the land, and serves, by encouraging competition, to distribute the products to every community of the nation.

In the development of our natural resources and the creation of industry, the locomotive has created commerce in the United States. Commercial centers have been created and developed at centers of distribution, such as railroad centers, and at points of change from one means of transportation to another, such as seaports.

By its very nature, railroad development encourages development in other means of transportation. Thus the commerce of America has been built up until it has reached tremendous proportions, and the locomotive has been one of the greatest factors in its development.

Labor is needed in commerce and industry and the locomotive is a vital factor in supplying the demand for it. It permits a wide distribution of labor and supplies easy and quick transportation of labor from place to place as needed. It also supplies a market for various kinds of labor. The locomotive has facilitated immigration by transporting the immigrant to new lands where his labor is most needed. It is noticeable that the number of immigrants increased tremendously with the advent of the railroad. The locomotive has helped to make the standards and conditions of labor uniform throughout the country. In this manner labor has become a united force to serve the nation's industries.

IMMIGRATION BY DECADES
FROM 1820 TO 1890

| 1821-1830 | 143,439 | 1841-1850 | 1,713,251 |
| 1831-1840 | 599,125 | 1881-1890 | 5,246,613 |

Another field of economic importance in which the influence of the locomotive has been felt is that of finance. The locomotive has not only created and developed wealth, but has also influenced its distribution. The development of corporations for financing large-scale operations came with the locomotive. It also aids in the distribution of money and facilitates its movement from place to place, thus tending to prevent panics. It enables business enterprises to operate over a vast territory with ease. The railroads themselves form a very significant part of the total wealth of the nation, of which the locomotive has been an important factor in developing.

"The effects of railroad construction are far-reaching." It is hard to overestimate the influence of the locomotive upon the development of our natural resources, industry, commerce, labor, and advances into a well-organized economic system. Certainly it may be said that this, the economic unity of America, owes much to the locomotive.

SOCIAL UNITY

The locomotive has been very influential in the development of social unity in America. In fact, the history of the locomotive is closely allied with the modern development of civilization. Better communication has brought better understanding and knowledge between peoples and is doing away with sectionalism in social thought and placing national social unity in its stead. The locomotive is of great aid in relieving suffering in times of distress. Modern travel has become a pleasure in itself. All these tend toward national peace, prosperity, and happiness, and

Fig. E. No. 91. Atchison, Topeka & Santa Fe Railway, 4-4-0 Type. Built by Baldwin Locomotive Works, Philadelphia, 1879. Builder's No. 4613. Typical of the early locomotives which pushed the frontier westward until, in 1887, with the completion of the last trans-continental railroad, it disappeared forever in the Pacific Ocean.

H. L. Broadbelt Collection.

in this the locomotive is an important factor.

Modern civilization has advanced farthest in those places where the locomotive is seen most often. The locomotive is its keynote, for it introduces modern art into the community. It encourages religion, education, and good government, while it is noticeable that bigotry, illiteracy, and lawlessness are found where railroads are not. The locomotive promotes progress in civilization among the people.

Better communication as afforded by the locomotive has several effects beneficial to a greater social unity in our country. The locomotive enables peoples of different communities to become better acquainted with one another. The customs and manners of one become better known and understood by the other. One of the greatest means of accomplishing this end is the "convention," which itself has been made possible to a great extent by the locomotive. Every year thousands of people are gathered together from all parts of the country in various places. Although various fields of endeavor are represented and many ideas are exchanged, it is the social contact at these conventions that does the most to promote a better understanding between peoples and communities.

Not only does better communication encourage better knowledge of society, but it tends to unite society in America with national bonds. Through better acquaintance, ideas, customs and manners, and views on common problems are exchanged, with the result that national ideas, national customs and manners, and national views are developed. Religion, education and government become national in character. The locomotive is preventing and eradicating the growth of dialects in America and is thus establishing a common language. Because it is the mail carrier of the nation and sends and brings the messages of the people, the locomotive provides a cheap form of communication which is an important factor in the development of social unity. The nation is united even in its emotions, for the mourning of the death of a president is as spontaneous as the celebration of the announcement of peace.

The locomotive is of great aid in times of distress. A flood on the Ohio, a tornado in Kansas, a fire in Chicago, or an earthquake in San Francisco, and the locomotive immediately rushes aid from all parts of the country to the distressed sufferers. A famine in any locality is nowadays almost impossible, for the locomotive soon relieves a shortage in any commodity, no matter what the season may be.

Modern conveniences have added to the work of the locomotive to make modern travel a pleasure. One is now able to visit all parts of the country with ease and comfort, and at little expense. By this means the locomotive enables the citizen to obtain a broader knowledge of his native land and at the same time to enjoy her beauties. Thus the locomotive is not only able to relieve man of his sorrow, but it has added new pleasures to increase his contentment in America.

No country in the world is as prosperous as America. Its people have an abundance of food, clothes, and wealth, and comfortable homes in which to live. They are happy and peace reigns among them. The locomotive has had a tremendous influence in bringing prosperity and contentment to America. Truly, as James J. Hill has said, "The railway, next after the Christian religion and the public school, has been the largest single contributing factor to the welfare and happiness of the people."

Modern transportation is a great benefit to society. It develops its civilization, increases its scope, knits it together more firmly, relieves its sorrows, and adds new pleasures for its enjoyment. It promotes prosperity and contentment among its members. The locomotive, which has made cheap and easy communication possible, has thus been a vital factor in establishing social unity in America.

CONCLUSION

It is just a century and a half since the Union had its humble yet determined beginning. With less than a century of existence the locomotive has had a tremendous influence in the accomplishment of a great and unparalleled achievement. Not only has the Union been increased, the national domain extended, and the population multiplied many times, but the nation has wealth and her people are prosperous and contented. But above all, the locomotive has given political, economic and social unity to America. It is recognized, however, that these three types of unity are by no means entirely separable. In fact, they are quite inseparable, for each one is involved in the other two to a great extent, and it is only when taken together that they make up the unity of our country.

Today a network of railroads covers the United States. Every community is united to every other community with bonds of steel. As to the future, the locomotive can be confident of more than holding its place in transportation. No other means of transportation can compare with the locomotive in efficiently supplying cheap and quick transportation of goods and men wherever needed. Just as past experience has shown the locomotive to exceed all expectations, so for the future it is safe to say that the locomotive will continue to be of the greatest influence in preserving the unity of our country.

CHAPTER 3
THE DEVELOPMENT OF STEAM
PASSENGER MOTIVE POWER ON THE
PENNSYLVANIA RAIL ROAD*

THE fourth quarter of the 19th Century witnessed keen competition for railroad passenger traffic between New York City and Chicago. The principal competitors were the Pennsylvania Rail Road and the New York Central & Hudson River —Lake Shore & Michigan Southern joint operation. Each road tried to surpass the other by providing fast, deluxe, through trains. In the early stages of the intense rivalry, the normal consist of those trains was four light-weight wooden cars, the interiors of which were finished and furnished in the height of luxury. Those trains became very popular with the traveling public, and their number was increased along with an increase in the number of cars per train. Schedules were reduced as competition became keener. (Figs. 1 and 2).

The first "Limited" train on the Pennsylvania was inaugurated in 1876 — it was limited to four cars, and gave limited service to a relatively small number of passengers. Its popularity definitely established the fact that there was a need for such service.

On October 26, 1881, the PENNSYLVANIA LIMITED commenced operation on a schedule of 26 hours 40 minutes between Jersey City and Chicago. The finest deluxe equipment available was assigned to that train, and only five stops were made en route. That train was continued in service for many years because of its popularity. The schedule was soon reduced to 24 hours. That was the first train in the world to be fully equipped with electric lights, and it made its first run with the improved lighting system in June 1887. (Fig. 3).

In 1893 the Pennsylvania began the operation of THE 20-HOUR SPECIAL between Jersey City and Chicago to provide de luxe transportation for passengers going to, or returning from, the World's Columbian Exposition held in Chicago that year. The Transportation Exhibit at the Exposition was very complete and of great interest to all who were concerned with the progress and developments which had been made in the railroad industry up to that time. THE 20-HOUR SPECIAL was continued in service after the Exposition closed on October 31, 1893.

Up to the end of 1893, the limited trains had been powered by light American (4-4-0) type locomotives, the largest of which were the Classes D13 and D14, built at Altoona Shops in 1893. (Fig. 4). Their tractive effort was 17,970 lbs. with 68-inch driving wheels, and 15,660 lbs. with 78-inch driving wheels. Increasing train weights necessitated the design and construction, beginning in 1895, of five sub-classes of Class D16, some of which had 68-inch driving wheels for service on divisions with heavy grades, while others had 80-inch driving wheels for service on divisions having comparatively flat profiles. The Pennsylvania built 429 Class D16 locomotives between 1895 and 1910. They were the largest Pennsylvania locomotives of the 4-4-0 type, and were built with Belpaire boilers, which had been the standard boiler on the Pennsylvania since 1885, when it was first applied to the Class R (H3) Consolidation (2-8-0) type locomotives built at Altoona. The Belpaire boiler continued to be the standard on the Pennsylvania to the end of steam with very few exceptions, notably the huge Class J1 and J1a Texas (2-10-4) type

*(See Appendix for Specifications of all locomotives illustrated).

locomotives, of which 125 were built at Juniata Shops between 1942 and 1944. Their fireboxes had radial staying.

Thus, up to the end of the 19th Century, passenger trains on the Pennsylvania had been moved by a large fleet of American (4-4-0) type locomotives which had been developed and improved through many years of service, and which included several classes lettered from A to P, reclassified D1 to D16 in 1895. (Figs. 5 and 6).

The Class D16 locomotives were essentially similar in design, although they differed in minor details. Those with 68-inch driving wheels developed 20,850 lbs. tractive effort, while the 80-inch driving wheels reduced the tractive effort to 17,500 lbs. Obviously, their tonnage rating was quite low.

On June 15, 1902, THE PENNSYLVANIA SPECIAL made its first run between Jersey City and Chicago as a new de luxe train on a 20 hour schedule. The four luxurious cars of that train were moved by a Class D16 locomotive. The train catered to an elite clientele and became immensely popular. Before long, the name was changed to THE PENNSYLVANIA LIMITED, and, on November 24, 1912, it was renamed THE BROAD WAY LIMITED, not for the famous Manhattan street, but for the broad, four-track way of the Pennsylvania over which it operated. The name was soon condensed to THE BROADWAY LIMITED, and this has been its name throughout the ensuing years. (Figs. 7 and 8).

THE PENNSYLVANIA SPECIAL was withdrawn from the time card in February, 1903, because of freight congestion, but it was reinstated on June 11, 1905, on an 18-hour schedule. On November 24, 1912, the schedule was increased to 20 hours. (Figs. 9 and 10).

On the initial west-bound trip on the 18-hour schedule, THE PENNSYLVANIA SPECIAL arrived at Crestline, Ohio, somewhat behind schedule. Class E2 Atlantic (4-4-2) type locomotive No. 7002 was coupled to the train and her engineer, Jerry McCarthy, was instructed to make up as much time as possible between Crestline and Fort Wayne. He followed his instructions literally. On a 3-mile stretch between AY Tower and Elida, Ohio, he whipped the 7002 up to an average of 127.1 miles per hour, a feat which won world-wide fame for the engineer, the train, and the locomotive. That American record still stands for steam power. (Fig. 11).

Because of heavy war-time traffic during World War I, THE BROADWAY LIMITED was discontinued between December 10, 1917, and May 25, 1919. In 1938, this train was operated on a schedule of 16 hours between New York and Chicago. Completion of the tunnels under the North River at New York City and the new Pennsylvania passenger terminal in the City permitted the operation of all passenger trains from and to the new terminal, beginning in 1910. (Figs. 44 and 45).

At the turn of the Century, the Pennsylvania had introduced Atlantic (4-4-2) type locomotives of Classes E2 and E3 in main line passenger service. (Figs. 12 and 13). Those locomotives were superior in power output to the Class D16 4-4-0 type locomotives which had been the mainstay of passenger train service for several years. The introduction of steel passenger train equipment in 1906, and its operation in high-speed service, beginning in 1907, required some double-heading with the Atlantic type locomotives, because of the increasing train weights. (Fig. 14). The result was a demand from the Traffic Department for locomotives of greater starting tractive effort and boiler capacity than was available in the Atlantics, without increasing the weight on the driving wheels beyond that which was considered safe. (Fig. 15).

The first step toward providing more powerful passenger locomotives was an order placed with the Pittsburgh Works of American Locomotive Company for an experimental Pacific (4-6-2) type locomotive.* That locomotive, No. 7067, designated Class K28, was built in April 1907, and was the first Pacific type locomotive to be operated by the Pennsylvania. (Fig. 16). In comparison with the Classes E2 and E3 Atlantics she looked like a monster, and the nickname "Fat Annie" was given to her by the engine crews. The 7067 was subjected to exhaustive road tests, providing data from which the Pennsylvania developed its own design for an enlarged and improved Pacific type locomotive, designated Class K2. (Figs. 17 and 18). Juniata Shops built 153 locomotives of that design in 1910 and 1911. Some of those locomotives were built with superheaters as Class K2s. (Figs. 22 and 23). Later, all saturated K2 locomotives were superheated.

Between 1911 and 1913, Juniata Shops built 62 Pacifics of Class K2a, and American Locomotive Company built 10 of that class in 1912. They were practically duplicates of the K2, with minor alterations to boilers and cylinders. (Fig. 19). All of the Class K2 Pacifics were built with 80-inch driving wheels. When superheated, they became Class K2sa.

American Locomotive Company built 12 Pacific type locomotives for the old Vandalia Line between 1911 and 1913. They were inherited in 1916 when the Vandalia Line was absorbed by the Pennsylvania, and were designated Class K21s. They were smaller than the K28, although similar in some respects. They were never adopted as a standard design by the Pennsylvania. (Fig. 20).

*(See Appendix for List of Pacific Type Locomotives on the Pennsylvania).

In 1911, Juniata Shops built 2 Pacifics of Class K2b, Nos. 3371 and 3375, with 72-inch driving wheels and KW style trailing trucks. They were later superheated and became Class K2sb. (Fig. 21).

From studies and tests of the K28 and the variations of the K2, the Pennsylvania developed Class K3s design. Thirty locomotives of that class were built by Baldwin Locomotive Works in 1913. One of that group, No. 8661, carried Baldwin Construction Number 40,000 on her builder's plate. Those locomotives were similar to Class K2, but they had 26-inch instead of 24-inch cylinders, Crawford underfeed stokers, (later removed), and superheaters. (Fig. 24 and 25).

Another experimental Pacific type locomotive was built at Schenectady Works of American Locomotive Company in November 1911. That locomotive, No. 3395, designated Class K29s, was designed for maximum power with minimum weight, and was equipped with a Schmidt superheater, Crawford underfeed stoker, brick arch, radial stay firebox, cylinders 27 inches by 28 inches, 80-inch driving wheels, outside steam pipes, screw reverse gear, and other contemporary innovations. (Fig. 26).

Before being placed in regular service, the 3395, considered one of the most successful experimental locomotives ever built, was operated on the Altoona Locomotive Test Plant. Those tests provided data for the development of a more advanced Pacific design. The 3395 was definitely the prototype for the famous Class K4s Pacific type locomotives designed and built by the Pennsylvania.

A total of 271 Pacific type locomotives had been built by or for the Pennsylvania prior to 1914. All, including the experimental locomotives, were considered very successful, but increasingly difficult traffic requirements exceeded their capacity, and heavier, more powerful locomotives were urgently needed.

The Pennsylvania designed and built Class K4s Pacific type locomotive No. 1737, which was delivered by Juniata Shops in May, 1914. It was quite evident that the 1737 was capable of producing outstanding performance, but at that time they did not realize her full capabilities. Three years of exhaustive testing on the Altoona Test Plant and in heavy main line service, hauling the limited trains, gave convincing proof that the late Mr. J. T. Wallis, Chief of Motive Power, and his Staff, had produced an outstanding locomotive— a Masterpiece. During the years 1917 to 1928, 424 duplicates of the 1737 were built, 75 by Baldwin, and the others by Juniata Shops, with only minor variations in details. (Figs. 27, 28 and 29).

In 1929, the Pennsylvania acquired 2 experimental Class K5 Pacific type locomotives, Nos. 5698 and 5699, which were larger and more powerful than the Class K4s Pacifics in almost every detail except their 80-inch driving wheels and their 70 sq. ft. of grate area. The 5698 was built by Juniata Shop with piston valves and Walschaert valve gear, while the 5699 was built by Baldwin Locomotive Works with poppet valves and Caprotti valve gear. Later, the Caprotti gear was removed and the 5699 was equipped with new piston valve cylinders and Walschaert valve gear. The advent of the Mountain (4-8-2) type locomotives in 1930 stopped all further development of the Pacific type locomotive on the Pennsylvania. (Figs. 30, 31, 32 and 33).

Even the Mountain type was not the last word in steam passenger power. In 1942, the Pennsylvania received 2 Baldwin experimental Duplex (4-4-4-4) type locomotives, designated Class T1. They were a radical departure from accepted locomotive design, but road tests, and tests on the Altoona Test Plant, indicated a promising future for them. Fifty additional locomotives of this class were built in 1945 and 1946; 25 complete locomotives plus 25 additional tenders at Juniata shops, and 25 locomotives without tenders by Baldwin. Their performance on the road was outstanding, but serious difficulties in operation and maintenance developed. It was too late to find remedies for those difficulties, although that might have been done had steam operation continued a few years longer. The rapid adoption of the diesel-electric locomotive put an end to steam operation on the Pennsylvania, and the T1's were rapidly down-graded to less important service, and were soon retired. They were the final step in the development of steam power on the Pennsylvania, and had disappeared by the late 1950's. (Fig. 34)

The Pennsylvania Rail Road had operated a total of 698 Pacific type steam locomotives between 1907 and the end of the wonderful Age of Steam. The K4s Pacific type steam locomotive was the most outstandingly successful and the most widely known of any of the outstanding power developed by the Pennsylvania. It would require a book to cover adequately the characteristics and performance of that superb steam locomotive. Here, however, we are concerned with the performance of 5 of those locomotives while serving as the motive power on one specific run of THE BROADWAY LIMITED, and the story is based on the personal observations of the author while riding in the cabs of those locomotives throughout the entire run from New York to Chicago, a total of 908 miles, in one continuous trip, with only operating stops to interrupt the run.

Fig. 1. No. 274. Pennsylvania Rail Road. Class C (D3) 4-4-0 Type. Built by Pennsylvania R. R. at Altoona, September 1875. Builder's No. 287. An early passenger locomotive.
George M. Hart Collection.

Fig. 2. No. 10 ("Old Long-legged No. 10"). Pennsylvania Rail Road. Class K (D6) 4-4-0 Type. Built by Pennsylvania R. R. at Altoona, March 25, 1881. An early passenger locomotive. This was the first locomotive to be equipped with a power reverse gear, a steam-hydraulic device mounted on the right side of the firebox ahead of the cab.
George M. Hart Collection.

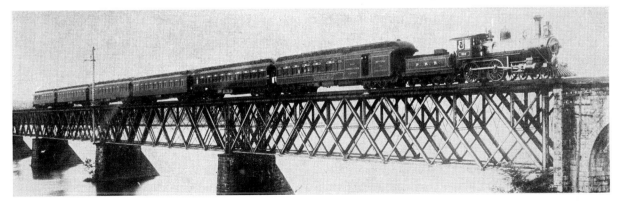

Fig. 3. No. 568. Pennsylvania Rail Road. Class O (D10a) 4-4-0 Type. Built by Pennsylvania R. R. at Altoona, June 1891. Builder's No. 1645. Shown about 1892 with THE PENN-SYLVANIA LIMITED crossing the iron truss bridge which carried the tracks of the Middle Division across the Susquehanna River at Rockville, near Harrisburg, from 1877 to 1902.
George M. Hart Collection.

Fig. 4. No. 1639. Pennsylvania Rail Road. Class P (D13c) 4-4-0 Type. Built by Pennsylvania R. R. at Altoona, May 1893. Builder's No. 1846. Assigned to THE PENNSYLVANIA SPECIAL.

George M. Hart Collection.

Fig. 5. No. 1659. Pennsylvania Rail Road. Class P (D14) 4-4-0 Type. Built by Pennsylvania R. R. at Altoona, 1893, for service on THE PENNSYLVANIA SPECIAL.

George M. Hart Collection.

Fig. 6. No. 88. Pennsylvania Rail Road. Class P (L) (D16a) 4-4-0 Type. Built by Pennsylvania R. R. at Altoona, 1895. The first locomotive of the D16 group, and the ultimate development of the 4-4-0 Type for service on the Limited trains.

George M. Hart Collection.

Fig. 7.   No. 296. Pennsylvania Rail Road. Class D16a 4-4-0 Type. THE PENNSYLVANIA LIM-
ITED in action on the Philadelphia Division near Merion, Pa., in 1899.

BALDWIN LOCOMOTIVES.

Fig. 8.   No. 101. Pennsylvania Rail Road. Class L (D16a) 4-4-0 Type. Built by Pennsylvania
R. R. at Altoona, 1895. Builder's No. 371. This class became famous as a result of
its excellent performance on the Limited trains.

Pennsylvania R. R.

Fig. 9.   No. 1395. Pennsylvania Rail Road. Class D16a 4-4-0 Type. Built by Pennsylvania R. R. at Juniata Shops, 1896. Shown here with THE PENNSYLVANIA SPECIAL, with Engineer Martin H. Lee at the throttle, speeding through Morrisville, Pa., at 85 miles per hour on June 16, 1902, on the second west-bound trip of the new de luxe train on the 20-hour schedule.

Frederick Westing Collection.

Fig. 10.   No. 955. Pennsylvania Rail Road. Class D16a 4-4-0 Type. An interesting action shot.
Harold C. Zieber Collection.

Fig. 11. No. 7002. Pennsylvania Rail Road. Class E7sa 4-4-2 Type. Built by Pennsylvania R. R. at Juniata Shops, 1902, as No. 2, Pittsburgh, Fort Wayne & Chicago R. R., Class E2. Builder's No. 877. Renumbered 7002. The original 7002 was scrapped before her historical value was recognized. The locomotive shown here was originally No. 8063, built at Juniata Shops, 1902, as Class E2a, later converted to Class E7sa as shown. This engine was preserved as No. 7002 at Northumberland, Pa.

Howard G. Hill Photo.

Fig. 12. No. 1968. Pennsylvania Rail Road. Class E2 4-4-2 Type. Built by Pennsylvania R. R. at Juniata Shops, 1901. Builder's No. 829. Equipped with radial-stayed firebox, slide valves and Stephenson valve gear.

Pennsylvania R. R.

Fig. 13. No. 2024. Pennsylvania Rail Road. Class E3a 4-4-2 Type. Built by Pennsylvania R. R. at Juniata Shops, 1902. Builder's No. 907. Equipped with Belpaire firebox and larger (22") cylinders, but retaining the balanced slide valves and Stephenson valve gear.
Pennsylvania R. R.

Fig. 14. No. 7374. Pennsylvania Rail Road. Class E2b 4-4-2 Type. Built by American Locomotive Co., Schenectady Works, 1903, as Class E2a with Belpaire firebox, slide valves, and Stephenson valve gear. Builder's No. 26780. Converted in 1904 to Class E2b with inside piston valves for Stephenson valve gear, as shown above. Converted in 1916 to Class E7s with outside piston valves, Walschaert valve gear, and superheater. Renumbered 9716.

Harold C. Zieber Collection.

Fig. 15. A view of the Pennsylvania Rail Road's West Philadelphia Engine Terminal in the early 1900's.

Frederick Westing Collection.

Fig. 16. No. 7067. Pennsylvania Rail Road. Class K28 4-6-2 Type. Built by American Locomotive Co., Pittsburgh Works, April 1907. Builder's No. 41525. This was the first Pacific (4-6-2) Type locomotive on the Pennsylvania R. R.

American Locomotive Co. Photo.

Fig. 17. No. 3337. Pennsylvania Rail Road. Class K2 4-6-2 Type. Built by Pennsylvania R. R. at Juniata Shops, 1910. This design was developed by the Pennsylvania R. R. from the Class K28 experimental design.

Frederick Westing Collection.

Fig. 18. No. 3379. Pennsylvania Rail Road. Class K2 4-6-2 Type. Built by Pennsylvania R. R. at Juniata Shops, 1911.

BALDWIN LOCOMOTIVES.

Fig. 19. No. 7049. Pennsylvania Rail Road. Class K2a 4-6-2 Type. Built by American Locomotive Co., Schenectady Works, 1912. Superheated later as Class K2sa.
American Locomotive Co. Photo.

Fig. 20. No. 8704. Pennsylvania Rail Road. Class K21s 4-6-2 Type. Built by American Locomotive Co., Schenectady Works, October 1911, as No. 4, St. Louis, Vandalia & Terre Haute R. R., "The Vandalia Line." Renumbered 8704 in 1916 when the Vandalia Line was absorbed by Pennsylvania R. R. This was never a standard class on the Pennsylvania R. R.

Pennsylvania R. R.

Fig. 21. No. 3375. Pennsylvania Rail Road. Class K2sb 4-6-2 Type. Built by Pennsylvania R. R. at Juniata Shops, November 1911, as Class K2b with 72-inch driving wheels. Builder's No. 2333. Superheated later as Class K2sb.

C. B. Chaney Photo.
Smithsonian Institution.

Fig. 22. No. 150. Pennsylvania Rail Road. Class K2s 4-6-2 Type. Built by Pennsylvania R. R. at Juniata Shops, March 1910. Builder's No. 2001.

Lt. Col. T. M. Flattley, Jr., Photo.

Fig. 23. No. 9999. Pennsylvania Rail Road. Class K2s 4-6-2 Type. Built by Pennsylvania R. R. at Juniata Shops, January 1911. Builder's No. 2179. This was the highest regular number carried by any Pennsylvania locomotive.

Lt. Col. T. M. Flattley, Jr., Photo.

Fig. 24. No. 8661. Pennsylvania Rail Road. Class K3s 4-6-2 Type. Built by Baldwin Locomotive Works at Eddystone, July 1913. Builder's No. 40000.

Howard G. Hill Collection.

Fig. 25. No. 8662. Pennsylvania Rail Road. Class K3s 4-6-2 Type Built by Baldwin Locomotive Works at Eddystone, July 1913. Builder's No. 39995.

Lt. Col. T. M. Flattley, Jr., Photo.

Fig. 26. No. 3395. Pennsylvania Rail Road. Class K29s 4-6-2 Type. Built by American Locomotive Co., Schenectady Works, November 1911. Builder's No. 50186. A highly successful experimental locomotive from which the famous Class K4s design was developed by the Pennsylvania R. R.

Pennsylvania R. R.

41

Fig. 27. No. 1737. Pennsylvania Rail Road. Class K4s 4-6-2 Type. Designed by Pennsylvania R. R. and built at Juniata Shops, May 1914. Builder's No. 2825. This was the first of 425 Class K4s Pacific type locomotives built by or for Pennsylvania R. R. It was an outstanding design.

Pennsylvania R. R.

Fig. 28. No. 1737. Pennsylvania Rail Road. Class K4s 4-6-2 Type. After 4 decades of faithful service, the first Class K4s locomotive was stored at Northumberland Roundhouse, awaiting rehabilitation and permanent exhibition. Rapid deterioration and neglect brought her to the sad condition shown here on October 20, 1957, and resulted in the decision to scrap her. Her Keystone number plate and builder's plates were transferred to Class K4s locomotive No. 3750, built at Juniata Shops in 1920, for preservation. At least, a Class K4s locomotive has been saved for exhibition in a museum.
Howard G. Hill Photo.

Fig. 29. No. 5453. Pennsylvania Rail Road. Class K4s 4-6-2 Type. Built by Baldwin Locomotive Works at Eddystone, 1927. Equipped with a 25,000-gallon tender for test purposes.
Howard G. Hill Collection.

Fig. 30. No. 5698. Pennsylvania Rail Road. Class K5 4-6-2 Type. Built by Pennsylvania R. R. at Juniata Shops, March 1929. Builder's No. 4205. An experimental locomotive, larger than the Class K4s locomotives in almost every detail except grate area and diameter of driving wheels. Equipped with piston valves and Walschaert valve gear.

Pennsylvania R. R.

Fig. 31. No. 5699. Pennsylvania Rail Road. Class K5 4-6-2 Type. Built by Baldwin Locomotive Works at Eddystone, September 1929. Builder's No. 60660. An experimental locomotive which was a duplicate of Class K5 No. 5698, except that Caprotti valve gear and poppet valves were used instead of Walschaert valve gear and piston valves. In 1937 the Caprotti valve gear and poppet valves were removed and new piston valve cylinders and Walschaert valve gear were substituted. Only two Class K5 locomotives were built for test purposes.

H. L. Broadbelt Collection.

Fig. 32. No. 4700. Pennsylvania Rail Road. Class M1 4-8-2 Type. Built by Pennsylvania R. R. at Juniata Shops, 1923. Builder's No. 3819. The first Mountain (4-8-2) type locomotive on the Pennsylvania R. R.

BALDWIN LOCOMOTIVES.

45

Fig. 33. No. 6703. Pennsylvania Rail Road. Class M1a 4-8-2 Type. Built by Baldwin Locomotive Works at Eddystone, 1930. One of 300 Class M1a locomotives built by Baldwin, Juniata and Lima between 1926 and 1930. I rode in the cab of No. 6703 from Pittsburgh to Altoona, 113 miles, on March 15, 1931, hauling Train No. 66, THE AMERICAN, as part of a cab trip from St. Louis to New York.

Lt. Col. T. M. Flattley, Jr., Photo.

Fig. 34. No. 5533. Pennsylvania R. R. Class T1 4-4-4-4 Type. Built by Baldwin Locomotive Works at Eddystone in 1946. Two T1 experimental locomotives were built by Baldwin in 1942, to be followed by 50 duplicates in 1945-1946; 25 complete locomotives and 25 extra tenders from Juniata Shops, and 25 locomotives without tenders from Baldwin. On a cold winter night in March, 1947, I rode in the cab of No. 5545, hauling THE GENERAL, from Chicago to Fort Wayne, 148 miles, at 95 miles per hour over much of the run. Her performance was superb. Two weeks later, with the same train, she was wrecked at Columbia, Indiana, while moving through a cross-over at excessive speed. Glad I was not in her cab that night!

H. L. Broadbelt Collection.

CHAPTER 4
RIDING THE BROADWAY LIMITED'S
K4s PACIFICS*

My hat is off to Frederick Westing for his outstanding article on a superb steam locomotive — the Pennsylvania Rail Road's Class K4s Pacific (4-6-2) type steam passenger locomotive! His splendid description (TRAINS Magazine, August 1956) of the history, development and characteristics of that beautiful locomotive was of great interest to me because of my close association with it during a brief period in 1931, when I had the rare privilege of riding in the cabs of several of them. Having studied a large volume of data on the K4s, including Altoona Locomotive Test Plant bulletins, and with numerous photographs and drawings of them in my library, it was a particularly thrilling experience to ride in a K4s cab from New York to Chicago, hauling THE BROADWAY LIMITED. It all came about in this way.

For several years after I resigned my position as Mechanical Engineer with the Southern Pacific Lines — Texas and Louisiana — I had been with the Railway Sales Department of The Texas Company as Engineer of Tests on railroad equipment lubrication problems. One of the difficult and troublesome problems of those days was the lubrication of the driving journal bearings on a large group of heavy Mallet (2-8-8-2) type articulated compound locomotives on the Norfolk and Western Railway, which were used to move heavy tonnage coal trains from the mines to tidewater, and to the Lakes region, over grades of up to 2.2%. (Figs. 35 and 36). That problem was also encountered on the heavy USRA Mountain (4-8-2) type locomotives used in passenger service in the same region. Overheated driving journal bearings were the rule rather than the exception, and, as a result, engine failures and train delays were frequent, and maintenance expenses were mounting. (Fig. 37).

*(See Appendix for Details of Performance of this Trip.)

The driving journal compound then in use, known as "cold-set grease," whose base was a soda soap, and which contained from 8% to 15% water held in suspension, would not provide satisfactory lubrication for over-heated bearings, because a bearing operating temperature in excess of 212° F. caused evaporation of the water in the grease. This caused the grease to assume a spongy mass, and the pressure plate under the grease cake quickly pushed the hot, soft grease out of the driving box grease cellar. In a few miles the lack of lubrication resulted in a badly scored and damaged bearing and journal, and, frequently, an engine failure with its attendant evils. The situation had become so critical all over the country, particularly on roads using heavy power, that a remedy was imperative.

The remedy appeared in the late spring of 1923 in the form of a new "dehydrated" driving journal compound which, instead of being processed in water-jacketed kettles to maintain a low temperature, was heated to about 485° F. The high temperature evaporated the water which formed during the manufacturing process, thus eliminating it from the finished grease. The new dehydrated grease, called Driving Journal Compound "M," was covered by a United States patent issued to my company. It was claimed that this new grease was a great new discovery — the result of intensive research in the laboratory. Actually, its discovery was more in the nature of an accident. Because of the serious difficulties resulting from the failure of the old grease, our Railway Department had become rather desperate, and the heat was on the laboratory to produce a satisfactory grease — or else! One of the young chemists at the laboratory made what seemed like a wild suggestion — put some of the old water grease and some "Crater Compound" into a kettle together and cook them, and see what comes out. "Crater Compound" was a very viscous residue from one of the refining processes and was considered of no value, and it had been discarded by burning it, mixed with a lighter fuel, in specially constructed fireboxes under some of the stills.

One fine day, a salesman, with unusual vision, made the statement that he could push the world around with one hand if they would put rollers lubricated with "Crater Compound" under it. This led to the wide use of "Crater Compound" as a lubricant for heavily loaded bearings, such as driving gears and bearings of rolling mills, driving gears in electric locomotives, steam locomotive crosshead guides and driving wheel hub faces, and many other types of heavily loaded bearings.

Examination of the original cooked sample, after it had cooled and congealed, revealed an entirely different texture from that of the old "cold-set" grease. Tiny pockets of oil were dispersed closely and uniformly throughout the grease, and it was believed that this feature would provide greatly improved journal lubrication. Accordingly, the decision was made to prepare a larger batch for road tests. In June 1923, I was assigned to make extensive road tests of the new "M" grease, beginning on the Mallet and Mountain type locomotives on the Norfolk and Western Railway, operating out of Roanoke, Va.

The initial road tests which I conducted with the "M" grease showed promise of outstanding performance. Its use was quickly extended to a large number of heavy Mallet and Mountain type locomotives operating on mountain grades and on divisions with comparatively flat profiles. The results were almost unbelievable. Many of those locomotives were returned to regular service without reconditioning the driving journals or bearings which had been damaged by repeated failures of the old type of grease. With the "M' grease, locomotives formerly assigned to runs of only 100 miles, were operated successfully on runs of 300 miles or more. Engine failures and train delays were almost eliminated, and locomotive availability was greatly increased. So was my work — I had to spread myself pretty thin to keep up with all of the activities and all of the territory involved in extending rapidly the use of the new grease on several railroads. But it was fun and a source of great satisfaction to be able to play a vital part in the solution of what had been a serious problem. Lack of sleep and long hours in engine cabs and in roundhouses seemed of little consequence as long as we were getting results. (Figs. 38 and 39).

News of the outstanding success of the new "M" grease spread rapidly, and, naturally, our success with it engendered the development of competitive products by other companies. Those competitive greases resulted, late in 1930, in patent litigation, in which I was involved as an expert witness for the plaintiff, The Texas Company, since I personally had made all of the original service tests of the "M" grease during the summer and fall of 1923. I had also supervised its application, during the period 1923 to 1928, on many railroads to eliminate the difficulties then being experienced with the old type of grease.

The trial began late in 1930 in the United States District Court for the Southern District of New York, in the Woolworth Building in New York City. As a part of the exhibits introduced by the plaintiff, I had prepared a set of photographs, to the same scale, of typical steam locomotives of each wheelbase type to illustrate their growth, in size and power, during the period 1890 to 1930. That growth had been accompanied by increasing difficulty in the lubrication of the driving journal bearings of heavy modern locomotives, and emphasized the need for an improved driving journal lubricant. That need had been fulfilled by our new dehydrated "M" grease.

To digress a moment — during the preparation for the trial, I attended the December 1930 annual dinner of the New York Railroad Club at Hotel Commodore in New York City. At that dinner I had the pleasure of meeting the late Mr. Fred W. Hankins, then Chief of Motive Power, Pennsylvania Rail Road, with whom I had a very interesting conversation about Pennsylvania motive power. (Fig. 40). During our conversation, I mentioned that I had long admired the Pennsylvania's Class K4s Pacific type locomotives and hoped that someday I might have the privilege of riding in the cab of one of them. (Fig. 41). Mr. Hankins replied, "When you get ready, let me know, and I will set up arrangements for you to ride one of the K4s." That was the opportunity of a lifetime, and I naturally planned to "let him know" on my next trip to Chicago. That came about much sooner than I had expected.

Returning now to the photographic exhibits which I had prepared — one was a large photograph, about 10 inches by 24 inches, of locomotive No. 5400, the first of the 1927 group of 75 K4's built by Baldwin Locomotive Works for the Pennsylvania. (See end of this Chapter.)

The photograph of K4s No. 5400 was a full view of the left side of the locomotive, but only the forward quarter of the tender appeared in the picture. Thus, the name "PENNSYLVANIA" on the side of the tank, near the center, did not show. That photograph was introduced to illustrate a typical modern, heavy, high-speed passenger locomotive, and the name of the railroad owning or operating it was "irrelevant and immaterial" —or so we thought! I do not recall that the elimination of the word "PENNSYLVANIA" from that photograph was a premeditated act on my part. It just happened that way, and apparently was done to emphasize the locomotive and not the tender. At any rate, it certainly worked out to my personal advantage, as will soon be evident. (Fig. 43).

One thing we had overlooked was the fact that the class symbol "K4s" on the builder's plate on the smokebox was clearly discernible in the photograph without the aid of a magnifying glass. Of course, even without that class symbol, any student of locomotive design would instantly recognize the subject of the photograph as a Pennsylvania K4s Pacific. The Belpaire firebox, light design of Walschaert valve gear, rod design, location and style of headlight and drifting valves, trailing truck frame, and cab and tender truck design, to mention only a few of the typically Pennsylvania features, placed those beautiful locomotives unmistakably in a design class by themselves, one which would be quickly identified by an expert.

After the photograph of "a typical modern, heavy, high-speed passenger locomotive" had been introduced in evidence, it was handed to opposing counsel for study. At first it made no apparent impression on them. (Who would suspect that a group of attorneys would recognize the locomotive represented by that photograph?) But alas! Our suspense was short-lived. One of the young attorneys (he must have been a rail fan!) suddenly exclaimed, sotto voce, and pointed to the smokebox. I knew then that he had discovered the "K4s" on the builder's plate and that he must have recognized it as one of the identifying marks of the Pennsylvania's famous Pacifics.

So what? Well, it so happened that, at that time, the Pennsylvania was using the old type of driving journal compound on all heavy power, and opposing counsel tried to prove that that fact nullified our claim that our new driving journal compound "M" was the only type of grease which would successfully lubricate the driving journal bearings of heavy, high-speed locomotives. They tried to make us admit that the "5400", illustrated in the photograph which had been submitted in evidence, was a Pennsylvania locomotive. Not one of our witnesses had ever seen the bill of sale trans-

ferring ownership of that locomotive from Baldwin Locomotive Works to Pennsylvania Rail Road, or to the bank or insurance company which may have held the equipment trust certificates with which the locomotive was purchased, so how could we testify under oath that the locomotive belonged to, or was operated by, the Pennsylvania Rail Road?

One of our witnesses, a well-known consulting chemist, was called to the witness stand. Opposing counsel hammered at him unmercifully in an attempt to persuade him to testify that the "5400" was a locomotive owned and/or operated by the Pennsylvania Rail Road. He withstood the onslaught successfully. When I was on the stand later, I was subjected to the same sharp questioning, but I was not in a position to enlighten the gentlemen of the opposition regarding the ownership of the "5400."

At that point, one of our attorneys, who knew of Mr. Hankins' promise to let me ride in the cab of a K4s, said to me, "Now is the time for you to ride a K4s and study journal lubrication to find out if the old type of grease is performing satisfactorily on those locomotives. You will then be qualified to testify under oath as an expert regarding Pennsylvania lubrication practice and performance."

It was hardly necessary for him to repeat those instructions! I immediately called Mr. Hankins' office in Philadelphia and talked with Mr. Charles Atkinson, his assistant. I explained Mr. Hankins' promise to let me ride a K4s, and told him I planned to leave New York on Train No. 29, THE BROADWAY LIMITED, the following afternoon, February 5, 1931, for Chicago, and intended to return to New York on Train No. 78, THE GOLDEN ARROW, on February 6. I asked him to set up arrangements for me to ride in the cabs of the locomotives on Train No. 29 the entire distance from New York to Chicago. That was back in the days of the 20-hour schedule, and it meant riding in a locomotive cab from 3:00 PM EST on the 5th until 10:00 AM CST on the 6th, covering a distance of 908 miles. Mr. Atkinson stated that he would make the necessary arrangements, and that I could pick up the required documents at the office of Mr. Sidney Kerl, Station Master at Pennsylvania Station, New York, on the day of departure. (Figs. 44 and 45).

Promptly at 2:30 pm on the 5th, I called on Mr. Kerl, and was very courteously received. I signed the required release and was given a letter authorizing me to ride in the locomotive cabs of Train No. 29 that day from New York to Chicago. I could hardly believe that I held in my hand the key to that coveted privilege — but there it was! Mr. Kerl, who retired as Manager, Washington Terminal Company, on July 1, 1956, sent one of his assistants to escort me down to the train.

When we reached the station platform on the lower level, there, on a track lined for the westward tunnel track, stood THE BROADWAY LIMITED in all her glory, ten glistening tuscan-red cars, weighing about 810 tons. This was a luxurious all-Pullman train, with club, diner and observation cars. On the head end, Class L5 (later Class L5pdw) electric locomotive No. 3924, built at Juniata Shops in 1924, stood ready to move the train through the tunnel to Manhattan Transfer. (Fig. 46). She weighed approximately 194 tons, and was of the 2-4-4-2 type, the four pairs of 80-inch driving wheels being held in the same rigid wheelbase, but independently coupled in two groups of two pairs each. There were four single-phase Westinghouse motors, two placed near each end of the locomotive. Each pair of motors was geared to a jack-shaft, which in turn was coupled to the adjacent group of driving wheels.

At the top of the rail, near the center of the train, the elvation was 9 feet below mean high water level of the North River. From that point the track sloped downward to both the east and the west on a 0.04% grade, so the train was straddling the hump on a long vertical curve.

After meeting the enginemen and a traveling engineer, I was given a seat on the left side of the cab, and sat down to wait in tense anticipation for the moment of departure. I did not have long to wait.

Three o'clock! The signal at the end of the platform changed from red to yellow; the 3924 began to speak through her bell, proclaiming to all within earshot that she was about to start THE BROADWAY LIMITED on her 20-hour dash to Chicago; and the conductor raised his lantern in the familiar "highball."

Simultaneously, the engineer pulled the controller handle back a notch, then another notch, and, with a shudder and a grinding hum, the 3924 began to move slowly forward — THE BROADWAY LIMITED was rolling! We left the gloom of the station quickly, moved out from under the Post Office building, rolled under the 9th Avenue viaduct, crossed about 800 ft. of open space surrounded by high buildings, and entered the east portal of the tunnel under the North River. By that time we were on the 1.93% descending grade, and our speed increased rapidly as we roared through the darkness of the tunnel. About 1 mile west of the east portal of the tunnel we were

on the vertical curve at the lowest point in the tunnel, where the tops of the rails are 93 ft. below mean high water level. That would be 84 ft. below the highest point on the vertical curve back in the station.

From the low point under the deepest part of the river, we started the ascent of 8,400 ft. of 1.3% grade. The 3924 walked up that grade as if it were level track. We rolled under Bergen Hill and burst out into the bright sunshine 2.54 miles west of the east portal, crossed the bridge over the Erie and Susquehanna Railroads, and rolled at high speed across Hackensack Meadows. We stopped at Manhattan Transfer at 3:14 pm, having averaged 38.5 miles per hour over that 9-mile section.

I left the cab of the 3924 before she was cut off and moved ahead. The 5439, a K4s built by Baldwin in 1927, was quickly backed onto our track and coupled to our train, hose connections were coupled between tender and first car, and the brakes were tested. I climbed into a K4s cab for the first time, met the enginemen and a traveling fireman who rode the engine to North Philadelphia, and settled down on the left seatbox in anticipation of the thrill of a lifetime! (Fig. 47).

Four minutes elapsed during the engine and crew change. The conductor gave us the "highball" at 3:18 pm. The engineer cracked the throttle, and those 80-inch driving wheels began to roll, slowly at first, but gaining speed with every revolution as we moved through the cross-over to the westward high-speed track, crossed the Passaic River bridge, and rolled into Newark Station for a one-minute stop to pick up passengers.

The 5439 was equipped with cab signals which became operative just after we left Manhattan Transfer. Those signals gave us a continuous indication in the cab of the indication displayed by the next wayside signal in advance, so we always knew the situation in regard to track occupancy in the block ahead of us. If the indication of the next signal changed to a more restrictive indication after we entered the block, we immediately received the same indication on the cab signal. That was an outstanding safety feature, especially in bad weather.

At 3:24 PM the conductor raised his lantern and the 5439 started the train smoothly. We now had the open road ahead of us and were ready to roll on schedule. It was quite a thrill to ride the electric locomotive through the tunnel and across Hackensack Meadows, but that was mild compared with the thrill I experienced as I watched that beautiful big Pacific ease the train out of Newark Station and quickly attain a mile-a-minute speed! As I leaned out of the left cab window and watched the flashing rods, the flying "monkey motion," and those huge driving wheels rolling faster every minute, I was watching one of the most beautiful examples of mechanical motion in the world!

The riding qualities of the 5439 were remarkably smooth and steady at all speeds. There was a noticeable absence of rolling and nosing, and no longitudinal or vertical oscillations due to unbalanced forces in the driving mechanism. Evidently those locomotives were very carefully and accurately counterbalanced. The smooth riding was also due to a large extent to the 152-lb. rails and nearly 2 ft. of rock ballast under the ties, and to accurate lining and surfacing of the rails. That was truly the Standard Railroad of the World!

As we glided smoothly and swiftly around a long radius curve a few miles east of New Brunswick, we could see the rear end of a west-bound freight train running ahead of us on the 'slow-speed' track. That train was running about 60 miles per hour. We trailed it for several miles, but did not overtake it until it reduced speed for the bridge and station at New Brunswick. Our speed was also reduced to 45 miles per hour at that point, but we passed the freight train there because of our faster acceleration.

About 10 miles east of Trenton we were about 4 minutes behind schedule, and the engineer pulled the throttle lever back to the end of the quadrant. The big K4s really leaped ahead and was soon running 85 miles per hour, still remarkably smooth and steady. It was really thrilling to be in the cab of that big Pacific at that speed. Her performance was superb, and the engineer handled her with great skill, apparently enjoying coaxing this burst of speed and power out of her as much as I was enjoying watching her performance. Her exhaust was almost a constant roar, and her rods and valve gear looked like a blurred frenzy of glistening steel. We were covering each mile in 42 seconds, and the 80-inch driving wheels were turning 357 revolutions per minute. The piston speed was 1,666 ft. per minute, and, with 205 lbs. per sq. in. on the steam gauge, her 27-inch by 28-inch cylinders were developing about 8,320 lbs. drawbar pull and about 1,888 drawbar horsepower, according to Test Plant data. Her maximum output on the Altoona Locomotive Test Plant had been 3,016 drawbar horsepower at 47.3 miles per hour and 65% cutoff. K4s No. 5399, after being rebuilt in 1939 with Franklin oscillating cam poppet valve gear, produced a maximum of 4,267 indicated horsepower on the Test Plant at 75 miles per

hour, and 4,099 indicated horsepower at 100 miles per hour. Those figures reflect the remarkable capabilities of the K4s.

We passed Trenton 2 minutes late without reducing speed, and were on time at Bristol and HJ Tower, which we passed at 4:30 PM. We stopped at North Philadelphia at 4:38 PM to pick up passengers. Our average speed from Newark to North Philadelphia, start to stop, was 60.8 miles per hour.

As soon as we stopped, I hit the platform just as the station-master walked up to the engine to ask me if everything was all right, and if he could do anything for me. I thanked him and told him that everything was wonderful—that a ride in a K4s cab had put me up on Cloud 9! While we were talking, I snapped a picture of the 5439 and her crew. (Fig. 48). At the same time, a waiter from the dining car brought me a sliced chicken sandwich and a thermos bottle full of hot coffee—a life-saving act of courtesy if I ever saw one, because there would be no opportunity to get anything to eat at any station during the trip—the stops would be too short. My next full meal would be about noon next day after completion of the trip. It was just such courtesies at North Philadelphia and other stops which gave me a very high regard for Pennsylvania personnel.

Leaving North Philadelphia on time at 4:40 PM, we crossed the Schuylkill River and started the 9-mile climb to Bryn Mawr. The fireman had been running a few years, but had just been set back to firing, and that was his first trip with a scoop. He was a man about 55 years of age and of slight build. He worked hard, but the 5439 was also working very hard to lift the train up the hill at about 35 miles per hour. She did not get enough fuel to maintain 205 lbs. steam pressure on the gauge. The needle dropped back to 140 lbs. This condition lasted only a few minutes — not long enough for the brakes to leak on — and there was no serious delay. We soon tipped over the top at Bryn Mawr and started the long, easy descent on a beautiful stretch of 4-track line. The fireman soon had the needle back on 205 again and had no more difficulty keeping it there, as this engine was a very free steamer. It really took muscle and stamina to keep those engines hot, as I found out later. Our speed increased quickly to 85 miles per hour, which was maintained most of the way to Harrisburg.

There was considerably more curvature on that section of the line, but the 5439 took the curves with remarkable smoothness at all speeds. There was a marked absence of lurching of the engine as she entered the curves. Due to the speed and smoothness of operation, that was the most thrilling part of the entire trip. After we started down hill from Bryn Mawr, Mr. Lighty, the engineer, invited me to sit on the right seatbox in front of him until we approached Harrisburg, and I indulged in a thrilling dream — I was running that beautiful machine! (They cannot shoot you for dreaming, you know.) The setting sun made the tops of the rails of the four tracks shine like eight twisting streaks of gold ahead of us as they curved to the right or left, with tangents of varying lengths connecting the curves. I know of no experience equal to a ride in the cab of one of those superb locomotives under the conditions existing during that trip. It was unforgettable.

We passed Paoli, Malvern, Coatesville (where the famous Jacobs-Shupert sectional firebox was tested to destruction by Dr. W. F. M. Goss in 1912), Lancaster and Middletown like a freight train passes a tramp, with hardly a slow-down for those and smaller towns. All trains were very careful to clear the time of Train No. 29 — to delay that train would be unpardonable — and all signals governing our movement were clear. We stopped at Harrisburg at 6:44 PM, having averaged 53.2 miles per hour from North Philadelphia.

As soon as we stopped, I slid down the handrail and had time to feel the ends of the driving axles on both sides of the engine before the 5439 was cut off. All were cool, which indicated very good lubrication, considering the high speed at which the engine had been operating. Class K4s locomotive No. 5417, another one of the 1927 Baldwin group, was then coupled to the train, and I "mounted to the cabin with my permit in my hand." (Shades of Casey Jones! What would the immortal Casey have thought of the K4s locomotives? He would have loved them — as I did, and he would have made some marvelous runs with them.) (Fig. 49).

Leaving Harrisburg at 6:55 pm, we started the 131-mile climb to Altoona on an undulating profile, with the grade predominantly ascending for westward trains. That was the run on which the 5075, Class E6 non-superheated prototype of the superb Class E6s Atlantic type locomotive of the Pennsylvania, produced outstanding performance during her preliminary road trials on the Middle Division in 1911. She made up lost time while hauling Train No. 29, THE PENNSYLVANIA SPECIAL, (renamed THE BROADWAY LIMITED on November 24, 1912), on a run from Harrisburg to Altoona with eight all-steel Pullman cars weighing about 600 tons. That was claimed to be a record on that division at that time. (Figs. 50 and 51).

At Rockville, about five miles out, we crossed the 4-track stone arch bridge over the Susquehanna River, the longest and widest stone arch bridge in the world. It is 3,820 ft. long, 52 ft. wide, and has 48 spans, each 70 ft. long. Just beyond the bridge, we climbed a short 0.8% grade and tipped over the top near Marysville. After a short dash downhill, we started the long climb on generally ascending grades where there was little opportunity for speeds above 60 miles per hour. It was mostly hard work, and, under skillful handling by the engineer and expert firing, the 5417 did a beautiful job throughout the run. The line follows the valley of the Juniata River for nearly 100 miles, crossing and recrossing it several times, and then follows the Little Juniata River for several miles. We were in curves most of the time. So far the grade had not exceeded 0.39% ascending westward, but about 4 miles west of Warrior Ridge it increased to 0.47% for a 9-mile climb, near the middle of which we roared through Spruce Creek Tunnel. As we approached Tyrone, the grade increased to 0.51% for about 10 miles. The last 5 miles into Altoona were on a 1.0% ascending grade, and the 5417 really talked to us with some beautiful stack music during that climb! We stopped at Altoona at 9:36 PM, having lifted the train non-stop from about 315 ft. elevation at Harrisburg to about 1,170 ft. elevation at Altoona in 131 miles, at an average speed of 48.8 miles per hour. The dining car was cut out at Altoona.

I dropped down to inspect the bearings and found them barely warm after the grueling grind. Class K4s locomotive No. 7116, built at Juniata Shops in July, 1918, was coupled on the head end to double-head up "the hill" to Gallitzin. I decided to ride up "the hill" in her cab. Believe me, I was very glad to have a few minutes for rest and relaxation before we started the climb. (Fig. 52).

We left Altoona at 9:51 PM, 1 minute late, and headed west for the mountain. The line soon began to rise to the ascent of the 1.8% grade, climbing by a succession of heavy grades and sharp curves, which testify to the skill of the engineers who laid out the route. After passing up the side of a hill for about 6 miles, the valley separates, forming two chasms, each of which was scaled by means of a very heavy fill, forming, together with the connecting sweep, the celebrated Horseshoe Curve. By this means the summit was reached at Gallitzin, where a tunnel 3,612 ft. long pierces the mountain at an elevation of 2,161 ft., at the western end of the bore. (Figs. 53 and 54).

As we stormed up the 1.8% grade, I leaned out of the left cab window to listen to the sharp rythmic exhaust of both locomotives as they blasted the cold night air — it was the sweetest music in the world! The two big Pacifics were working almost at maximum capacity — a beautiful display of power. Looking eastward down the valley from Kittaning Point, I could see the reflection of the full moon on the ice on Altoona's city water supply reservoirs — quite a sight to see from the cab of a K4s as she pounded up the grade. As we passed the helper engines, and, soon afterward, the I1s road engine on a westward freight train on the outside track, the combined exhausts from the engines on both trains was deafening. An eastward freight train and several helper engines running light down the grade helped to complete a fascinating panorama of a busy 4-track mountain railroad which has no equal anywhere in the world. That hill can be pretty busy at times with its four tracks working to capacity.

The 7116 was working beautifully, and there was no difficulty in lifting the train up the grade and around the curves except above Allegrippus, near the summit, where 7116's driving wheels slipped several times, due to "whiskers" on the rails.

At Kittaning Point, located at about the midpoint of the Horseshoe Curve, the Pennsylvania recently placed Class K4s locomotive No. 1361 in a small park beside the track on the east side as a permanent monument to that magnificent class of locomotive. (Fig. 55). No. 1361 was built at Juniata Shops in May 1918, builder's number 3475. She stands on a short length of standard track and is surrounded by a high steel fence to protect her from vandalism. It is fervently hoped that she will remain there in her present condition, in order that future generations may see an outstanding example of the steam locomotive, the machine which played a most important part in building our country from a wilderness to the great nation which it is today.

We stopped 1 minute at Gallitzin at 10:20 PM, near the east portal of the tunnel, to cut off the 7116. We had averaged 24.8 miles per hour up the 12-mile grade, and had lifted the train a little over 1,000 ft. in that distance. I had just time enough to slide down the handrail and run back to climb into the cab of the 5417. It was pretty cold when I left the 7116's cab, but the exhaust steam and gas filled the tunnel, and we were pretty well cooked and gassed before we rolled through that 3,612-ft. tunnel at slow speed. Riding in the cab of a steam locomotive through a tunnel with the throttle open is not very pleasant, but I have survived many such trips.

West of the tunnel, the grade was about 1.0% descending, and we drifted downhill at fairly high speed, alternately working steam and drifting, through Johnstown and other cities, and finally drifted into the yards at Pittsburgh. Just before we reached the station, we were stopped by a red signal behind a preceding train, but the signal cleared immediately and we proceeded to the station, stopping there at 12:35 AM. All driving journals on the 5417 were cool. We had averaged 45.2 miles per hour from Gallitzin to Pittsburgh. The 5417 was cut off and Class K4s No. 5373 was coupled to the train. She was one of a group of 50 Class K4s locomotives built at Juniata Shops in 1924. (Fig. 56).

Leaving Pittsburgh at 12:45 AM, we crossed the Allegheny River and ran at medium speed for several miles through the crowded industrial district along the north bank of the Ohio River. The steel mill furnaces were casting a brilliant glow into the darkened sky, and the constantly changing scene was fascinating. After climbing the grade above Beaver Falls, we ran at high speed over most of the distance to Alliance, where we stopped at 2:38 AM. We took water while a dining car was being cut into the train. That was the only point at which we took water from a roadside tank. At all other points, water was picked up on the run from track pans after reducing speed to 45 miles per hour, thus avoiding water stops. All driving journals were cold at Alliance. We had averaged 44.1 miles per hour from Pittsburgh to Alliance.

Leaving Alliance at 2:50 AM, the 5373 accelerated the train rapidly and ran at better than 60 miles per hour over most of the distance to Crestline, as there were no severe grades on that portion of the run. We stopped at Crestline at 5:11 AM, having averaged 45.1 miles per hour from Alliance to Crestline. All journals on the 5373 were cold. She was cut off, and the 3878 was coupled to the train. She was one of a group of 57 Class K4s locomotives built at Juniata Shops in 1923. (Fig. 57).

We left Crestline at 5:18 AM EST, 6 minutes late, but by "beating the stack off the old girl," the engineer soon whipped her up to over 70 miles per hour. We covered the 30 miles from Crestline to Upper Sandusky, start to pass, in 30 minutes flat. That was an excellent example of the fast acceleration and speed available in those high-wheeled Pacifics, and the 3878 really showed us her capabilities in beautiful style. She appeared to be the smoothest running and easiest riding engine of the five used on that trip. She was worked at about 25% cut-off and full throttle, and rode with remarkable steadiness. There was no pounding in her rods or driving boxes, and the entire machine appeared to be in almost perfect adjustment.

Obviously, I was rather tired and sleepy by that time. The smooth steady working of the engine lulled me to sleep several times for very brief periods. I actually lost consciousness for a few seconds at at time, sitting upright on the left seat-box, which I occupied alone most of the time, since the fireman was on the deck, bailing the "real estate" into the firebox. Those brief moments of relaxation revived me, and I was able to stay alert during the remainder of the trip.

All track previously covered had been in excellent condition, but the track from Crestline to Chicago appeared to be especially smooth. The 3878 rode as steady as a Pullman car. Since we were on schedule, the speed was somewhat reduced after we left Upper Sandusky, and there was no further opportunity for the 3878 to show what she could do at high speed, as the 5439 had done east of Harrisburg. We stopped at the Fort Wayne coaling station at 6:30 AM CST for fuel. All journals were cold. We left that point at 6:31 AM and stopped at Fort Wayne Station at 6:35 AM for passengers and to change crews. We had averaged 58.2 miles per hour from Crestline to Fort Wayne.

Leaving Fort Wayne at 6:45 AM, we were just getting under way when the train signal whistle in the cab sounded twice. We stopped at 6:47 AM with the rear end of the train near the west end of the station platform. We soon received a 'high-ball' from the rear end and started moving again at 6:50 AM. I was told later that the conductor had been left behind when we first left the station. Evidently the flagman saw him running out of the station and pulled the signal cord to stop us. (Fine way to tie up THE BROADWAY, eh?)

We were now on the "racetrack" of the Lines West, but we were on time and the schedule did not call for any fast running, so the 3878 did not have an opportunity to show us what she could really do. (Fig. 58). A couple of miles out of Fort Wayne brought us to a 0.51% ascending grade about 5 miles long. A few miles further west we climbed about 10 miles of 0.38% ascending grade, but from the summit at Larwill the grade was generally descending, with only short stretches of 0.4% or less ascending grades against westward traffic, so the 3878 just rolled smoothly along, working at short cut-off and light throttle most of the time. There was not sufficient force to the exhaust to lift the smoke, so one side or the other of the cab was smothered in trailing smoke and steam a good bit of the time. That was not too good when you were trying to watch the track and signals ahead. (That was not cab signal territory at that time.)

The condition was made worse by the cold, damp and practically stationary early morning atmosphere.

A few miles out of Englewood, I took the scoop and fired the 3878 about 5 miles. That white-hot firebox, 80 inches wide and 126 inches long, with its 70 sq. ft. of grate area, looked awfully big, and it took all of my strength to throw the coal to the front corners. I had done most of my firing on oil-burning locomotives on the Southern Pacific Lines in Texas and Louisiana prior to 1920. They say that is a job for a strong mind and a weak back, while hand-firing a coal-burning locomotive is a job for a weak mind and a strong back! (No offense to the coal-burner fireman intended, of course!) Since I had had no sleep for 24 hours, (except brief cat-naps in the cab), and no food for 12 hours, my mind may have been a bit weak and my back was certainly not very strong at that stage of the game, and I could not last at that job more than about 5 miles. So I surrendered the scoop to the fireman as we approached Englewood. At least I can say that I fired a K4s Pacific hauling THE BROADWAY LIMITED, and that is a rare privilege enjoyed by few men except the regular engine crews assigned to that run! We stopped at Englewood at 9:28 AM to discharge passengers. We had averaged 53.5 miles per hour from Fort Wayne to Englewood.

Leaving Englewood at 9:35 AM, we dropped down about 3 miles of 0.8% grade and threaded our way slowly and smoothly through the maze of tracks in the approach to Chicago Union Station. We rolled smoothly to a final stop in the station at 9:51 AM, 9 minutes ahead of the scheduled arrival time. That was a memorable moment to me—THE BROADWAY LIMITED had successfully completed her 20-hour run from New York to Chicago—and I had realized my ambition to ride in the cabs of five Class K4s Pacific type steam locomotives the entire distance, except for the first 9 miles in the cab of an electric locomotive. It was a marvelous experience, the memory of which will remain with me as long as I live.

As soon as we stopped, I slid down the hand-rail to the platform to inspect the bearings. They were cool. Just then a gentleman walked up to me and, apparently thinking I was one of the enginemen, asked, "Did you have a visitor on the engine with you on this trip?" I answered, "I am the visitor, at least what is left of him, after 20 hours in the engine cab." He introduced himself as a representative of the General Manager, Lines West, and invited me to accompany him to that official's office to give them my impression of the trip. I asked for time to shed my overalls and dig the cinders out of my eyes and ears. He very kindly showed me to the very fine marble showers in the station, where a hot shower and fresh clothes revived me considerably.

I then called on Mr. J. A. Appleton, General Manager, Lines West, (later Brigadier General, U. S. Army Transportation Corps, during World War II), who was very much interested in my comments on the trip. When I mentioned that I thought the 3878 gave a better over-all performance than the other locomotives assigned to that run, he took me to see Mr. J. A. Sheedy, Superintendent Motive Power, Lines West. Mr. Sheedy was particularly pleased by my comments on the performance of the 3878, one of his locomotives. They arranged for a room for me on Train No. 78, THE GOLDEN ARROW, that afternoon, and, later, escorted me to the Pullman, instructing the conductor and train secretary to see to it that I was made comfortable during the trip back to New York. Shortly after leaving Chicago, I was served dinner in my room, after which I turned in and slept soundly until after we passed North Philadelphia next morning. I really needed that sleep!

Nine days later, on February 15, The Pennsylvania News, published by the Lines West, devoted a full column on the front page to an account of my trip, stating that I had "probably won the distinction of being the only man to make the entire, continuous 908-mile trip between Manhattan and the Windy City in an engine cab. Pennsylvania officers at Chicago were unable to recall a previous case in which it was necessary or desirable for anyone to undertake a similar trip."

Reviewing the entire trip, it was my impression that the performance of the K4s locomotives used on that run was outstanding in every respect. Those locomotives demonstrated very effectively their capacity for smooth starting, rapid acceleration, sustained high speed, and exceptionally steady riding qualities at all speeds on both tangent and curved track. They were expertly operated by the enginemen and firemen. The air brakes were expertly operated by the enginemen to cause smooth braking for station stops, and to control speed on descending grades. I think it was one of the finest examples of locomotive operation and train control I had ever observed. Having ridden in locomotive cabs all over this country, and having run locomotives myself in this and nine other countries, I have had some wonderful opportunities to observe many different types of locomotives in operation. In my opinion, those K4s Pacifics topped them all.

In addition, I received the most courteous treatment from all officials and employees of the Pennsylvania Rail Road with whom I came in contact during the trip, all of which made it one of the pleasantest and most instructive experiences of the kind I have ever had.

The Pennsylvania's Class K4s Pacific type steam locomotive was a brilliant example of the Age of Steam at its zenith. Its passing from the American scene leaves an aching void in the hearts of all who knew and loved that beautiful locomotive. I consider myself most fortunate to have been privileged to spend a few brief but wonderful hours in their cabs, learning to know them intimately as they performed their mission in a superb manner. I shall be forever grateful to Mr. Hankins for making it possible for me to have that wonderful experience!

According to shop officials, the Pennsylvania had experienced considerable difficulty due to the failure of the "cold-set" grease under the driving journals of heavy power. By setting up rigid maintenance standards and shop practice, and by rigid inspection and frequent changing of the grease in the driving journal lubricators, the trouble was considerably reduced, but servicing costs were increased. In addition, certain operating conditions were also conductive to the satisfactory driving journal lubrication which I observed on several trips on their locomotives.

It may be of interest to note here that the patent specification for the new dehydrated "M" grease contained a calculated analysis showing 4.76% glycerin in the finished product. The defendant proved that he was not making the grease of the patent, because his grease contained only a trace of glycerin. It was brought out that the "M" grease also contained only a trace of glycerin. It appeared that the glycerin had been evaporated and lost during the cooking process. On the basis of this technicality, the court handed down a decision in favor of the defendant.

SOME HEAVY PACIFICS

Railroad	Class	Builder	Date Built	Weight on Drivers	Notes
C&O	F-19	American	1926	200,000#	
B&O	P-7	Baldwin	1927	201,000#	
PRR	K4s	Baldwin	1927	201,830#	Hand-fired
LV	K-5½	Baldwin	1918	204,560#	
CRRofNJ	G-4s	Baldwin	1930	205,900#	
C&O	F-20	Baldwin	1927	208,000#	
PRR	K4s	Baldwin	1927	209,300#	Stoker-fired
PRR	K5	Baldwin	1929	209,410#	Experimental
B&M	P-4a	Lima	1937	209,500#	
B&M	P-4b	Lima	1937	209,800#	
CStPM&O	E-3	American	1930	210,000#	
PRR	K4s	Juniata	1920	223,000#	Streamlined

Later, numerous Hudson type locomotives carried from 201,800# to 219,500# on six-coupled drivers.

Fig. 35. No. 900. United States Railroad Administration. Built for Virginian Railway but delivered instead (with 4 others) to Norfolk and Western Railway as No. 2000 (2000-2004). Builder's Nos. 59853-59857. Built in 1919 by American Locomotive Co., Schenectady Works. They were the heavy USRA 2-8-8-2 type Mallet articulated compound locomotives, of which 106 were built during 1919. Fifty were delivered to Norfolk and Western Railway during 1919 as Class Y-3, Nos. 2000-2049. The first extensive road tests of Texaco Driving Journal Compound "M" were conducted by the author on No. 2038 between Roanoke and Crewe, beginning in June 1923.

H. L. Broadbelt Collection.

Fig. 36. No. 2056. Norfolk and Western Railway. Class Y-3a 2-8-8-2 Type. Built by American Locomotive Co., Richmond Works, 1923. These were practically duplicates of the Class Y-3 locomotives built in 1919.

Harry Beichert Photo.

Fig. 37. No. 132. Norfolk and Western Railway. Class K-2a 4-8-2 Type. Built by Baldwin Locomotive Works at Eddystone, 1923. Design based on heavy USRA 4-8-2 type locomotives, 10 of which were built for Norfolk and Western Ry. by American Locomotive Co., Brooks Works, May 1919. These locomotives were used in the initial road tests of Texaco Driving Journal Compound "M" in 1923, with great success.

H. L. Broadbelt Collection.

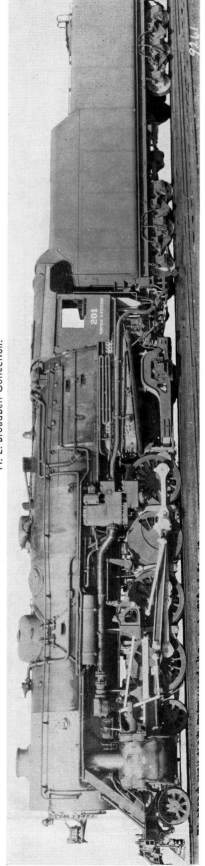

Fig. 38. No. 201. Norfolk and Western Railway. Class K-3 4-8-2 Type. Designed and built at Roanoke Shops by Norfolk and Western Ry., 1926. Operated in time freight service between Roanoke and Norfolk. Overheated driving journal bearings were the cause of many delays and much expense with these locomotives, but the use of Texaco Driving Journal Compound "M" resulted in a great improvement.

Howard G. Hill Collection.

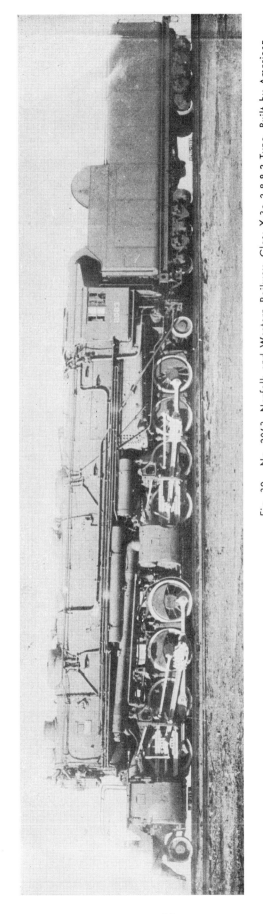

Fig. 39. No. 2063. Norfolk and Western Railway. Class Y-3a 2-8-8-2 Type. Built by American Locomotive Co., Richmond Works, April 1923. Several of this group were out of service in July 1923 with damaged driving journal bearings, due to lubrication failures. The use of "M" grease on the damaged bearings permitted their return to regular service without dropping the wheels for repairs.

Howard G. Hill Collection.

Fig. 40. The late Frederick W. Hankins, who was appointed Chief of Motive Power, Pennsylvania Rail Road System, on March 1, 1927. He authorized my trips in the K4s locomotive cabs.

RAILWAY AGE.

Fig. 41. No. 5400. Pennsylvania Rail Road. Class K-4s 4-6-2 Type. One of 75 Class K-4s locomotives built by Baldwin Locomotive Works at Eddystone, January 1927. Builder's No. 59761.

Pennsylvania Rail Road.

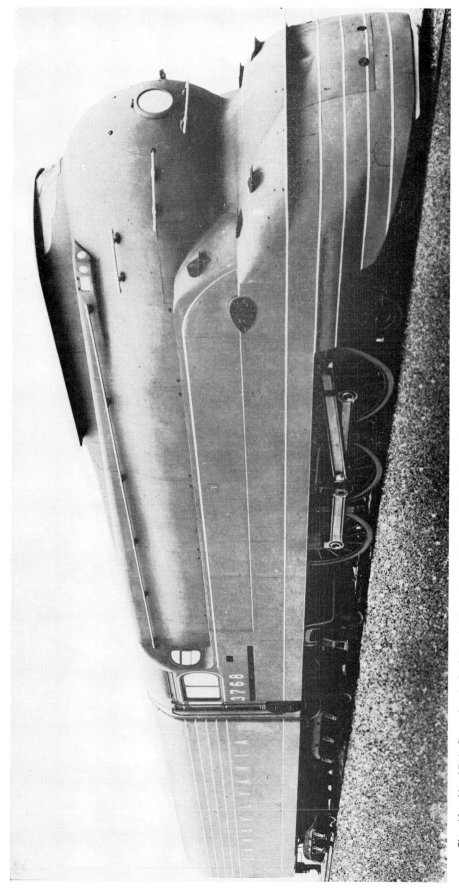

Fig. 42. No. 3768. Pennsylvania Rail Road. Class K4s 4-6-2 Type. Built by Pennsylvania R. R. at Juniata Shops, May 1920. Builder's No. 3721. Streamlined in 1936, with weight on driving wheels increased from 201,830 lbs to 223,000 lbs. The streamlining was later removed.

H. L. Broadbelt Collection.

Fig. 43. No. 5400. "A TYPICAL MODERN HEAVY HIGH-SPEED PASSENGER LOCOMOTIVE."
This photograph was the cause of extended arguments at the trial, and resulted in my
trips in the Class K4s locomotive cabs.

H. L. Broadbelt Collection.

Fig. 44. "Penn Station," New York City passenger terminal of Pennsylvania Rail Road. A classic example of railroad architecture. Torn down in 1968-69 and replaced by a modern office building and a huge sports arena. The underground trackage arrangement, somewhat modernized and rearranged, with new passenger facilities, still serves the Penn Central and Long Island passenger traffic.

Pennsylvania Rail Road.

Fig. 45. Passenger Concourse, above track level, Pennsylvania Station, New York City.
RAILWAY GAZETTE, London

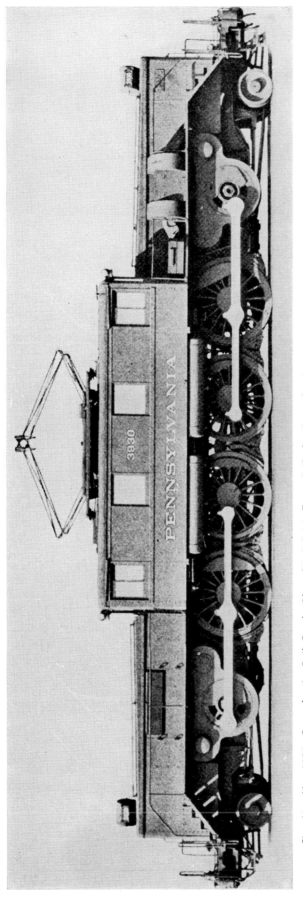

Fig. 46. No. 3930. Pennsylvania Rail Road. Class L5 2-4-4-2 Type. Built by Pennsylvania R. R. at Juniata Shops, 1924. This locomotive was used in freight service in the Philadelphia area. The 3924, Class L5a, in whose cab I rode on February 5, 1931, was geared for passenger service through the North River Tunnels between New York City and Manhattan Transfer, N. J., 9 miles.

BALDWIN LOCOMOTIVES.

Fig. 47. No. 5439. Pennsylvania Rail Road. Class K4s 4-6-2 Type. Built by Baldwin Locomotive Works at Eddystone, 1927. I rode in the cab of this locomotive from Manhattan Transfer, N. J., to Harrisburg, Pa., 186 miles, on Train No. 29, THE BROADWAY LIMITED, February 5, 1931.

Clarence R. Weaver Photo.

Fig. 48. No. 5439. Pennsylvania Rail Road. Class K4s 4-6-2 Type. Standing at North Philadelphia Station with THE BROADWAY LIMITED on February 5, 1931. Left to right— Fireman Pratt in gangway, a Traveling Fireman, and Engineer Lighty next to engine.
Howard G. Hill Photo.

Fig. 49.   No. 5417. Pennsylvania Rail Road. Class K4s 4-6-2 Type. Built by Baldwin Locomotive Works, Eddystone, 1927. I rode in her cab from Harrisburg to Pittsburgh, 220 miles, (except 12 miles in the cab of Class K4s helper No. 7116 from Altoona to Gallitzin), on February 5-6, 1931, hauling THE BROADWAY LIMITED.   Clarence R. Weaver Photo.

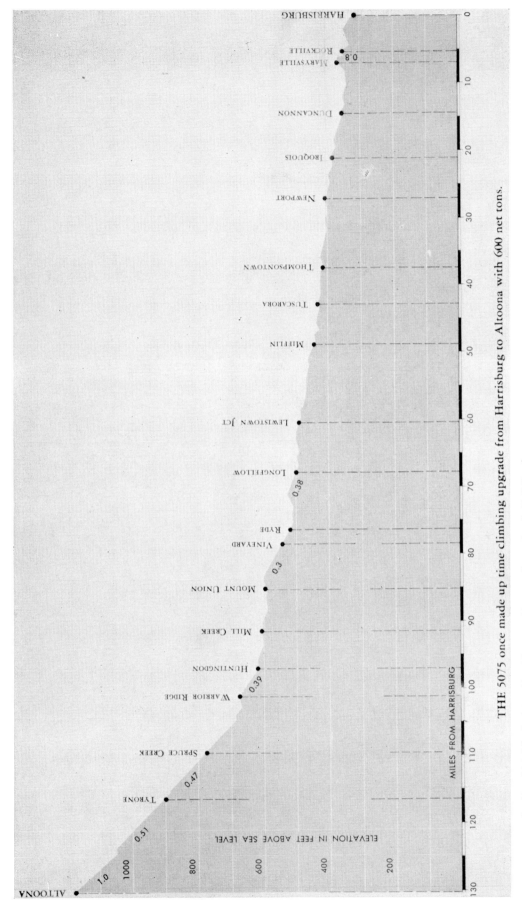

THE 5075 once made up time climbing upgrade from Harrisburg to Altoona with 600 net tons.

Fig. 50. Profile of Middle Division, Harrisburg to Altoona. Pennsylvania Rail Road.
From "Apex of the Atlantics."
Frederick Westing, 1963.
Kalmbach Publishing Co.
Copyright 1963.

Fig. 51. No. 5075. Pennsylvania Rail Road. Class E6 non-superheated 4-4-2 Type. Built by Pennsylvania R. R. at Juniata Shops, December 1910. Builder's No. 2159. This locomotive produced outstanding performance on the Middle Division between Harrisburg and Altoona. When superheated later, and renumbered 1067, she became the prototype of the famous Class E6s Atlantics, of which 80 were built in 1914.

Frederick Westing Collection.

Fig. 52. No. 7116. Pennsylvania Rail Road. Class K4s 4-6-2 Type. One of 110 Class K4s locomotives built by Pennsylvania R. R., Juniata Shops, 1918. Builder's No. 3512. This was the helper locomotive in whose cab I rode on Train No. 29, THE BROADWAY LIMITED, from Altoona to Gallitzin, 12 miles, February 5, 1931.

Lt. Col. T. M. Flattley, Jr., Photo.

Fig. 53. A scene on the famous Horseshoe Curve, Pennsylvania Rail Road, in 1870, when it was a 2-track railroad.

BALDWIN LOCOMOTIVES.

Fig. 54. A modern view of Horseshoe Curve in 1924, showing the 4 tracks, with Train No. 2, THE PENNSYLVANIA LIMITED, descending eastbound, with 2 Class K4s locomotives on the point.

C. B. Chaney Photo.
BALDWIN LOCOMOTIVES

Fig. 55. No. 1361. Pennsylvania Rail Road. Class K4s 4-6-2 Type. Built by Pennsylvania R. R. at Juniata Shops, May 1918. Builder's No. 3475. This locomotive has been placed on exhibition at Kittaning Point, near the mid-point of Horseshoe Curve, as a permanent monument to this famous class of locomotives.

Richard J. Dent Collection.

Fig. 56. No. 5373. Pennsylvania Rail Road. Class K4s 4-6-2 Type. Built by Pennsylvania R. R. at Juniata Shops, 1924. Builder's No. 3897. I rode in the cab of this locomotive from Pittsburgh, Pa. to Crestline, Ohio, 189 miles, on February 6, 1931, hauling THE BROADWAY LIMITED, Train No. 29.

Lt. Col. T. M. Flattley, Jr., Photo

Fig. 57. No. 3878. Pennsylvania Rail Road. Class K4s 4-6-2 Type. Built by Pennsylvania R. R. at Juniata Shops, 1923. Builder's No. 3774. I rode in the cab of this locomotive from Crestline, Ohio, to Chicago, Illinois, 280 miles, on February 6, 1931, the last lap of the February 5-6, 1931, run of Train No. 29, THE BROADWAY LIMITED, from New York to Chicago, 908 miles in 20 hours.

Lt. Col. T. M. Flattley, Jr., Photo

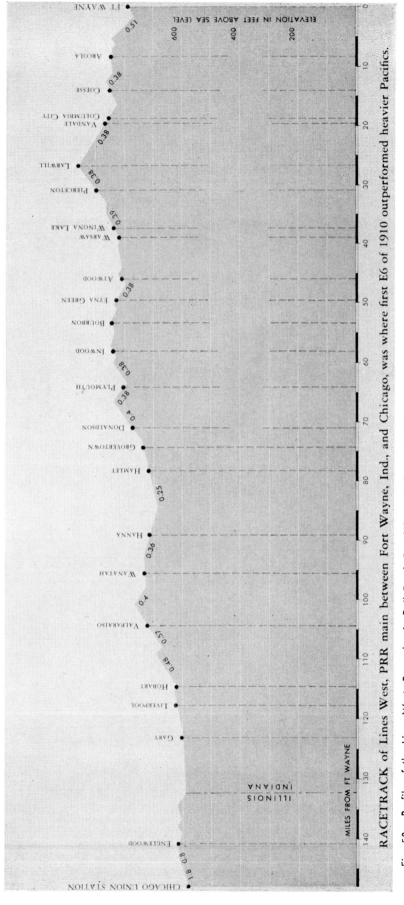

Fig. 58. Profile of the Lines West, Pennsylvania Rail Road, Fort Wayne, Indiana, to Chicago, Illinois, where some fast running has been performed by both the Atlantic and Pacific types of locomotives.

From "Apex of the Atlantics."
By Frederick Westing, 1963.
Kalmbach Publishing Co.
Copyright 1963.

CHAPTER 5
THE DEVELOPMENT OF
STEAM PASSENGER MOTIVE POWER
ON THE NEW YORK CENTRAL LINES*

By 1875, Commodore Cornelius Vanderbilt had welded the Hudson River Rail Road, the New York Central Rail Road, and the Lake Shore & Michigan Southern Railway into a through line from New York to Chicago, all under his control. He had improved those properties, and they were making money by moving many passengers and much tonnage. After his death in January, 1897, his son, William H. Vanderbilt, succeeded him as the guiding genius of the expanding system.

Early in 1875, plans were under way for a fast mail train to be operated by the Pennsylvania Rail Road and its affiliated lines between New York and Chicago. Not to be outdone by a rival, the New York Central decided to inaugurate a competitive service. In order to determine the feasibility of a high-speed through train, a special 3-car train was operated from New York to Chicago in 28 hours 30 minutes, leaving New York at 2:30 AM on Sunday, July 4, 1875, and arriving at Chicago at 8:00 AM on Monday. A special train was run on that schedule on each of the eight following Sundays. (Fig. 59).

The successful performance of those special trains was followed by the establishment of the most outstanding express train ever attempted by any American railroad up to that time. That train was known as THE FAST MAIL, and it was the result of the cooperative efforts of the New York Central and Lake Shore railroads and the United States Post Office Department. Daily operation of that train in both directions commenced on September 14, 1875, with four specially constructed and equipped mail cars which made it possible to sort mail en route. Those cars were painted white, with buff striping. Lettering and trimming were in gold. Streaking along at 75 miles per hour in some places, that train must have been a spectacular sight! Known initially as THE NEW YORK CENTRAL AND LAKE SHORE

RAILROAD POST OFFICE (later abbreviated to FAST MAIL), that train made the run to Chicago in 27 hours 12 minutes, and thus established the first regular, fast, through service between New York and Chicago. A similar eastbound schedule was set up at the same time. (Fig. 60).

A similar train was started by the Pennsylvania on September 24, 1875. There was keen competition between those two railroads and their two fast mail trains. Those trains were operated about ten months, when, as a result of dissatisfaction on the part of the railroads with the unsatisfactory compensation paid for that service by the Post Office Department, both trains were discontinued on July 22, 1876.

On Monday, October 31, 1881, the New York Central inaugurated a new LIMITED passenger train which provided luxury service between New York and Chicago on a fast schedule of 26 hours 40 minutes. That train averaged 40 miles per hour on the NYC and 35 miles per hour on the LS&MS. Because of the luxury service provided by that train, its popularity increased rapidly, and the train was continued in service.

On May 28, 1893, THE EXPOSITION FLYER was inaugurated to provide a de luxe service to and from Chicago to serve the World's Columbian Exposition. That train was operated on a 20-hour schedule between New York and Chicago, and was immensely popular. It was withdrawn on November 19, 1893, because it was not believed that there would be sufficient traffic to justify its continued operation, partly as a result of the panic of 1893. (Fig. 61).

During the early '90's, the New York Central was operating several fast trains between New York and Chicago, among them THE CHICAGO LIMITED, via NYC-LS&MS; THE WORLD'S FAIR SPECIAL (or EXPOSITION FLYER,

*(See Appendix for Specifications of All Locomotives Illustrated).

already mentioned), via NYC-LS&MS; and THE NORTH SHORE LIMITED, via NYC-MC. Those trains, and others which followed within a few years, became immensely popular with the traveling public, and they set the standard for reliability and luxury travel which was followed closely by other railroads. (Fig. 62 and 63).

The ultimate in luxurious travel and reliability of service was established on June 15, 1902, when the New York Central added Trains 25 and 26, THE TWENTIETH CENTURY, to the time card. The name was changed to THE TWENTIETH CENTURY LIMITED five days later, on June 20, and that was the name under which it was operated daily, almost continuously, until it made its last run on December 2, 1967, after 65 years of outstanding service and performance. (Fig. 64).

The initial consist of THE TWENTIETH CENTURY LIMITED was four luxurious Pullman cars, and the number of cars was gradually increased as the traffic demanded. The original cars were of wooden construction, with elaborate finish and furnishings inside, and decorated with gold lettering and striping outside. A decidedly modern touch was added in 1910, when all-steel cars were substituted for the wooden cars. The interior finish of the new cars was much less ornate than that of the old cars, but a dignified atmosphere was maintained in spite of the lack of elaborate decoration. In 1938, the open section Pullmans gave way to the all-room cars of streamlined design, and those cars gave passengers the ultimate in comfort and privacy.

The early limited trains were moved behind 4-4-0 type locomotives similar to No. 567 (Fig. 59) between New York and Buffalo. Between Buffalo and Chicago, 4-4-0 type locomotives similar to No. 317 (Fig. 60) and No. 160 (Fig. 61), and 4-6-0 type locomotives similar to No. 107 (Fig. 66), provided the power.

The first run of Train No. 25, THE TWENTIETH CENTURY, behind No. 2960, a Class I Atlantic (4-4-2) type locomotive, departed on June 15, 1902, from Track 20 of the old Grand Central Depot at 42nd Street and Park Avenue in New York City. Train No. 26, the opposite run, started from La Salle Street Depot in Chicago on the same date. The 2900-series Atlantics were assigned to Trains 25 and 26 between New York and Buffalo, and they powered those runs until the Pacifics arrived about five years later. (Fig. 65).

Locomotives of Class J-40 Prairie (2-6-2) type, and Classes F-51 and F-52 Ten Wheel (4-6-0) type, powered THE CENTURY between Buffalo and Chicago. The Prairies and Ten Wheelers had driving wheels 80 inches in diameter. The Atlantics, Prairies and heavy Ten Wheelers handled THE CENTURY until the appearance of the Pacific (4-6-2) type locomotives on the NYC&HR and LS&MS in 1907. (Figs. 67, 68, 69 and 70).

In 1903, 15 light Pacific type locomotives of Classes K and K-1 were built for the NYC&HR RR, but they were assigned to the Boston & Albany and were not operated on the main line of the NYC&HR RR. Thus, they did not handle the CENTURY on the main line. (Fig. 71.)

From 1904 to 1912, the Michigan Central and the Canada Southern received 70 Class K-80 Pacifics, of 14 sub-classes, from Schenectady, Brooks and Beech Grove Shops. They were operated on the Boston & Albany and the Cleveland, Cincinnati, Chicago & St. Louis R. R. (Big Four). (Fig. 72.)

The urgent need for heavier power on the New York-Chicago runs resulted in the construction by Schenectady, between 1907 and 1910, of 192 Class K-2 Pacifics, of 12 sub-classes. They were the first Pacifics to be operated on the NYC&HR-LS&MS through limited trains, and they were of somewhat greater proportions and capacity than the Pacifics then in service on other portions of the System. (Fig. 73.)

The K-2 Class was successful, and, as succeeding sub-classes were built, improvements were made in details of design and specialties, until 1911, when a locomotive of more improved proportions, capacity, and greater starting tractive effort and drawbar pull at higher speeds was built. It was designated Class K-3. 276 Class K-3 locomotives, of 17 sub-classes, were built between 1911 and 1925. During this period, minor changes in dimensions and numerous improvements were made. The application of the trailing truck booster presented one of the most desired improvements, an increase of 9,700 lbs. starting tractive effort, without exceeding the limit in axle loading for this class of locomotive. The following comparison of the K-2 and K-3 shows considerable improvement in the K-3:

	K-2a	K-3q
Cylinders, diam. & stroke, ins.	22x28	23½x28
Driving wheels, diam., ins.	79	79
Boiler pressure, psi,	200	200
Starting tractive effort, lbs.	29,160	40,610 (incl. booster)
Weight, working order, lbs.		
on front truck	46,500	44,000
on drivers	171,500	194,500
on trailing truck	48,000	57,000
total, engine	266,000	298,800

In this development from the original K-2 to the K-3q, there was an increase of 39.2% in starting tractive effort, 16% in drawbar pull at 50 miles per hour, and 14% in total weight of locomotive. During that period, one of the most important improvements in the locomotive boiler was made — the application of the superheater. The K-3 boiler had the same firebox heating surface and grate area as the K-2, with a reduction in the heating surface of the tubes and flues and an increase in the superheating surface. (Figs. 75, 76, 77 and 78).

In 1924, it became evident that a passenger locomotive of much greater starting capacity and increased horsepower output was required to meet the demand of increasingly heavier trains, with sufficient reserve power for the most severe operating conditions. Operating statistics for 1924 revealed the fact that in that year the total passenger train-miles for the New York Central Railroad, which was considered representative for the Lines, was 26% greater than that of 1919, with an increase of 33% in Pullman equipment car-miles, whereas, there was an increase of only 3½% in passenger car-miles (day coach). Those figures showed the rapid gain in service of the heavier Pullman equipment.

A Pacific heavier than the K-3 was required, of such design as would meet the constantly increasing load and schedule conditions. Class K-5 experimental locomotive was built in 1924. During 1925-1926, 35 Pacifics of the new design, known as Classes K-5a and K-5b, were placed in service on the Big Four, Michigan Central, and Pittsburgh & Lake Erie. With 25-inch by 28-inch cylinders, 79-inch drivers, and a working pressure of 200 psi, they developed a maximum starting tractive effort, with booster, of 47,300 lbs., representing an increase of 16½% in starting tractive effort, and a corresponding improvement in boiler capacity by the application of a mechanical stoker and the increased heating surface and grate area. (Fig. 79).

Because of more severe operating conditions on the Boston & Albany, the K-5 design was slightly modified with 26-inch by 28-inch cylinders and 75-inch driving wheels, resulting in a starting tractive effort, with booster, of 52,620 lbs. Ten of the K-6 Class were delivered in 1925-1926.

It soon became evident that even the heavier Pacifics did not have sufficient capacity for the operation of some of the heavier trains to which they were assigned. Train loads were constantly increasing. In 1926 it was found that passenger traffic was increasing in a greater ratio than was provided for in locomotive design. The increased tonnage of the Pullman equipment was accompanied by the use of observation and lounge cars, and the service of two diners in certain trains — all of which greatly increased train loads. New fast limited trains were added. Schedules of trains were reduced. The task of the locomotive was increasing steadily.

Prior to this progressive era, it was considered impractical to operate a locomotive over more than one division. With such practice the locomotive would be idle at a terminal up to three times longer than its actual service period. As a result of trials, the economy and increased efficiency obtainable by operating engines over three to five divisions were soon realized. Such operation required the best possible design, inspection and maintenance to meet the demands of this severe service.

Larger capacity tenders, introduced to eliminate coal and water stops on the long runs, also represented an appreciable addition to the engine load.

In 1926, an analysis of train loads and operating conditions, with due consideration for future demands, resulted in the definite conclusion that a passenger locomotive of an entirely new design must be developed. A design was required which would provide much greater starting tractive effort and increased boiler proportions to produce increased cylinder horsepower capacity, with maximum output at higher speeds, but with weight distribution so limited as to keep rail stresses and bridge loads lower than had previously been observed. The design must meet clearance limits for all parts of the Lines. Long continuous runs required improved designs of wearing parts and standardization of operation and maintenance over the entire System.

Since the K-5 Pacific presented the maximum desired limit in weight for that type, any increase in total weight required an entirely new design and wheel arrangement. After several preliminary designs were prepared, it was decided that the conditions could best be met by the 4-6-4 wheel arrangement and 79-inch diameter driving wheels. Upon completion of a general design, a complete diagram and specification, covering the major characteristics, were prepared, and an order for the construction of one sample locomotive was placed with the American Locomotive Company.

This new type of passenger locomotive was designated as the "Hudson" type, and sample engine No. 5200 was the first 4-6-4 to be built in America. The 5200 was received from the builder's plant at Schenectady, N.Y., on February 14, 1927. The actual weights of the engine were found to be satisfactory. They were: 63,500 lbs. on the front truck, 182,000 lbs. on drivers, 44,000 lbs. on the front axle and 53,500 lbs. on the rear axle, supporting the booster, of the 4-wheel trailing truck.

Official tests of the 5200 were started in March 1927, using the NYC Dynamometer Car under everyday operating conditions, hauling up to 25 main line steel passenger cars, totaling 1,696 tons. The results showed that the Hudson type locomotive exceeded the expectations of design and performance of all other System locomotives ever tested for thermal efficiency, maximum horsepower, fuel and water consumption per horsepower, and weight per horsepower. The J-1 produced 16% greater actual maximum starting tractive effort, without booster, over the K-5, 27% greater cylinder horsepower at 22% higher speed, 22% greater thermal efficiency at the drawbar than the K-5, and a decrease of 11% in total engine weight per cylinder horsepower. In actual train service, the Hudsons handled, without difficulty, 16 to 18 cars on Pullman equipment trains on any NYC schedule, including continuous runs ranging from 403 to 925 miles. (Figs. 80, 81 and 82).

The New York Central Lines' final attempt to develop a super-power steam locomotive for passenger service produced the following magnificent Niagara (4-8-4) type locomotives:

Eng. No.	Class	Date Built	Cylinders	Drivers	Weight, Eng.	Retired
6000	S-1a	2-1945	25″x32″	75″*	471,000#	1956
6001-6025	S-1a	1945-46	25½″x32″	79″	471,000#	1955-56
5500	S-2a	6-1946	25½″x32″+	79″	485,000#	1951

*Later changed to 79″. +Franklin Poppet Valves.

They were built as dual purpose locomotives, and they produced outstanding performance at the head end of the limited trains, including **THE TWENTIETH CENTURY LIMITED**. They could match or exceed the performance of any diesel-electric locomotive, and were the pinnacle of New York Central's steam power. Their only draw-back was that they were steam locomotives, and time was fast running out for steam locomotives when they were built. (Fig. 83).

Fig. 59. No. 567. New York Central & Hudson River Rail Road. (NYC). Class C-9 4-4-0 Type. Built by Schenectady Locomotive Works, 1877. Typical of the locomotives which hauled the fast passenger trains between New York and Buffalo from 1875 to about 1890, when larger power was substituted.

New York Central Lines.
W. D. Edson Collection.

THE MAIL CARRIER OF 100 YEARS AGO.

The FLIGHT of the FAST MAIL on the
LAKE SHORE *and* MICHIGAN SOUTHERN RY.
The Popular Passenger Route between the EAST and WEST.
UNION DEPOTS, NO FERRY TRANSFERS, NO DELAYS.

Fig. 60.   No. 317. Lake Shore & Michigan Southern Railway. (NYC). 4-4-0 Type. Built by
LS&MS Ry., 1871. An artist's conception of THE FAST MAIL, which began operation
on September 14, 1875, on a schedule of 27 hours 12 minutes, the first regular, fast,
through service in both directions between New York and Chicago.

Penn Central Rail Road.

Fig. 61. No. 160. Lake Shore & Michigan Southern Railway. (NYC). Class Q (C-53) 4-4-0 Type. Built by Brooks Locomotive Works, 1893. An artist's conception of THE EX-POSITION FLYER which operated from May 29 to November 19, 1893, making the run between New York and Chicago, 980 miles, in 20 hours, the fastest regular train in the world for the distance. One of the first luxury trains.

Penn Central Rail Road.

Fig. 62. No. 862. New York Central & Hudson River Rail Road (NYC) Class I 4-4-0 Type. Built by Schenectady Locomotive Works, 1890. Builder's No. 3057. Shown at the head end of one of the Limited trains on the NYC&HR RR.

Howard G. Hill Collection.

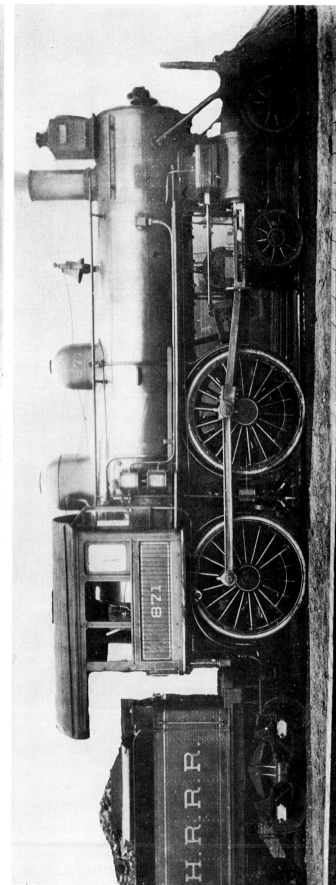

Fig. 63. No. 871. New York Central & Hudson River Rail Road. (NYC) Class I (Ca) 4-4-0 Type. Built by Schenectady Locomotive Works, 1890. Builder's No. 3066. Designed by William Buchanan, SMP&RS, NYC&HR RR, Albany, N.Y., for Limited train service New York City to Buffalo.

Penn Central Rail Road.

Fig. 64. The Train Shed of the Old Grand Central Depot at 42nd Street and Park Avenue, New York City. THE TWENTIETH CENTURY LIMITED departed daily from Track 20 behind steam until the new electrified station was built. By February 1907, all regular trains between this station and High Bridge were moved by electric locomotives. Later, the electrified run was extended to Harmon, 32.7 miles from New York, where the change to steam locomotives was made.

Penn Central Rail Road.

Fig. 65. No. 2960. New York Central & Hudson River Rail Road. (NYC). Class I 4-4-2 Type. Built by American Locomotive Co., Schenectady Works, May 1902. Builder's No. 25028. Shown with Train No. 26, THE TWENTIETH CENTURY, between Albany and New York City on the morning of June 16, 1902, on the first eastward trip, with Thomas Sherwood at the throttle and Thomas Jordan handling the scoop. Jordan is momentarily drinking in a few breaths of unpolluted fresh country air as they roll smoothly along on the left-hand track not far from New York City.

New York Central Lines.

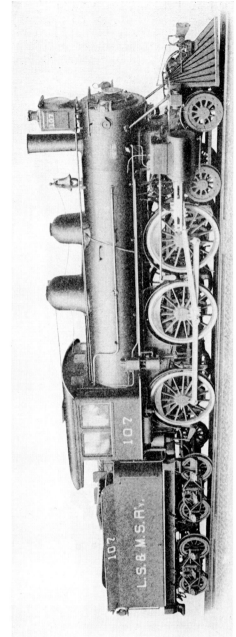

Fig. 66. No. 107. Lake Shore & Michigan Southern Railway. (NYC). Class F 4-6-0 Type. Built by Schenectady Locomotive Works, 1896. Builder's No. 4512. Powered the early Limited trains between Buffalo and Chicago, but soon superseded by heavier power.

Howard G. Hill Collection.

Fig. 67. No. 660. Lake Shore & Michigan Southern Railway. (NYC). Class J-40b 2-6-2 Type. Built by Brooks Locomotive Works, 1901. Builder's No. 3817. This class hauled THE TWENTIETH CENTURY LIMITED between Buffalo and Chicago.

Howard G. Hill Collection.

Fig. 68. No. 4670. Lake Shore & Michigan Southern Railway. (NYC). Class J-40c 2-6-2 Type. Built by American Locomotive Co., Brooks Works, 1902. Builder's No. 26442. Shown at the head end of THE TWENTIETH CENTURY LIMITED after the renumbering in 1905. Original number 670.

New York Central Lines.

Fig. 69. No. 613. Lake Shore & Michigan Southern Railway. (NYC). Class I-1 4-6-0 Type. Built by Brooks Locomotive Works, August 1900. Builder's No. 3606. A 10-wheeler with 80-inch drivers was indeed a rarity! Powered THE TWENTIETH CENTURY LIMITED between Buffalo and Chicago.

Howard G. Hill Collection.

Fig. 70. No. 604. Lake Shore & Michigan Southern Railway. (NYC). Class I 4-6-0 Type. Built by Brooks Locomotive Works, October 1899. Builder's No. 3335. Shown westbound with THE TWENTIETH CENTURY LIMITED prior to the renumbering in 1905. Was there ever a prouder-looking, more beautiful 10-wheeler, with those huge 80-inch drivers? No.

New York Central Lines.

Fig. 71. No. 2701. New York Central & Hudson River R. R. (NYC). Class K-1 4-6-2 Type. Built December, 1903, by American Locomotive Co., Schenectady Works. Builder's No. 28961. This was the first group of Pacific type locomotives on the NYC&HR RR, but they were assigned to the Boston & Albany R. R. Not used on NYC main line.

Frederick Westing Collection

Fig. 72. No. 8452. Michigan Central R. R. (NYC). Class K-80b 4-6-2 Type. Built 1905 by American Locomotive Co., Schenectady Works. Builder's No. 30778. One of 70 Class K-80 Pacifics used on the Michigan Central and the Canada Southern, but not on the main line. Looks like the 8452 developed a hot right main crank pin, and the lady had to go up to the head end to make sure the "hogger" got it cooled down properly! Note the pressure reducing valve, part of the Westinghouse High Speed Automatic Air Brake, under the running board just below the right boiler check valve. Photographed at Niles, Michigan, in 1908.

C. B. Chaney Collection.
From William D. Edson

Fig. 73. No. 3565. New York Central & Hudson River R. R. (NYC). Class K-2e 4-6-2 Type. Built 1908 by American Locomotive Co., Schenectady Works. Builder's No. 45254. The K-2 Class were the first Pacifics operated on the NYC&HR-LS&MS through runs.

Howard G. Hill Collection.

Fig. 74. Nos. (left to right) 4854, 4863, 4858, 4871 and 4868. Lake Shore & Michigan Southern Railway (NYC). Class K-21 4-6-2 Type. Built 1910 by American Locomotive Co., Schenectady Works. Five sections of Train No. 26, THE TWENTIETH CENTURY LIMITED, lined up for departure from La Salle Street Depot, Chicago, to New York. No. 4863, second from left, will run as the fifth section of Train No. 26. Photographed in 1927.

Penn Central Rail Road.

Fig. 75. No. 3426. New York Central & Hudson River Rail Road. (NYC). Class K3a 4-6-2 Type. Built by American Locomotive Co., Schenectady Works, 1911. Builder's No. 49457. One of the first of 276 very successful Class K-3 locomotives used in main line service on the Limited trains.

Fig. 76. No. 4723. New York Central Lines. Class K-41a 4-6-2 Type. Built by American Locomotive Co., Brooks Works, 1905, as Class J-41a 2-6-2 type for LS&MS Ry. Builder's No. 37719. Rebuilt by NYC Lines between 1915-1919 as Class K-41a 4-6-2 type.
William D. Edson Collection.

Fig. 77. No. 3406. New York Central & Hudson River Rail Road. (NYC). Class K-3c 4-6-2 Type. Built by Baldwin Locomotive Works, Philadelphia, 1912. Builder's No. 37431. 20 of these locomotives were built for heavy passenger service on the main line.
H. L. Broadbelt Collection.

Fig. 78. No. 3359. New York Central & Hudson River Rail Road. (NYC). Class K-3g 4-6-2 Type. Built by American Locomotive Co., Schenectady Works, September 1913. Builder's No. 54045. A further development of the Class K-3, some of which served for 38 years — the last one was retired in 1953.
Howard G. Hill Collection.

Fig. 79. No. 6510. Cleveland, Cincinnati, Chicago & St. Louis Rail Road. (NYC). Class K-5b 4-6-2 Type. Built by American Locomotive Co., Schenectady Works, November 1926. Builder's No. 67114. Another step in the development of a more powerful Pacific.
William D. Edson Collection.

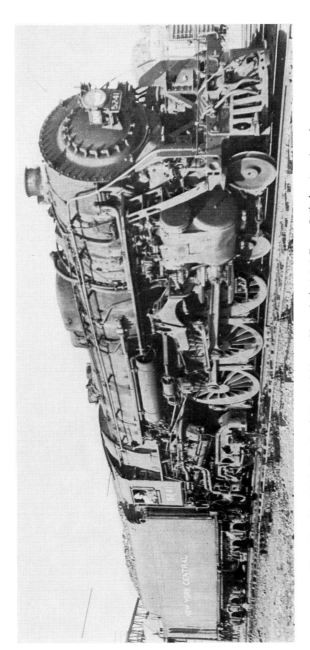

Fig. 80. No. 5241. New York Central Lines. Class J-1b 4-6-4 Type. Built by American Locomotive Co., Schenectady Works, October 1927. Builder's No. 67472. One of 59 Class J-1b locomotives built in 1927. They were essentially duplicates of Class J-1a No. 5200 with minor improvements.
Arnold Haas Photo.

Fig. 81. No. 5442, New York Central Lines, Class J-3a 4-6-4 Type. Built by American Locomotive Co., Schenectady Works, November 1937. Builder's No. 68876. One of the final group of Hudson type locomotives on the NYC.

Arnold Haas Photo.

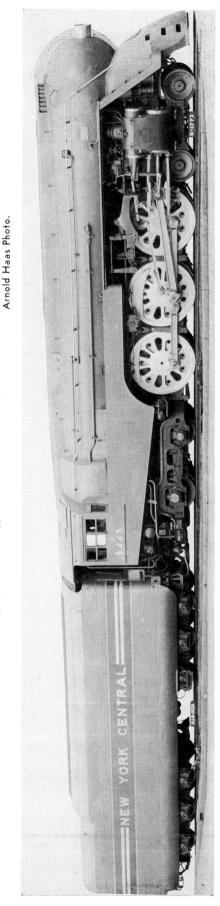

Fig. 82. No. 5445. New York Central Lines, Class J-3a 4-6-4 Type. Built by American Locomotive Co. Schenectady Works, March 1938. Builder's No. 68879. Nos. 5445-5454 were streamlined until 1947 for service on THE TWENTIETH CENTURY LIMITED and other Limited trains.

Howard G. Hill Collection.

Fig. 83. No. 6001. New York Central Lines. Class S-1b 4-8-4 Type. Built by American Locomotive Co., Schenectady Works, 1945. The final attempt by the New York Central Lines to develop a super-power dual-purpose steam locomotive. They were exceptionally fine machines, but time was fast running out for the steam locomotive when they were built, and they lived only about ten years.

Charles M. Smith Collection.

CHAPTER 6
RIDING THE J-1 LOCOMOTIVES
ON THE CENTURY *

AS already related, I had the rare privilege of riding in the cabs of several Class K-4s Pacific type locomotives hauling the Pennsylvania Rail Road's BROADWAY LIMITED from New York (Manhattan Transfer) through to Chicago, a thrilling experience. After that trip I felt that it would be very interesting and instructive to ride in the cabs of the Class J-1 Hudson (4-6-4) type locomotives which hauled THE TWENTIETH CENTURY LIMITED on the New York Central Lines. My request for that rare privilege was very kindly granted by one of the Central's Vice Presidents at New York.

On Tuesday, February 17, 1931, the four-faced clock at the Information Booth on the Concourse, **Grand Central Terminal, New York City**, proclaimed the hour as 2:30 PM. (Fig. 84). The daily ritual which preceded the departure of Train No. 25, THE TWENTIETH CENTURY LIMITED, was already in full swing. The elite clientele of the New York Central Lines had congregated at Gate 27 while their transportation was checked. (Fig. 85). I was in that group, and soon passed through the gate to start the long walk down the red-and-gray carpeted platform beside which twelve gleaming dark-green Pullman cars stood in majestic dignity. I shall not attempt to describe that famous train here — that has already been done by several well-known authors. On that particular trip I was concerned primarily with the performance of THE CENTURY's steam locomotives.

The other passengers boarded the immaculate Pullmans to which they had been assigned, and settled comfortably in the drawing rooms, compartments or sections, and in the club and observation cars. Such luxury was not to be enjoyed by me that night. There would be no relaxation or sleep for me — no gourmet dinner in the dining car that evening — no breakfast next morning

after a refreshing night's sleep in a gently swaying Pullman berth. I was to spend twenty consecutive hours, covering 961.2 miles, in the locomotive cabs on that famous train. (Fig. 86). So I proceeded forward along the platform, and found Class T-3a electric locomotive No. 1176 on the point. (Fig. 87). She was built in 1926 by American Locomotive Company — General Electric Company at Schenectady, builder's number 66708. She was of the B-B+B-B type, with four 4-wheeled motor-driven trucks under the articulated frame which supported the cab. Those locomotives were rated at 2,488 horsepower, and could run 75 miles per hour, but they were restricted to 55 miles per hour between New York and Harmon, 32.7 miles. They weighed 146.3 tons.

On that particular day, travel was light, and Train No. 25 was to operate in only one section, instead of the usual two to seven sections, so we were to make all of the scheduled stops normally made only by the last of two or more sections. After meeting the engine crew and showing my credentials, I settled down on the left seat-box behind the fireman and waited impatiently for the moment of departure.

Two-forty-five. Gate 27 closed quietly. The conductor raised his lantern. Car platform doors closed. A dwarf signal just ahead of the 1176 changed from red to yellow, authorizing THE TWENTIETH CENTURY LIMITED to begin her 20-hour dash to Chicago. (Fig. 88). The engineer notched the controller handle back slowly and deliberately. The start was barely perceptible, so smoothly was that operation handled in every detail. A line of dwarf signals up ahead changed progressively from red to yellow as the towerman lined our route to the westward main track. We rolled along very smoothly as our speed quickly increased to the 35 miles per hour maximum allowed in the underground yard. Just after we

*(See Appendix for details of performance of this trip.)

passed the 51st Street tower, the 42 yard tracks converged at the "throat" to form the four main line tracks.

Two-forty-eight. We saw a friendly green signal up ahead in the gloom of the underground yard. THE CENTURY left the yard and rolled onto the main track. Speed increased smoothly and rapidly. Even at that early stage of the run, the engineer was checking his watch frequently, controlling the speed accurately, and passing each mile post exactly on time. It was a very precise operation.

Two-fifty-one. We were now out of the tunnel and were rolling on the long viaduct through Harlem. The fireman had started the fire in the oil-burning train-heating boiler. Four minutes later we passed the 125th Street Station without reducing speed. Green signals let us through the Harlem River bridge. Before three o'clock we rolled through the long curve to the left, just south of Mott Haven Yard, and entered the Hudson River Division. Speed was then increased to 55 miles per hour as we rolled along the east bank of the Hudson River, a very scenic ride, especially when you can view it, as I did, through the front and side windows of a speeding electric locomotive. The 1176 rode as smoothly as a Pullman car. (Fig. 89).

We stopped at Harmon at 3:30 PM, having averaged 43.6 miles per hour over that portion of the run. The 1176 was cut off quickly and moved into a siding just ahead. A cross-over switch was lined for the main track, and the 5302 backed onto the train, with the coupling operation completed within a few seconds. Now THE CENTURY was complete — twelve luxurious Pullmans with steam on the head end! She was the Central's pride and joy, complete and ready for a superb example of locomotive and train operation. (Fig. 90).

The 5302 was one of those beautiful new Class J-1d Hudson type locomotives built at Schenectady in 1930, builder's number 68180. She was the last word in steam locomotive design and construction at that time. Paul Kiefer certainly packed the ultimate in power, stamina, speed and beauty into what was then the crowning achievement in the development of the six-coupled steam passenger locomotive. She was a thing of beauty and a joy to behold. And I was going to ride in a J-1 cab for almost 1,000 miles! To top that off, the famous Bob Butterfield was to handle the 5302 on that run from Harmon to Albany, and he put the 5302 through her paces in the most outstanding demonstration of expertise in steam locomotive running it had ever been my privilege to witness. (Figs. 91 and 92).

There was time for only a fleeting glance over the massive lines of that beautiful locomotive as she backed onto the train. The feeling of exhilar-

ation which swept over me as I climbed into the cab of the 5302 cannot be described. I introduced myself to Bob Butterfield and showed him my engine permit. With his usual pleasant smile, he invited me to take a seat on the fireman's seatbox. Since those locomotives were stoker-fired, I had to share the seat with the fireman except when he was on the deck using the firehook or operating the water scoop. (Fig. 93).

With the "highball" at 3:39 PM, four minutes late, Bob Butterfield released the engine brakes, cut in the booster, opened the sander valve, and cracked the pilot valve in the front end throttle. (Figs. 94 and 95). The 79-inch drivers bit into the sand, and, in a couple of seconds, THE TWENTIETH CENTURY LIMITED was moving behind steam! The throttle was opened wider, and, slowly and smoothly, with increasingly sharp blasts from the stack, the 5302 increased her speed, and the train was soon rolling along smoothly at about 50 miles per hour — smoothly, that is, as long as the drivers held the rails. A drizzling rain was falling, and the rails were very slippery. Even with a factor of adhesion of 4.58, the driving wheels slipped frequently, causing slight slow-downs, and it was necessary to use sand almost constantly, with frequent easing off on the throttle. The schedule was very tight along the river, with a 65-mile speed limit. With frequent curves, short tangents, several slow orders for track work (where they were completing the four-tracking of the Division), and a wet rail, it required extremely skillful handling of the locomotive to maintain the schedule. ((Fig. 96).

Bob Butterfield had 119 minutes for the 110 miles to Albany, and he had to use every second of that time to best advantage. That did not leave any time for loafing along the way. He was too good and loyal an engineer to exceed the 65-mile limit, so he had to take advantage of every opportunity to crowd the limit on the short tangents, but had to pinch the wheels a bit for the many curves. He played a tune with the throttle, the reverse wheel, the sander valve, and the brake valves, with an obligato by the whistle, which reminds me of some of the exhibitions I witnessed later in England, during World War II, as I sat beside some of the most noted cathedral organists and watched them perform on their marvelous 4- and 5-manual pipe organs. Some of those organs had up to 9,000 pipes, with 146 speaking stops and 30 couplers. I've often said, "Next to a steam locomotive, I love a pipe organ best!" They both produce the sweetest music in the world! Bob Butterfield produced superb music as he sat at the controls of the 5302 that day. (Fig. 97). His left hand flashed back and forth from the throttle lever to the automatic brake valve handle, while his right hand released the engine brakes and operated the sander valve to prevent, not suddenly stop, the slight slipping of the driving wheels which occurred with distracting frequency. Through it all, his attitude was one of calm, unruffled competence.

With all of this constant activity, he checked his watch frequently, splitting the seconds in his quick mental calculations to determine where he could make up a few seconds. He had established an enviable reputation for "On Time" performance with that train, and he had no intention of spoiling his record that day because of a little rain and a delayed departure from Harmon.

There were two track pans between Harmon and Albany at which the fireman dropped the water scoop to pick up hundreds of gallons of water on the run, but that meant reducing speed to 45 miles per hour, as we could not pass a pan 1,800 ft. long in less than 27 seconds. (Fig. 98). Then there would be the 20-mile limit, later, through the double curve around the base of the bluff whereon the city of Hudson stands. In spite of those handicaps, the skillful hand of Bob Butterfield soon had the 5302 crowding 65 again.

After passing Anthony's Nose and the Bear Mountain bridge, we roared through a short tunnel and emerged onto about five miles of comparatively straight track past the Highlands and up to the tight curve around the nose of Breakneck, where trackwork again put a dent in our schedule. As we came out of the short tunnel at the foot of Breakneck, the throttle was opened wider so we could take advantage of the many long tangents ahead, with fewer curves, although we were still following the river bank closely. We soon roared past Beacon and hardly noticed the short tunnel at New Hamburg. The track pan at Clinton Point gave us additional water, but it cost us several seconds. Poughkeepsie and the high bridge were soon behind us, and Hyde Park, Staatsburg and Rhinecliff flashed by as Bob Butterfield took advantage of the long tangents and easy curves of one of the most perfect stretches of four-track main line railroad I have ever seen. He soon had the 5302 erasing the lost minutes by some beautiful flashes of speed along the tangents. There was another slow-down for the Tivoli track pan where the 5302 took her last drink on the run before reaching Albany. (Fig. 99).

After the slow order through the double curve at the base of the bluff near Hudson, there was another burst of speed. Darkness had settled over the land, and a shaft of light from the 5302's electric eye stabbed the gloom ahead. All the way up the river, the fireman had kept his Duplex stoker operating steadily, varying the speed slightly as the steam demand varied, and adjusting the steam jets to distribute the coal evenly over the 81.5 sq. ft. of grate area. He kept the needle within

a pound or two of 225 all the way, and carried the water near the middle of the glass. The pyrometer indicated a superheated steam temperature of 660° to 700° F. At the latter figure, the superheater was producing about 310° of superheat, and the exhausts were very sharp. (Fig. 100).

Until we reached the long tangents, the fireman had kept a sharp lookout ahead, calling the signal indications across the cab when he could see them first, and repeating them when Bob Butterfield called them first. After reaching the long tangents, he frequently took the squirt hose to wet down the coal and lay the dust. He also trimmed the coal pile in the tender so it would feed steadily into the screw conveyor which delivered the coal to the crusher and thence to the elevators in the cab. He timed his absences from the left side carefully so he would not miss any signals on his side of a curve. He was not a "tourist" — he was skillfully working his way over the railroad.

At Castleton-on-Hudson we rolled rapidly under the high-level A. H. Smith Memorial Bridge which carries New York Central freight traffic over the main line and the river. We could now see the glow from the lights of Albany shimmering faintly in the misty distance about eight miles ahead. As we approached Rensselaer Yard, a service application of the brakes reduced our speed. A signal ahead changed from red to yellow, then to green. The brakes were released and our speed picked up a little. We rattled through the interlocking at the junction of the Boston & Albany main line from Boston, rolled across the big double-track bridge over the Hudson River, through a tight curve to the right, and, after another heavy service application of the brakes, rolled majestically, slowly—still slower—almost down to a walk—through the station, and at just the right spot, near the north end of the platform, the 5302, with her twelve cars, came to an almost imperceptible stop. Bob Butterfield quickly pulled out his watch, glanced at it, and said, with a smile of justifiable pride, "Five-thirty-eight—we're on time!" He had averaged 55.2 miles per hour by running the 110 miles from Harmon to Albany in 119 minutes, start to stop, and had successfully completed his run after a superb demonstration of expert locomotive operation and train control. He was Master of the Machine — a skilled "throttle artist" of top rank. He was one of those rare souls who possessed a delicate touch and a keen intuition which enabled him to sense every motion—every sound— in his locomotive, and to operate it with consummate skill and precision. Only those who have personally observed that performance can appreciate the beauty of such an outstanding example of steam locomotive running and performance. Bob Butterfield was, indeed, a very fortunate man to be blessed with such skill and the privilege of exercising that skill while running those beautiful Hudsons almost daily, hauling THE TWENTIETH CENTURY LIMITED between Harmon and Albany, over a very difficult division, and on a very tight schedule! I consider myself most fortunate to have had the rare privilege of riding in the cab of a J-1 Hudson type locomotive with such an outstanding locomotive engineer at the throttle.

While changing crews, two Pullmans from Boston were cut into the train ahead of the observation car. With the switch engine coupled to the rear end of the fourteenth car to help us up Albany Hill, a short distance west of the station, we started pulling at 5:51 PM, on time. The 5302 made some beautiful stack music as she blasted up the hill, even though she had a helper engine at the rear end. When the switch engine reached the top of the hill, her fireman pulled a lever in the cab which lifted the pin in the front coupler, thus permitting the switch engine to uncouple without stopping THE CENTURY.

From the top of Albany Hill to Chicago, the line was a succession of long tangents connected by curves of long radius which permitted the maximum speed, with few exceptions. The profile was predominantly level, with a few easy grades, some of which reduced our speed slightly. Over such a line, the 5302 gave a beautiful demonstration of her capabilities for sustained high speed and power by moving her 1,350-ton train, including the 5302, at from 60 to 75 miles per hour. Track pans required frequent speed reductions to 45 miles per hour, but much of the time we were crowding the 75-mile speed limit.

With Albany Hill behind us, our speed quickly increased to about 65 miles per hour and was maintained at about that figure until we approached Utica, where we stopped 1 minute to pick up passengers, leaving 1 minute late at 7:46 PM. We had averaged 49.8 miles per hour between Albany and Utica. (The speeds quoted were read from the speed recorder in the cab). The engineer had to take slack when starting from Utica, the only point of the entire trip where this was necessary.

Once under way, however, we were soon running 65 miles per hour, with the pyrometer indicating a steam temperature of about 650° F. in the right steam pipe just above the piston valve chamber. The nature of the terrain and track were such that the remainder of the run to Chicago resolved itself into steady slugging under more or less constant conditions, with little of the frequent fine adjustments of throttle, reverse wheel and brakes which had been necessary back on the Hudson River Division. Nevertheless, it was a revelation to study the performance of that beautiful big Hudson as she produced 77,992 gross ton-miles per train-hour for more than ten hours! It was a superb performance.

Our speed was reduced at 8:38 PM for the movement through the yard limits of Syracuse, and we stopped at the station at 8:47 PM for 15 minutes to pick up passengers, and to cut out the dining car. That left 13 cars in the consist from Syracuse to Toledo. We had averaged 52.1 miles per hour from Utica to Syracuse.

Leaving Syracuse at 9:02 PM, 6 minutes late, the 5302 showed us some outstanding acceleration by hitting 75 miles per hour in less than 15 miles. Here I got the worst scare I ever experienced in my life. We were on a long tangent on Track 1, and were hitting 75 miles per hour as we passed a long west-bound freight train on Track 3, on our right. That train appeared to be standing. I was standing beside the engineer, watching him intently as he made fine adjustments of throttle and cut-off to adhere closely to the 75-mile limit. (Bob Butterfield had told me that the 5302 could run 100 miles per hour with that train if he had a long, level tangent to run on, but 75 was the limit west of Albany. I wish I could have ridden one of those Hudsons at 100 miles per hour.)

When we were about one car length from the engine of the freight train, a lighted red fusee was suddenly thrust out of the left cab window of the engine, literally in our faces! We got only an instantaneous flashing glimpse of it—and we were by the other engine. Quick as a flash, the engineer moved the automatic brake valve handle to service application position and left it there, thus causing a heavy service application of the brakes, as he closed the throttle. An emergency application of the brakes under those conditions might have had serious results—at best, every wheel in the train might have been slid flat, and that would have meant buying a new train at the next terminal!

We would normally expect to feel immediately the retarding effect of a heavy service application of the brakes—at least, within a few seconds—but in this case, it seemed that the brakes were not taking hold. Of course, from 75 miles per hour you do not stop on a dime! I do not mind admitting that I was scared—and both engineer and fireman appeared unusually tense and alert. They both stood up and leaned out of their respective cab windows as they tried to see what lay ahead of us.

I stepped to the right gangway and looked ahead. I could see two marker lights, but the atmosphere was so hazy that it was impossible to determine if the left one was yellow, which would indicate to us that the train ahead was on Track 3, and therefore, clear of our track. After what seemed to be several minutes, although it was undoubtedly only a few seconds, we could feel the brakes take hold, and our speed began to drop. We could soon observe that the left-hand marker on the caboose ahead was yellow—she was on Track 3. We finally stopped a few feet behind the caboose. As we ground to a halt, the engineer turned to me and said, "I thought those brakes would never take hold!" I knew then that I was not imagining the situation. The three of us in the cab heaved mighty sighs of relief when we realized that our train was safe.

We were near Jordan, about 17 miles west of Syracuse, when we stopped. Within a couple of minutes, the flagman of the freight train ahead climbed into the cab of the 5302 and told us that his train had been stopped by an emergency application of the brakes, and he did not know whether or not his train was scattered all over the right-of-way—he had to hustle back to protect his train against the following train, as required by Rule 99. He suggested that we run by his train slowly, prepared to stop short of any obstruction on Track 1. We then proceeded at slow speed, and found that the freight train had broken in two in two places, but all equipment was still on the rails. IF we had not seen that red fusee — IF that freight train had been scattered all over the right-of-way—but the Good Lord was looking after us that night! We got a little scare, and lost about 6 minutes, but we did not mind that when we found the way clear.

After passing the disabled train, our speed was increased to Wayneport, where we stopped 4 minutes for coal, and then continued to Rochester, where we stopped at 10:38 PM for passengers. Our average speed from Syracuse to Rochester had been 56 miles per hour for the actual running time.

We left Rochester 14 minutes late, running 70 miles per hour or more on the level and lighter grades, but were slowed down a little by the heavier grades and track pans. A heavy snow was falling between Rochester and Buffalo, and slippery rails caused considerable slipping of the driving wheels. The engineer had to handle the throttle and sander valve very skillfully to overcome the slipping, in spite of which we arrived at Buffalo on time at 11:50 PM, having averaged 57.4 miles per hour from Rochester to Buffalo, where crews were changed.

Just as we stopped at Buffalo, an operator ran up to the engine to ask the engineer what he had been doing along the line—this in spite of the fact that we had arrived exactly on time. That was a good illustration of the close attention which the dispatcher gave to the minute-by-minute progress of that train along the line.

Leaving Buffalo at 11:59 PM, 6 minutes late, the 5302 ran the 178.1 miles to Collinwood nonstop in 2 hours 51 minutes, averaging 62.4 miles per hour, with brief reductions in speed for the track pans and some of the larger cities along the line. That was a beautiful example of the capacity of those locomotives for sustained high speed and power. The 5302 was cut off at Collinwood after running 581.3 miles in 10 hours 20 minutes actual running time, at an average speed of 56.3 miles per hour. She had produced 804,887 gross ton-miles, or 77,992 gross ton-miles per train-hour.

In spite of my keen interest in studying the splendid over-all performance of the 5302, it was quite a relief to leave her cab just before she was cut off at Collinwood. She was a very hard-riding engine. That was not so noticeable on the Hudson River Division, but when she began to stretch out at high speed on the long tangents west of Albany, she developed a severe pounding between engine and tender. That appeared to be due to excessive slack in the Franklin Radial Buffer between engine and tender. Unbalanced reciprocating forces caused violent longitudinal movement of the engine which reversed itself with every revolution of the driving wheels, or 636 times each minute at 75 miles per hour. That constant pounding between engine and tender was extremely unpleasant, especially when it had to be endured, as I endured it, for 9 consecutive hours, with no let-up except for 7 brief station stops, the emergency stop near Jordan, and the fuel stop at Wayneport, totaling 51 minutes.

From Collinwood through Cleveland Union Terminal to Linndale, 13.2 miles, I rode in the cab of CUT electric locomotive No. 1061, Class P-1a, a very easy riding machine of the 4-6-6-4 type, with a rating of 2,635 horsepower. (Fig. 101). She was built at Schenectady in 1929, by American Locomotive Company—General Electric Company, builder's number 67690. It was quite a relief to glide smoothly down a slight grade to the underground terminal in that smooth-running locomotive after the rough ride on the 5302. We stopped at the underground terminal station at 3:10 AM for 5 minutes, and then ascended a steep grade to Linndale, where we stopped at 3:28 AM to cut off the 1061.

The 5246, a Class J-1b Hudson built by American Locomotive Company at Schenectady in 1927, builder's number 67477, was coupled to THE CENTURY for the remainder of the run to Chicago. (Fig. 102). She was one of the group of 49 J-1b's built shortly after the trials of the original Class J-1a No. 5200, which was placed in service on February 14, 1927, to be followed during the next 11 years by 274 additional locomotives of that type. They were a phenomenal success.

We left Linndale at 3:35 AM and were soon running from 60 to 65 miles per hour, and maintained that speed to Toledo, where we stopped at 5:18 AM EST for 17 minutes to change crews and to pick up two dining cars. We had averaged 57.7 miles per hour from Linndale to Toledo, on a non-stop run of 100.4 miles.

While we were standing at Toledo, the conductor came up to the engine with the train orders for the engineer. When he saw me in the cab, he asked what I was doing up there. I told him I was riding the engine to Chicago. He then asked what I was riding on, and I told him that I had a permit from one of the Vice Presidents in New York, but that the conductor out of Albany had lifted it. I had assumed that it would be passed on to the other conductors along the line. He said that I could not ride in the cab unless he could see my authority. I was pretty tired by that time, and in no mood to argue the matter, so I said, "I have ridden all the way from New York in the engine cab by authority of the Vice President, and I guess I can go the rest of the way in the cab." He was about to throw me off the engine when the engineer said, "He is O.K. Let him stay up here." The conductor went back to the train without further argument, and I completed the trip in the 5246's cab. So, I almost had the dubious distinction of being thrown off the engine of THE TWENTIETH CENTURY LIMITED!

We left Toledo at 4:35 AM CST with 15 cars and ran between 60 and 75 miles per hour non-stop to Elkhart, 133 miles, in 2 hours 25 minutes, start to stop, averaging 54.9 miles per hour. The 12-minute stop at Elkhart was for a crew change.

Leaving Elkhart at 7:12 AM, our speed varied from 40 to 75 miles per hour, and we ran the 93.9 miles to Englewood non-stop in 2 hours 1 minute, averaging 46.7 miles per hour. We stopped at Englewood at 9:13 AM to discharge passengers, and were delayed there about 3 minutes while waiting for the eastbound GOLDEN STATE LIMITED of the Rock Island Lines to clear the station. After a slow run of 6.7 miles through Chicago Terminals, we arrived at La Salle Street Depot at 9:32 AM CST, which was 13 minutes ahead of the scheduled arrival time for that train. That was normal "On Time" performance when THE

TWENTIETH CENTURY LIMITED was operated in only one section. When more than one section was operated, the stops at Utica, Rochester and Cleveland would have been made by the last section only, and there would be two additional non-stop runs of approximately 146 miles each for the locomotives of the preceding sections, except for the fuel stop at Wayneport.

The movement of Train No. 25 as related above involved the production of 1,354,168 gross ton-miles, or 77,440 gross ton-miles per train-hour. The best performance of the 5302 was 85,925 gross ton-miles per train-hour between Buffalo and Collinwood. The best performance of the 5246 was 84,636 gross ton-miles per train-hour between Toledo and Elkhart. The approximate total weight of locomotive and train over the various divisions on that run varied from 1116 tons to 1540 tons.

The 5246 rode very much more smoothly than the 5302, as there was none of the pounding between engine and tender like that in the 5302. However, the stoker on the 5246 was sluggish in its action, and there was some difficulty in maintaining 225 lbs. pressure on the steam gauge. It was not serious enough, however, to cause any delay. The overall performance of both locomotives was superb, and the privilege of riding in their cabs over the entire run of each locomotive was a rare and thrilling experience, especially since they were hauling THE TWENTIETH CENTURY LIMITED.

When I rode in the cabs of the locomotives hauling THE BROADWAY LIMITED 12 days earlier, the K4s Pacifics produced 929,190 gross ton-miles, or 51,110 gross ton-miles per train-hour. Thus the work done by the Hudsons was 40.0% greater than that done by the Pacifics, and they produced 52.0% more gross ton-miles per train-hour over their entire run than the Pacifics produced. The best performance by the 5302, 85,925 gross ton-miles per train-hour, was 34.2% better than the best performance by the K4s Pacific No. 5439, which was 64,024 gross ton-miles per train-hour. The approximate total weight of the locomotives and train of THE BROADWAY LIMITED varied from 960 tons to 1200 tons. It is obvious that the Hudsons had to produce greater power output over the entire run than was the case with the Pacifics. The Hudsons were reported to have developed 4,075 horsepower at 66 miles per hour. All things being considered, each of those two classes of locomotives produced outstanding performance in its respective sphere of operation.

Fig. 84. The Main Concourse, Grand Central Terminal, New York City.

New York Central Lines.

Fig. 85.   The daily scene at Gate 27, Grand Central Terminal, New York City, just prior
to the departure of THE TWENTIETH CENTURY LIMITED.

Penn Central Rail Road.

Fig. 86. A CENTURY departure quay at Grand Central Terminal. The red-and-gray carpet on the quay paves the way to the immaculate TWENTIETH CENTURY LIMITED.
New York Central Lines.

Fig. 88. No. 1153. New York Central Lines. Class T-1b B-B+B-B Type. Built by American Locomotive Co.-General Electric Co., Schenectady Works, 1913. Builder's No. 53785. Standing at the north end of the train shed at Grand Central Terminal with THE TWENTIETH CENTURY LIMITED in 1914, ready to depart for Chicago.
New York Central Photo.

Fig. 87. No. 1174. New York Central Lines. Class T-3a B-B+B-B Type. Built by American Locomotive Co.-General Electric Co., Schenectady Works, 1926. Builder's No. 66706. These locomotives were operated in passenger service between Grand Central Terminal and Harmon, 32.7 miles. No. 1176, in whose cab I rode on February 17, 1931, hauling THE TWENTIETH CENTURY LIMITED, was one of the same class, built 1926, Builder's No. 66708.

New York Central Lines.

Fig. 89. No. 1166. New York Central Lines. Class T-2b B-B+B-B Type. Built by General Electric Co., Erie Works, 1917. Builder's No. 5863. Hauling Train No. 25, THE TWENTIETH CENTURY LIMITED, on the main line just north of New York City, before the arrival of air-conditioned cars.

New York Central Lines.

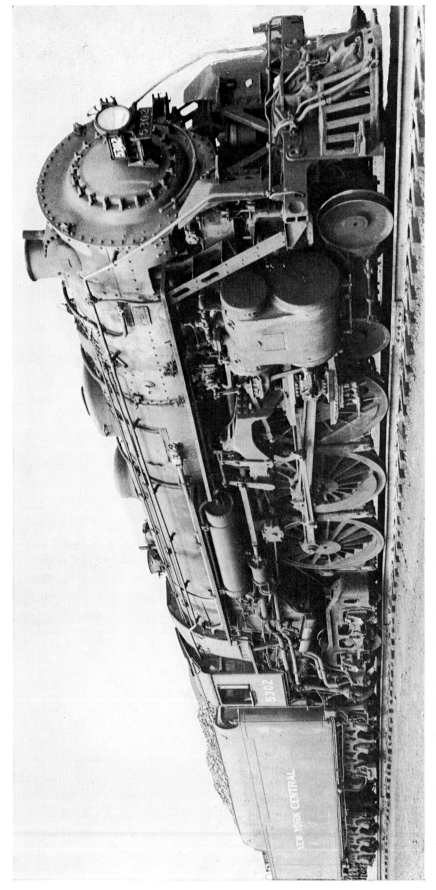

Fig. 90. No. 5302. New York Central Lines. Class J-1d 4-6-4 Type. Built by American Locomotive Co., Schenectady Works, January 1930. Builder's No. 68180. I rode in the cab of this locomotive from Harmon, N.Y., to Collinwood, Ohio, 581.3 miles, on Train No. 25, THE TWENTIETH CENTURY LIMITED, on February 17, 1931.

Edward L. May Photo.

Fig. 91. Bob Butterfield, a famous New York Central Lines Locomotive Engineer on the Hudson River Division, Harmon to Albany. He succeeded Charles Hogan at the throttle of the famous 4-4-0 type locomotvie No. 999 on THE EMPIRE STATE EXPRESS, and he handled the throttle of the 5302 when I rode in the cab of that locomotive on THE TWENTIETH CENTURY LIMITED on February 17, 1931. His handling of the locomotive and train was outstanding!

Fred J. Smith Photo.
American Magazine, May 1931.

Fig. 92.   Bob Butterfield oiling the shoes and wedges of a Hudson type locomotive before his
run with THE TWENTIETH CENTURY LIMITED from Harmon to Albany.

New York Central Lines.

Fig. 93.   Bob Butterfield at the throttle of No. 5200, New York Central Lines, Class J-la 4-6-4 Type (the first Hudson in the U.S.), ready to leave Harmon with Train No. 25, THE TWENTIETH CENTURY LIMITED.

New York Central Lines.

Fig. 94.   No. 5215. New York Central Lines. Class J-lb 4-6-4 Type. Built by American Locomotive Co., Schenectady Works, September 1927. Builder's No. 67446. Ready to leave Harmon with Train No. 25, THE TWENTIETH CENTURY LIMITED.

New York Central Lines.

Fig. 95. Two sections of Train No. 25, THE TWENTIETH CENTURY LIMITED, at Harmon for the change from electric to steam locomotives. The section on the right is ready to leave.

Penn Central Rail Road.

Fig. 96. No. 5271. New York Central Lines. Class J-1c 4-6-4 Type. Built by American Locomotive Co., Schenectady Works, January 1929. Builder's No. 67733. Photographed near Cold Spring, N. Y., with THE TWENTIETH CENTURY LIMITED when both engine and train were new.

Arnold Haas Collection.

Fig. 98. No. 5240. New York Central Lines. Class J-1b 4-6-4 Type. Built by American Locomotive Co., Schenectady Works, October 1927. Builder's No. 67471. Taking water from the track pan while running 45 miles per hour with THE TWENTIETH CENTURY LIMITED.

New York Central Lines.

Fig. 97. The controls in the cab of a New York Central Lines Hudson Type locomotive. Bob Butterfield produced a superb example of locomtive performance and train control while handling these controls on No. 5302 while hauling Train No. 25, THE TWEN-TIETH CENTURY LIMITED, from Harmon to Albany on February 5, 1931. I had the rare privilege of closely observing his work from the left seatbox.

New York Central Lines.

Fig. 99. No. 5214. New York Central Lines. Class J-1b 4-6-4 Type. Built by American Locomotive Co., Schenectady Works, September 1927. Builder's No. 67445. She looms up large and impressive as she dashes westward with THE TWENTIETH CENTURY LIMITED on the Hudson River Division.

New York Central Lines.

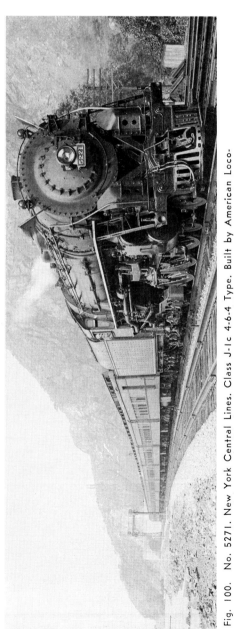

Fig. 100. No. 5271. New York Central Lines. Class J-1c 4-6-4 Type. Built by American Locomotive Co., Schenectady Works, January 1929. Builder's No. 67733. Headed east on the Hudson River Division with a section of Train No. 26, THE TWENTIETH CENTURY LIMITED.

Arnold Haas Collection.

Fig. 101. No. 1050. Cleveland Union Terminals Co. (NYC). Class P-1a 2-C-C-2 Type. Built by American Locomotive Co.-General Electric Co., Schenectady Works. November 1929. Builder's No. 67679. Nos. 1050-1071 moved passenger trains between Collinwood and Linndale through Cleveland Union Terminal Station. I made this run in the cab of No. 1061 on February 18, 1931, since Train No. 25, THE TWENTIETH CENTURY LIMITED, ran in only one section that night.

RAILWAY AGE.

Fig. 102. No. 5246. New York Central Lines. Class J-1b 4-6-4 Type. Built by American Locomotive Co., Schenectady Works, November 1927. Builder's No. 67477. I rode in the cab of this locomotive from Linndale, Ohio, to Chicago, Illinois, 334 miles, on February 18, 1931, hauling THE TWENTIETH CENTURY LIMITED on the last lap of a New York - Chicago cab trip.

Arnold Haas Photo.

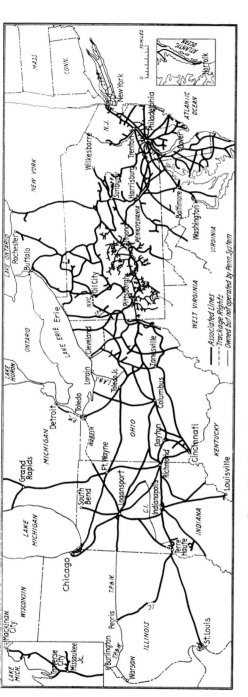

Fig. 103. Map of the Pennsylvania System, 1947.

RAILWAY AGE.

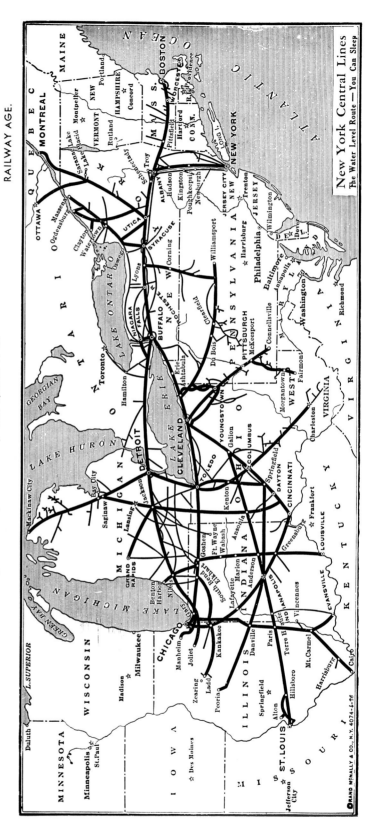

New York Central Lines
The Water Level Route — You Can Sleep

Rand McNally & Co.

Fig. 104. Map of the New York Central Lines, 1926.

EPILOGUE

FAREWELL TO THE CENTURY

ON the afternoon of December 2, 1967, I was relaxing in my library, browsing through some of my 700 books on railroads and locomotives which I have collected during the past 60 years. I picked up my copy of Lucius Beebe's "20TH CENTURY," an outstanding literary work which describes and illustrates the magnificent TWENTIETH CENTURY LIMITED throughout her career from 1902 to 1962. That book must be read through carefully to get the true picture of the characteristics and operation of that train. I have read it several times, and each reading is a fresh, new experience. Having ridden THE CENTURY several times, in addition to my thrilling trip in her locomotive cabs as related herein, Beebe's book helps me to live over again each of those trips, and I decided that afternoon to ride THE CENTURY again.

About 5:20 PM, while deeply engrossed in that fascinating story, I happened to overhear a radio newscast announcing the discontinuance of THE TWENTIETH CENTURY LIMITED, effective upon completion of the runs of Trains 25 and 26 commencing on that date! I was stunned by that announcement. I am sure many others were equally stunned. It did not seem possible that THE TWENTIETH CENTURY LIMITED was to disappear suddenly into history after 65 years of superb performance. I could not find words adequate to express my inner feelings over this loss, and I am sure there were many others who experienced the same heartache.

There is one man, however, who was able to express his feelings about this loss most eloquently in a beautiful epitaph to THE TWENTIETH CENTURY LIMITED. He is Mr. Mason Peters, Editorial Page Editor, "The Daily Advance," Elizabeth City, N.C. His beautiful tribute to THE TWENTIETH CENTURY LIMITED appeared in "The Daily Advance" on December 5, 1967, and is reprinted here through the courtesy of Mr. Loyal Phillips, General Manager of the paper.

SO LONG, "CENTURY"

The Obituary of a railroad train may seem totally out of place here but please permit a point of personal privilege for a mourner whose shameless love affair with the great steam locomotives ended not on a whimper but with the groan and whish of releasing Pullman brakes at exactly 6:00 PM last Saturday. And you may be sure it was precisely six o'clock when the Twentieth Century Limited pulled out of New York for the long, racketing run through the ,night to Chicago, where she arrived and died, a lovely faded old Floradora whose illness was sad and lingering and somehow an epitaph to an era. It was the Century's last run and now she is gone, buried by progress.

The wonderful New York Central train was both child and victim of her namesake century. For sixty-five storied years she was, in the jellied hearts of true lovers, The Train, the one and only. In 1928, when Hoover was in flower and you could buy the world on margin, she grossed 10-million dollars all by herself and remained every inch a lady though she hustled. No parvenu could equal her, though many tried . . . The Broadway Limited, the Chief, El Capitan, the Crescent Limited, the Orange Blossom Special, charmers all, as trains go, but without the essence of style and grace that in courtesans makes a Du Barry or a Montespan and on the High Iron made the Twentieth Century Limited.

Age began to catch up with the Century when she started running around with Diesels. Somehow her lovers openly admired the great steam locomotives that led her down the silver-ribboned path in the primrose years. The Diesels seemed almost like gigolos trying to make the old Grand Dame something she was no longer and the lovers were hurt and a little fickle, too. They fled away to keep memories intact and on the rebound caught the svelte but whining jades that jetted through the skies. No amount of rouge and makeup could hide the sagging face and the runover heels that clattered through the Catskill nights behind a yellow eye and a brazen Diesel throat, so alien and rude compared to the joyous basso profundo of the huge steam swains.

Long ago there was a little boy, trying hard to be a man, who used to sneak out of a darkened dormitory at a military school in Peekskill, N. Y., where the New York Central tracks follow at water's edge the great bend of the Hudson around Bear Mountain. With other young lunatics-in-love he would crouch along the mainline tracks below Peekskill, waiting in petrified anticipation for the Century, an hour out of New York and coming fast. It was best on the coldest of winter nights when the stars hung just overhead on icy threads and distant signal lights reflected tiny touches of red and green and amber on the silvery lines of steel that disappeared with the river. Then far, far away down the ghostly mainline, there came

the sound of that great voice, bellowing imperiously at the mountains, at Storm King and Dunderberg, which bellowed echoes right back across the dark water to chill all the more. And finally out of the night she came, the Century . . . Only the stoutest of young hearts could survive the absolute agony of excitement on that quaking roadbed. First the appalling white headlight, jerking and leaping in a kind of mad disembodiment in the night, and then the awful noises of a devil's thunder symphony rushing down, all crescendo.

There simply never was anything like the shattering explosion of sound when that great Four-Six-Four Hudson steam locomotive yanked the Century past through the night. It was all over in one flashing spasm of delight as the monstrous 84-inch (sic) drivers* hammered the High Iron and bounced transfigured boys clear off the nearby gravel. You tried to freeze forever in memory the vision of the huge connecting rods, lurid for an instant in the firebox glow, as they flailed away like the swords of giants gone mad in a doomsday duel. Then the Titan was passed, trailing behind in almost silent contrast the elegant Century Pullmans that seemed to make no more noise than a thousand lady-like high heels clickety-clicking over the tiepoints. Heady and intoxicating was the lingering perfume of oil and steam and cinders and, briefly, of ambrosia as the diner went by. Two red bullseyes on the observation car winked away into the gloom and then all sound seemed to be cut off with a knife and only a long line of articulated light curled silently around the curve under Bear Mountain. But always one last word came from the king and his trailing lady; that great final bellow, dopplered down and far away in darkness. Was there ever, ever another train like this? No.

(*The driving wheels on the Hudsons were 79 inches in diameter.)

APPENDIX
THE PENNSYLVANIA NEWS
Western Region of the Pennsylvania Railroad
Vol. X CHICAGO, ILLINOIS, FEBRUARY 15, 1931 No. 4

RIDES 20 HOURS CONTINUOUSLY IN BROADWAY'S CAB
H. G. Hill, Lubrication Expert, Probably First Man to Make 908-Mile Trip
PRAISES P. R. R. ENGINES

Riding the Broadway Limited's locomotives from New York to Chicago, arriving on Feb. 6, H. G. Hill, an officer of The Texas Company of Port Arthur, Texas, probably won the distinction of being the only man to make the entire, continuous 908-mile trip between Manhattan and the Windy City in an engine cab.

Pennsylvania officers at Chicago were unable to recall a previous case in which it was necessary or desirable for anyone to undertake a similar trip.

Under regular operating conditons, seven engine crews are required during the Broadway's trip.

Hill is Lubrication Expert

Mr. Hill is a lubrication engineer for the Texas concern and made the 20-hour journey to observe the locomotive's performance, particularly with regard to the lubricated parts.

"The performance of the locomotives used on the Broadway's trip was perfect," said Mr. Hill, who was formarly a fireman on the Southern Pacific. He has been a lubrication engineer for ten years.

"All bearings were not above normal running temperature throughout the entire trip," said the lubrication expert, with as much pride as a Pennsylvania Railroad engineman praising the performance of his iron horse. "At every stop I climbed down from the cab and felt the main driving box bearings, the engine truck bearings and other lubricated parts of the locomotive and every time they were cool."

Praises Engine Crew

Mr. Hill had much praise for the enginemen and firemen who handled the locomotives which he rode.

"The engine crews treated me as if I were the Prince of Wales," said Mr. Hill as he climbed down from the big K-4 at Chicago Union Station.

The Pennsylvania's K-4 engines came in for much praise from Mr. Hill and he commented particularly on locomotive No. 3878, the engine which handled the Broadway Limited on the Western Region, between Crestline and Chicago.

"I never thought a Pacific type of locomotive could be built so as to ride as well as your K-4 engines," Mr. Hill told members of the crews with which he rode and he repeated this to Western Region officials who met him in Chicago at the end of his run.

"No. 3878 Is Sweetest Riding"

"The 3878 is the sweetest riding locomotive I have ever been on, and in my business, I have ridden engines on nearly all the railroads of the country. The easy start, the steady pick-up and the smooth performance at all speeds made a big hit with me.

"We made the run from Crestline to Upper Sandusky in exactly 30 minutes and the performance was perfect," said Mr. Hill. (The distance from Crestline to Upper Sandusky is approximately 30 miles.)

He said that the most enjoyable part of his trip was between Crestline and Chicago. As he climbed down from the cab at Chicago, he said, he felt fine, being "not at all fatigued."

Mr. Hill was served sandwiches and coffee at various times on the trip by the dining car stewards.*

T. H. Sinclair, engineman, and W. C. Lopshire, fireman, handled Engine 3878 between Fort Wayne and Chicago. The crew from Crestline to Fort Wayne was composed of F. C. Welsh, engineman, and E. G. Ludwig, fireman.

(Reprinted by courtesy of Penn Central Rail Road)

*(This occurred only at North Philadelphia.—HGH)

TABLE 1

THE EXPOSITION FLYER

NYC&HR-LS&MS Train No. 41, New York to Chicago, September 26-27, 1893.

980 Miles in 20 Hours, as reported by Cy Warman in January, 1894.

From	To	Eng. No.	Type	Class Old	New	Date Built	Bldr.	C/N
New York	Albany	898	4-4-0	I	Ca	1891	Schen.	3588
Albany	Syracuse	907	4-4-0	I	Ca	1892	"	3645
Syracuse	Buffalo	896	4-4-0	I	Ca	1891	"	3586
Buffalo	Erie	293	4-4-0	R-2	C52b	1886	"	2066
Erie	Cleveland	559	4-6-0	E-4	F49b	1891	Brooks	1927
Cleveland	Toledo	Not reported						
Toledo	Elkhart	94	4-4-0	Q	C-53	1893	"	2256
Elkhart	Chicago	160	4-4-0	Q	C-53	1893	"	2257

Principal Dimensions of Locomotives Used on Train 41, 9-26/27-1893						
Engine No.	Type	Cylinders	Drivers Diam.	Boiler Pressure	Total Weight	Tractive Effort
898	4-4-0	19" x 24"	78"	180 psi	125,000	17,400
907	"	"	"	"	"	"
896	"	"	"	"	"	"
293	"	17" x 24"	69"	"	108,000	15,880
559	4-6-0	"	57"	160	"	17,200
94	4-4-0	"	73"	180	104,000	14,900
160	"	"	"	"	"	"

NYC&HR RR - New York to Buffalo; LS&MS Ry. - Buffalo to Chicago.

TABLE 2

PACIFIC TYPE LOCOMOTIVES OF THE PENNSYLVANIA RAIL ROAD

Number Built	Class	Numbers	Builder	Date Built	Built Sat. or Sup.	Reverse Gear	Driving Wheel Diam.
1	K28	7067	ALCO	1907	Sat.	Screw	80"
153	K2	7510+	Juniata	1910-11	"	"	"
62	K2a	86+	"	1911-13	"	"	"
2	K2b	3371, 3375	"	1911	"	"	72"
12	K21s	8701-8712	ALCO#	1911-13	Sup.	"	80"
1	K29	3395	"	1911	"	"	"
10	K2a	7049+	"	1912	Sat.	"	"
30	K3s	7546+	Baldwin	1913	Sup.	Lever	"
1	K4s	1737	Juniata	1914	"	Screw	"
40	K4s	12+	"	1917	"	"	"
18	K4s	3667-3684	"	1918	"	"	"
16	K4s	5334-5349	"	1918	"	"	"
76	K4s	8+	"	1918	"	"	"
17	K4s	7267+	"	1919	"	"	"
50	K4s	3726-3775	"	1920	"	"	"
2	K4	3800-3801	"	1923	"	Power	"
3	K4	3805-3807	"	1923	"	"	"
52	K4	3838-3889	"	1923	"	"	"
50	K4	5350-5399	"	1924	"	"	"
75	K4	5400-5474	Baldwin	1927	"	"	"
17	K4	5475-5491	Juniata	1927	"	"	"
8	K4	5492-5499	"	1928	"	"	"
1	K5	5698	"	1929	"	"	"
1	K5	5699*	Baldwin	1929	"	"	"
698 Total							

+ Number shown and assorted other numbers.

Originally Vandalia Line Nos. 1-12.

* Built with Caprotti Valve Gear and Poppet Valves; later changed to Piston Valve Cylinders and Walschaert Valve Gear.

s The use of the letter "s" in the classification indicated that the locomotive was equipped with a firetube superheater. The use of the letter "s" was discontinued for designs made after January 1, 1923, as the superheater was then standard equipment.

TABLE 3

PENNSYLVANIA RAIL ROAD CLASS K4s PACIFIC (4-6-2) TYPE LOCOMOTIVES

From W. D. Edson

Builder	Date Built	No. in Order	Numbers						
Juniata	1914	1	1737						
Juniata	1917	40	12	358	669	1188	1497	5058	5238
			20	359	719	1195	2034	5072	5243
			43	383	830	1395	2445	5077	5253
			122	422	920	1453	5022	5086	5296
			227	612	1120	1462	5038	5147	
			299	623	1139	1488	5041	5154	
Juniata	1918	110	8	850	1435	1980	7053	8181	8309
			16	911	1436	1981	7054	8195	8334
			225	945	1517	1983	7116	8212	8373
			262	949	1522	1984	7133	8218	8378
			269	958	1526	1985	7294	8225	3667-3684
			295	962	1531	2032	7914	8236	5334-5349
			389	1329	1533	2112	7938	8240	
			452	1330	1546	2665	8009	8242	
			518	1339	1551	2673	8085	8251	
			526	1361	1554	2761	8157	8261	
			646	1392	1588	3654	8161	8278	
			837	1433	1653	3655	8165	8281	
Juniata	1919	17	7267	7274	7279	7288	8114	8347	
			7270	7275	7280	8068	8122	8377	
			7273	7278	7287	8108	8137		
Juniata	1920	50	3726-3775						
Juniata	1923	57	3800, 3801, 3805-3807, 3838-3889						
Juniata	1924	50	5350-5399						
Baldwin	1927	75	5400-5474						
Juniata	1927	20	5475-5494						
Juniata	1928	5	5495-5499						
	Total	425							

TABLE 4

THE BROADWAY LIMITED
PENNSYLVANIA RAILROAD

LOG OF PERFORMANCE - Train No. 29 - February 5-6, 1931 - New York to

Chicago. Class L5pdw 2-4-4-2 Type Electric Locomotive No. 3924.

Class K4s Pacific (4-6-2) Type Steam Locomotives Nos. 5439, 5417,

7116, 5373 and 3878.

MILEAGE RUN BY INDIVIDUAL LOCOMOTIVES

Locomotive No.	From	To	Miles	Time h-m	Av'ge Speed MPH
3924	New York	Manhattan Transfer	9	0-14	38.5
5439	Manhattan Transfer	Harrisburg	186	3-23	54.9
5417	Harrisburg	Pittsburgh	244	5-24	45.1
5373	Pittsburgh	Crestline	189	4-14	44.6
3878	Crestline	Chicago	280	5-12	54.1
		Total	908	18-27	49.3
7116	Altoona (helper)	Gallitzin	12		

NON-STOP RUNS BY INDIVIDUAL LOCOMOTIVES

5439	Newark	North Philadelphia	74	1-14	60.8
	North Philadelphia	Harrisburg	110	2-04	53.2
5417	Harrisburg	Altoona	131	2-41	48.8
	Gallitzin	Pittsburgh	101	2-14	45.2
5373	Pittsburgh	Alliance	83	1-53	44.0
	Alliance	Crestline	106	2-21	45.1
3878	Crestline	Fort Wayne	132	2-16	58.2
	Fort Wayne	Englewood	141	2-38	53.5

TABLE 5

THE BROADWAY LIMITED
PENNSYLVANIA RAIL ROAD

LOG OF PERFORMANCE - TRAIN No. 29 - FEBRUARY 5-6, 1931 - NEW YORK TO CHICAGO. CLASS L5pdw 2-4-4-2 TYPE ELECTRIC LOCOMOTIVE No. 3924. CLASS K4s PACIFIC (4-6-2) TYPE STEAM LOCOMOTIVES Nos. 5439, 5417, 7116, 5373 and 3878.

	NOTES	NO. CARS	TONS (X)	MILES	TIME h-m	AV'GE SPEED MPH
2-5-1931						
No. 3924. Class L5pdw Electric Locomotive.						
New York to Manhattan Transfer	acd	10	810	9	0-14	38.5
Total & average, running time, no stops				9	0-14	38.5
Manhattan Transfer, engine and crew change					0-04	
No. 5439. Class K4s Steam Locomotive						
Manhattan Transfer to Newark - stop 1 min.	a	10	810	1	0-05	12.0
Newark to North Philadelphia - stop 2 min.	a	10	810	75	1-14	60.8
North Philadelphia to Harrisburg	acde	10	810	110	2-04	53.2
Total & average, running time only				186	3-23	54.9
Total & average, including 3 min. stops				186	3-26	54.1
Engine & crew change & station work, Harrisburg					0-11	
No. 5417. Class K4s Steam Locomotive.						
Harrisburg to Altoona - stop 15 min.	adef	10	810	131	2-41	48.8
Altoona to Gallitzin - stop 1 min.	h	9	720	12	0-29	24.8
Gallitzin to Pittsburgh	acde	9	720	101	2-14	45.2
Total & average, running time only				244	5-24	45.1
Total & average, including 16 min. stops				244	5-40	43.0
Engine & crew change & station work, Pittsburgh					0-10	
2-6-1931						
No. 5373. Class K4s Steam Locomotive.						
Pittsburgh to Alliance - stop 12 min.	egw	9	720	83	1-53	44.0
Alliance to Crestline	bcde	10	810	106	2-21	45.1
Total & average, running time only				189	4-14	44.6
Total & average, including 12 min. stops				189	4-26	42.6
Engine & crew change & station work, Crestline					0-07	
No. 3878. Class K4s Steam Locomotive.						
Crestline to Fort Wayne - stop 16 min.	bde	10	810	132	2-16	58.2
Fort Wayne to Englewood - 7 min. stop	b	10	810	141	2-38	53.5
Englewood to Chicago	b	10	810	7	0-16	26.9
Total & average, running time only				280	5-10	54.1
Total & average, including 23 min. stops				280	5-33	50.4
Total & average, running time only, entire trip				908	18-25	49.3
Total & average, including 1h. 26m. stops, entire trip				908	19-51	45.7

NOTES: (a) Receive passengers. (b) Discharge passengers. (c) Change engine. (d) Change crews. (e) Receive or discharge mail. (f) Cut out dining car. (g) Pick up dining car. (h) Engine 7116 doubleheaded Altoona to Gallitzin. (w) Take water at roadside tank. (X) Estimated train tonnage does not include locomotive weight. No. 3924 weighed 194 tons. Class K4s locomotives weighed 240 tons. Total train-miles - 908. Total locomotive-miles - 920. Total car-miles - 8,884. Gross ton-miles - 938,226. Gross ton-miles/train-hour - 50,962. GTM/Tr-Hr - No. 3924, 39,287; No. 5439, 57,729; No. 5417, 46,094; No. 5373, 45,116; No. 3878, 56,910.

TABLE 6

THE TWENTIETH CENTURY LIMITED
NEW YORK CENTRAL LINES

LOG OF PERFORMANCE - Train No. 25 - February 17-18, 1931 - New York to

Chicago. Class T-3a Electric Locomotive No. 1176; Class J-1d Hudson

(4-6-4) Type Steam Locomotive No. 5302: CUT Class P-1a Electric Loco-

motive No. 1061: Class J-1b Hudson (4-6-4) Type Steam Locomotive No. 5246.

MILEAGE RUN BY INDIVIDUAL LOCOMOTIVES

Locomotive No.	From	To	Miles	Time h-m	Av'ge Speed MPH
1176	New York	Harmon	32.7	0-45	43.6
5302	Harmon	Collinwood	581.3	10-20	56.2
1061	Collinwood	Linndale	13.2	0-28	28.0
5246	Linndale	Chicago	334.0	6-24	52.1
			961.2	17-57	53.5

NON-STOP RUNS BY INDIVIDUAL LOCOMOTIVES

5302	Harmon	Albany	109.5	1-59	55.2
5302	Albany	Utica	94.6	1-54	49.8
5302	Buffalo	Collinwood	178.1	2-51	62.4
5246	Linndale	Toledo	100.4	1-43	57.7
5246	Toledo	Elkhart	133.0	2-25	54.9
5246	Elkhart	Englewood	93.9	2-01	46.7

TABLE 7

THE TWENTIETH CENTURY LIMITED
NEW YORK CENTRAL LINES

LOG OF PERFORMANCE - TRAIN No. 25 - FEBRUARY 17-18, 1931 - NEW YORK TO CHICAGO.
CLASS T-3a ELECTRIC LOCOMOTIVE No. 1176; CLASS J-1d HUDSON (4-6-4) TYPE STEAM
LOCOMOTIVE No. 5302; CUT CLASS P-1a ELECTRIC LOCOMOTIVE No. 1061; CLASS J-1b
HUDSON (4-6-4) TYPE STEAM LOCOMOTIVE No. 5246.

2-17-1931	NOTES	No. CARS	TONS (k)	MILES	TIME h-m	AV'GE SPEED MPH
No. 1176 Class T-3a (1926)						
New York to Harmon	acd	12	960	32.7	0-45	43.6
Total & average, running time				32.7	0-45	43.6
Engine & crew change at Harmon					0-09	
No. 5302 Class J-1d (1930)						
Harmon to Albany	adfj	12	960	109.5	1-59	55.2
Albany to Utica	ac	14	1120	94.6	1-54	49.8
Utica to Syracuse	adeg	14	1120	52.8	1-01	52.1
Syracuse to Rochester	ai	13	1040	80.3	1-26	56.1
Rochester to Buffalo	ade	13	1040	66.0	1-09	57.4
Buffalo to Collinwood	cd	13	1040	178.1	2-51	62.4
Total & average, running time				581.3	10-20	56.2
Total & average, incl. 51 min. stops				581.3	11-11	51.9
Engine & crew change at Collinwood					0-05	
2-18-1931						
No. 1061 Class P-1a (1930)						
Collinwood to Cleveland (Un. Term.)	e	13	1040	7.0	0-15	28.0
Cleveland to Linndale	cd	13	1040	6.2	0-13	29.5
Total & average, running time				13.2	0-28	28.0
Total & average, incl 5 min. stop				13.2	0-33	24.0
Engine & crew change at Linndale					0-07	
No. 5246 Class J-1b (1927)						
Linndale to Toledo	deh	13	1040	100.4	1-43	57.7
Toledo to Elkhart	bde	15	1200	133.0	2-25	54.9
Elkhart to Englewood	b	15	1200	93.9	2-01	46.7
Englewood to Chicago	be	15	1200	6.7	0-15	26.8
Total & average, running time				334.0	6-24	52.1
Total & average, incl. 33 min. stops				334.0	6-57	48.0
Total & average, running time, entire run				961.2	17-57	53.5
Total & average, incl. 1h 50m stops, entire run				961.2	19-47	48.5

NOTES: (a) Receive passengers. (b) Discharge passengers. (c) Change engines.
(d) Change crews. (e) Receive or discharge mail. (f) Pick up 2 Pullman cars
from Boston. (g) Cut out dining car. (h) Pick up 2 dining cars. (i) Stop 6
minutes on flag and 4 minutes for fuel between Syracuse and Rochester. (j)
Helper engine on rear end to top of grade near West Albany Shops - cut off
without stopping train. (k) Tonnage shown is estimated weight of train.
Weight of No. 1176, 146.3 tons; No. 5302, 335 tons; No. 1061, 209.4 tons;
No. 5246, 320 tons. Train miles, 961.2; locomotive miles, 961.2: car miles,
12,967. Gross ton-miles, 1,354,168; gross ton-miles/train-hour, 77,440, (based
on running time). GTM/Tr-Hr, No. 1176, 48,657; No. 5302, 77,992; No. 1061,
35,869; No. 5246, 77,545.

TABLE 8

SUMMARY OF PERFORMANCE

PRR Train No. 29 - THE BROADWAY LIMITED - New York to Chicago - February 5-6, 1931.
NYC Train No. 25 - THE TWENTIETH CENTURY LIMITED - New York to Chicago - February 17-18, 1931.

Road	Loco. No.	From	To	Miles	Run'g Time Hours	Loco. Weight Tons	Train Weight Tons	Total Weight Tons	Gross Ton-Miles	GTM/Tr-Hr.
PRR #29	3924	New York	Man. Trans.	9	0.23	194	810	1004	9,036	39,287
	5439	Man. Trans.	Newark	1	0.08	240	810	1050	1,050	13,125
	5439	Newark	N. Phila.	75	1.23	240	810	1050	78,750	64,024
	5439	N. Phila.	Harrisburg	110	2.06	240	810	1050	115,500	55,797
	5417	Harrisburg	Altoona	131	2.68	240	810	1050	137,550	51,324
	5417	Altoona	Gallitzin	12	0.48	480	720	1200	14,400	30,000
7116	5417	Gallitzin	Pittsburgh	101	2.23	240	720	960	96,960	43,479
	5373	Pittsburgh	Alliance	83	1.88	240	720	960	79,680	42,383
	5373	Alliance	Crestline	106	2.35	240	810	1050	111,300	47,361
	3878	Crestline	Fort Wayne	132	2.26	240	810	1050	138,600	61,327
	3878	Fort Wayne	Englewood	141	2.62	240	810	1050	148,050	56,507
	3878	Englewood	Chicago	7	0.26	240	810	1050	7,350	28,269
				908	18.41				938,226	50,962
NYC #25	1176	New York	Harmon	32.7	0.75	146	970	1116	36,493	48,657
	5302	Harmon	Albany	109.5	1.98	335	970	1305	142,897	72,166
	5302	Albany	Utica	94.6	1.90	335	1130	1465	138,589	72,941
	5302	Utica	Syracuse	52.8	1.01	335	1130	1465	77,352	76,586
	5302	Syracuse	Rochester	80.3	1.43	335	1040	1375	110,412	77,210
	5302	Rochester	Buffalo	66.0	1.15	335	1040	1375	90,750	78,913
	5302	Buffalo	Collinwood	178.1	2.85	335	1040	1375	244,887	85,925
	1061	Collinwood	Cleveland	7.0	0.25	210	1040	1250	8,750	35,000
	1061	Cleveland	Linndale	6.2	0.21	210	1040	1250	7,750	36,905
	5246	Linndale	Toledo	100.4	1.72	320	1040	1360	136,544	79,386
	5246	Toledo	Elkhart	133.0	2.42	320	1220	1540	204,820	84,636
	5246	Elkhart	Englewood	93.9	2.01	320	1220	1540	144,606	71,943
	5246	Englewood	Chicago	6.7	0.25	320	1220	1540	10,318	41,272
				961.2	17.95				1,354,168	77,440

Locomotive weights from Railroad Companies' Diagram Books. Train weights based on 80 tons per Pullman car and 90 tons per dining car (approximate).

PRR #3924, Class L5pdw electric locomotive; Nos. 5439, 5417, 7116, 5373 and 3878, Class K4s Pacific type steam locomotives. NYC #1176 Class T-3a and #1061 Class P-1a electric locomotives; #5302 Class J-1d and #5246 Class J-1b Hudson (4-6-4) type steam locomotives.

TABLE 9
NEW YORK CENTRAL LINES CLASS J HUDSON (4-6-4) TYPE LOCOMOTIVES

Class	Bldr.	Date Built	No. in Order	Road	Original Nos.	1936 Nos.
J-1a	ALCo	1927	1	NYC	5200	5200
J-1b	ALCo	1927-28	49	NYC	5201-5249	5201-5249
J-1c	ALCo	1928-29	25	NYC	5250-5274	5250-5274
J-1d	ALCo	1929-30	40	NYC	5275-5314	5275-5314
J-1e	ALCo	1931	30	NYC	5315-5344	5315-5344
J-1b	ALCo	1927-28	10	MC	8200-8209	5345-5354
J-1c	ALCo	1929	5	MC	8210-8214	5355-5359
J-1d	ALCO	1929	15	MC	8215-8229	5360-5374
J-1d	ALCo	1929	10	CCC&StL	6600-6609	5375-5384
J-1d	ALCo	1930	10	CCC&StL	6610-6619	5385-5394
J-1e	ALCo	1931	10	CCC&StL	6620-6629	5395-5404
J-3a	ALCo	1937-38	50	NYC	5405-5454	5405-5454
J-2a	ALCo	1928	5	B&A	600-604	5455-5459
J-2b	ALCO	1930	5	B&A	605-609	5460-5464
J-2c	Lima	1931	10	B&A	610-619	5465-5474

Total   275

From "Locomotives of the New York Central Lines", 1966,
by Edward L. May and W. D. Edson.

LOCOMOTIVE SPECIFICATIONS

The following pages contain condensed specifications for the locomotives illustrated in this book. The data shown were taken primarily from the builders' specification cards, from the railroad companies' Locomotive Diagram Books, and from other sources in the author's Library which were believed to be authentic. The specifications are as complete as the availability of data permitted.

These specifications are included for the benefit of those readers who desire to study the details and design of the locomotives illustrated. It is sincerely hoped that the data will be of interest and value to all who read this book.

Compiled by COLONEL HOWARD G. HILL, USAR (Ret.)

Type ....

Page .... Class ....

Fig. 1.

No. 274 Name	Road Pennsylvania Rail Road	Type 4-4-0
Builder Pennsylvania R. R.	Boiler, type Wagon top	Wheelbase, Rigid 8' 6"
Works Altoona Machine Shops	" diam. 48-3/4" pressure 125 psi.	" , Driving 8' 6"
Date built 9-1875 Bldr's. No. 287	Firebox, type Crown bar - narrow	" , Engine 22' 5-5/8"
Builder's Class	" length 72-5/8" width 35"	" , Eng. & Tender 44' 6-1/8"
R.R. Class, Old C New D3	Combustion Chamber, length	Weight in Working Order, lbs.:
Bldr's. Order No. Neg. No.	Grate Area. 17.6 sq. ft.	Front Truck 28,150
No. in Order Orig. Nos	No. of Tubes 155 No. of Flues	Driving Wheels 50,950
Orig. No. this Engine 274	Diam. " 2¼" Diam "	Trailing
Gauge of Track 4' 8½"	Length, Tubes & Flues 10' 7-1/16"	Engine, total 79,100
Service Passenger & Fast Freight	Heating Surface, sq ft.:	Tender 59,900
Cylinder diam. H.P. 17" L.P.	" Tubes 966 Flues Total 966	Eng. & Tender 139,000
Stroke of Piston 24" No. of Cyls. 2	" Firebox 117 Arch Tubes	Tender, type Rectangular
Driving Wheels diam. 62"	" Syphons Total 1083	" No. of Wheels 8
Valves, type. H.P. Slide diam.	Superheater, type H.S.	Water, gals. 2,400 Coal, tons 4
" " L.P. diam.	Feedwater Heater	Fuel Oil, gals.
Valve Gear Stephenson	Stoker Brakes WAB	Max. Tractive Effort (a) 11,890 lbs.
Reverse Gear, Lever X Power	Throttle, type Dome	" " Booster (b) lbs.
Designer		Factor of Adhesion (a) 4.28 (b)
Source of Photo George M. Hart Collection.		Notes on back of this sheet
Disposition: Sold to		Retired or scrapped

An early Pennsylvania passenger locomotive. 6" air pump. Cam type driver brakes.

Fig. 2.   "Old Long-Legged No. 10"

No. 10 Name /	Road Pennsylvania Rail Road.	Type 4-4-0.
Builder Pennsylvania R. R.	Boiler, type Wagon top	Wheelbase, Rigid 7' 9"
Works Altoona Machine Shops	" diam. 49¼" pressure 140 psi.	" , Driving 7' 9"
Date built 3-25-1881 Bldr's. No. 532	Firebox, type Crown bar - narrow	" , Engine 22' 8"
Builder's Class	" length 119-7/8" width 41-3/4"	" , Eng. & Tender 47' 10"
R.R. Class, Old K New D6	Combustion Chamber, length	Weight in Working Order, lbs.:
Bldr's. Order No. Neg. No.	Grate Area. 34.7 sq. ft.	Front Truck 31,800
No. in Order 18 Orig. Nos Note	No. of Tubes 201 No. of Flues	Driving Wheels 64,900
Orig. No. this Engine 10	Diam. " 1-7/8" Diam "	Trailing
Gauge of Track 4' 8½"	Length, Tubes & Flues 10' 11-13/16"	Engine, total 96,700
Service Passenger	Heating Surface, sq ft.:	Tender 60,300
Cylinder diam. H.P. 18" L.P.	" Tubes 1085 Flues Total 1085	Eng. & Tender 157,000
Stroke of Piston 24" No. of Cyls. 2	" Firebox 145 Arch Tubes	Tender, type Rectangular
Driving Wheels diam. 78"	" Syphons Total 1230	" No. of Wheels 8
Valves, type. H.P. Slide diam.	Superheater, type H.S.	Water, gals. 2,400 Coal, tons 6
" " L.P. diam.	Feedwater Heater	Fuel Oil, gals.
Valve Gear Stephenson	Stoker Brakes WAB	Max. Tractive Effort (a) 11,860 lbs.
Reverse Gear, Lever Power X	Throttle, type Dome	" " Booster (b) lbs.
Designer		Factor of Adhesion (a) 5.47 (b)
Source of Photo George M. Hart Collection.		Notes on back of this sheet
Disposition: Sold to		Retired or scrapped

Note:- Nos. 1, 3, 10, 184, 260, 274, 317, 340, 341 built in 1881. No. 10 was the
first one. Nos. 956-959 followed in 1882, and Nos. 1066-1070 in 1883. No. 10 was
the first locomotive to be equipped with a power reverse gear, a steam-hydraulic
device. Cam type driver brakes. 6" air pump. Later Class K locomotives had extended smokeboxes and sloping firebox mud rings. All Class K locomotives were
eventually equipped with 68" or 72" drivers for local passenger service.

Fig. 3.

No. 568 Name	Road Pennsylvania Rail Road	Type 4-4-0
Builder Pennsylvania R. R.	Boiler, type Straight top	Wheelbase, Rigid
Works Altoona Machine Shops	" diam. pressure 160 psi	" , Driving
Date built 6-1891 Bldr's. No. 1645	Firebox, type Belpaire – narrow	" , Engine
Builder's Class	" length width	" , Eng. & Tender
R.R. Class, Old 0 New D10a	Combustion Chamber, length	Weight in Working Order, lbs.:
Bldr's. Order No. Neg. No.	Grate Area, 17.3 sq. ft.	Front Truck 36,600
No. in Order Orig. Nos	No. of Tubes No. of Flues	Driving Wheels 66,900
Orig. No. this Engine 568	Diam. " Diam "	Trailing
Gauge of Track 4' 8½"	Length, Tubes & Flues	Engine, total 103,500
Service Passenger	Heating Surface, sq. ft.:	Tender
Cylinder diam. H.P. 18" L.P.	" Tubes Flues Total	Eng. & Tender
Stroke of Piston 24" No. of Cyls. 2	" Firebox Arch Tubes	Tender, type Rectangular
Driving Wheels diam. 68"	" Syphons Total 1296	" No. of Wheels 8
Valves, type, H.P. Slide diam.	Superheater, type H.S.	Water, gals. Coal, tons
" " L.P. diam.	Feedwater Heater	Fuel Oil, gals.
Valve Gear Stephenson	Stoker Brakes WAB	Max. Tractive Effort (a) 15,550 lbs.
Reverse Gear, Lever X Power	Throttle, type Dome	" " Booster (b) lbs.
Designer		Factor of Adhesion (a) 4.3 (b)
Source of Photo George M. Hart Collection.		Notes on back of this sheet
Disposition: Sold to		Retired or scrapped

No. 568, with THE PENNSYLVANIA LIMITED, crossing the iron truss bridge which carried the tracks of the Middle Division across the Susquehanna River at Rockville, near Harrisburg, from 1877 to 1902. Photographed about 1902.

Fig. 4.

No. 1639 Name	Road Pennsylvania Rail Road	Type 4-4-0
Builder Pennsylvania R. R.	Boiler, type Straight top	Wheelbase, Rigid 7' 9"
Works Juniata	" diam. 56-1/8" pressure 175 psi	" , Driving 7' 9"
Date built 5-1893 Bldr's. No.	Firebox, type Belpaire – narrow	" , Engine 22' 8½"
Builder's Class	" length 119-5/8" width 40"	" , Eng. & Tender 48' 7¼"
R.R. Class, Old P New D13c	Combustion Chamber, length	Weight in Working Order, lbs.:
Bldr's. Order No. Neg. No.	Grate Area, 33.2 sq. ft.	Front Truck 35,000
No. in Order Orig. Nos	No. of Tubes 258 No. of Flues	Driving Wheels 79,500
Orig. No. this Engine 1639	Diam. " 1-7/8" Diam "	Trailing
Gauge of Track 4' 8½"	Length, Tubes & Flues 11' 3-7/8"	Engine, total 114,500
Service Passenger	Heating Surface, sq. ft.:	Tender 77,500
Cylinder diam. H.P. 18½" L.P.	" Tubes 1404 Flues Total 1404	Eng. & Tender 192,000
Stroke of Piston 24" No. of Cyls. 2	" Firebox 167 Arch Tubes	Tender, type Rectangular
Driving Wheels diam. 68"	" Syphons Total 1571	" No. of Wheels 8
Valves, type, H.P. Slide diam.	Superheater, type H.S.	Water, gals. 3,000 Coal, tons 7½
" " L.P. diam.	Feedwater Heater	Fuel Oil, gals.
Valve Gear Stephenson	Stoker Brakes WAB A-1	Max. Tractive Effort (a) 17,970 lbs.
Reverse Gear, Lever X Power	Throttle, type Dome	" " Booster (b) lbs.
Designer		Factor of Adhesion (a) 4.42 (b)
Source of Photo George M. Hart Collection		Notes on back of this sheet
Disposition: Sold to		Retired or scrapped

One of the locomotives built for service on THE PENNSYLVANIA SPECIAL.

Fig. 5.

No. 1659 Name	Road Pennsylvania Rail Road	Type 4-4-0
Builder Pennsylvania R. R.	Boiler, type Straight top	Wheelbase, Rigid
Works Juniata	" diam. pressure 175 psi.	" , Driving
Date built 1893 Bldr's. No.	Firebox, type Belpaire - narrow	" , Engine
Builder's Class	" length width	" , Eng. & Tender
R.R. Class, Old P New D14	Combustion Chamber, length	Weight in Working Order, lbs.:
Bldr's. Order No. Neg. No.	Grate Area, 33.2 sq. ft.	Front Truck 40,000
No. in Order Orig. Nos	No. of Tubes No. of Flues	Driving Wheels 82,600
Orig. No. this Engine 1659	Diam. " Diam "	Trailing
Gauge of Track 4' 8½"	Length, Tubes & Flues	Engine, total 122,600
Service Passenger	Heating Surface, sq ft.:	Tender
Cylinder diam. H.P. 18½" L.P.	" Tubes Flues Total	Eng. & Tender
Stroke of Piston 24" No. of Cyls. 2	" Firebox Arch Tubes	Tender, type Rectangular
Driving Wheels diam. 78"	" Syphons Total 1583	" No. of Wheels 8
Valves, type, H.P. Slide diam.	Superheater, type H.S.	Water, gals. Coal, tons
" " L.P. diam.	Feedwater Heater	Fuel Oil, gals.
Valve Gear Stephenson	Stoker Brakes WAB A-1	Max. Tractive Effort (a) 15,660 lbs.
Reverse Gear, Lever X Power	Throttle, type Dome	" " Booster (b) lbs.
Designer		Factor of Adhesion (a) 5.27 (b)
Source of Photo George M. Hart Collection		Notes on back of this sheet
Disposition: Sold to		Retired or scrapped

One of the locomotives built for THE PENNSYLVANIA SPECIAL. 8" air pump. Cam type driver brakes. Subsequently rebuilt with 68" drivers for local service.

Fig. 6.

No. 88 Name	Road Pennsylvania Rail Road	Type 4-4-0
Builder Pennsylvania R. R.	Boiler, type Conical	Wheelbase, Rigid 7' 9"
Works Juniata	" diam. 60" pressure 185 psi.	" , Driving 7' 9"
Date built 1895 Bldr's. No.	Firebox, type Belpaire - narrow	" , Engine 22' 9½"
Builder's Class	" length 19-5/8" width 40"	" , Eng. & Tender 55' 0¼"
R.R. Class, Old L New D16a	Combustion Chamber, length	Weight in Working Order, lbs.:
Bldr's. Order No. Neg. No. ME22C	Grate Area, 33.2 sq. ft.	Front Truck 40,000
No. in Order Orig. Nos	No. of Tubes 310 No. of Flues	Driving Wheels 93,000
Orig. No. this Engine 88	Diam. " 1-7/8" Diam "	Trailing
Gauge of Track 4' 8½"	Length, Tubes & Flues 11' 4-3/4"	Engine, total 133,000
Service Passenger	Heating Surface, sq ft.:	Tender 134,000
Cylinder diam. H.P. 18½" L.P.	" Tubes 1734 Flues Total 1734	Eng. & Tender 267,000
Stroke of Piston 26" No. of Cyls. 2	" Firebox 166 Arch Tubes	Tender, type Rectangular
Driving Wheels diam. 80"	" Syphons Total 1900	" No. of Wheels 8
Valves, type, H.P. Slide diam.	Superheater, type H.S.	Water, gals. 5,500 Coal, tons 12½
" " L.P. diam.	Feedwater Heater	Fuel Oil, gals.
Valve Gear Stephenson	Stoker Brakes WAB A-1	Max. Tractive Effort (a) 17,500 lbs.
Reverse Gear, Lever X Power	Throttle, type Dome	" " Booster (b) lbs.
Designer		Factor of Adhesion (a) 5.32 (b)
Source of Photo George M. Hart Collection		Notes on back of this sheet
Disposition: Sold to		Retired or scrapped

This was the first locomotive of the Class D16 groups - the ultimate in the 4-4-0 type saturated steam locomotives for service on the limited trains.

Fig. 7.

No. 296 Name	Road Pennsylvania Rail Road	Type 4-4-0
Builder Pennsylvania R. R.	Boiler, type Conical	Wheelbase, Rigid 7' 9"
Works Juniata	" diam. 60" pressure 185 psi.	", Driving 7' 9"
Date built 1895 Bldr's. No.	Firebox, type Belpaire - narrow	", Engine 22' 9½"
Builder's Class	" length 119-5/8" width 40"	", Eng. & Tender 55' 0¼"
R.R. Class, Old L New D16a	Combustion Chamber, length	Weight in Working Order, lbs.:
Bldr's. Order No. Neg. No.	Grate Area, 33.2 sq. ft.	Front Truck 40,000
No. in Order Orig. Nos	No. of Tubes 310 No. of Flues	Driving Wheels 93,000
Orig. No. this Engine 296	Diam. " 1-7/8" Diam "	Trailing
Gauge of Track 4' 8½"	Length, Tubes & Flues 11' 4-3/4"	Engine, total 133,000
Service Passenger	Heating Surface, sq ft.:	Tender 134,000
Cylinder diam. H.P. 18½" L.P.	" Tubes 1734 Flues Total 1734	Eng. & Tender 267,000
Stroke of Piston 26" No. of Cyls. 2	" Firebox 166 Arch Tubes	Tender, type Rectangular
Driving Wheels diam. 80"	" Syphons Total 1900	" No. of Wheels 8
Valves, type, H.P. Slide diam.	Superheater, type H.S.	Water, gals. 5,500 Coal, tons 12½
" " L.P. diam.	Feedwater Heater	Fuel Oil, gals.
Valve Gear Stephenson	Stoker Brakes WAB. A-1	Max. Tractive Effort (a) 17,500 lbs.
Reverse Gear, Lever X Power	Throttle, type Dome	" " Booster (b) lbs.
Designer		Factor of Adhesion (a) 5.32 (b)
Source of Photo BALDWIN LOCOMOTIVES		Notes on back of this sheet
Disposition: Sold to		Retired or scrapped

THE PENNSYLVANIA LIMITED on the Philadelphis Division, near Merion, Pa., in 1899.

LA-4.500. 3-70

Fig. 8.

No. 101 Name	Road Pennsylvania Rail Road	Type 4-4-0
Builder Pennsylvania R. R.	Boiler, type Conical	Wheelbase, Rigid 7' 9"
Works Juniata	" diam. 60" pressure 185 psi.	", Driving 7' 9"
Date built 1895 Bldr's. No. 371	Firebox, type Belpaire - narrow	", Engine 22' 9½"
Builder's Class	" length 119-5/8" width 40"	", Eng. & Tender 55' 0¼"
R.R. Class, Old L New D16a	Combustion Chamber, length	Weight in Working Order, lbs.:
Bldr's. Order No. Neg. No. ME3169A	Grate Area, 33.2 sq. ft.	Front Truck 40,000
No. in Order Orig. Nos	No. of Tubes 310 No. of Flues	Driving Wheels 93,000
Orig. No. this Engine 101	Diam. " 1-7/8" Diam "	Trailing
Gauge of Track 4' 8½"	Length, Tubes & Flues 11' 4-3/4"	Engine, total 133,000
Service Passenger	Heating Surface, sq ft.:	Tender 134,000
Cylinder diam. H.P. 18½" L.P.	" Tubes 1734 Flues Total 1734	Eng. & Tender 267,000
Stroke of Piston 26" No. of Cyls. 2	" Firebox 166 Arch Tubes	Tender, type Rectangular
Driving Wheels diam. 80"	" Syphons Total 1900	" No. of Wheels 8
Valves, type, H.P. Slide diam.	Superheater, type H.S.	Water, gals. 5,500 Coal, tons 12½
" " L.P. diam.	Feedwater Heater	Fuel Oil, gals.
Valve Gear Stephenson	Stoker Brakes WAB. A-1	Max. Tractive Effort (a) 17,500 lbs.
Reverse Gear, Lever X Power	Throttle, type Dome	" " Booster (b) lbs.
Designer		Factor of Adhesion (a) 5.32 (b)
Source of Photo Pennsylvania Rail Road.		Notes on back of this sheet
Disposition: Sold to		Retired or scrapped

American Equalized Driver Brakes. Engine truck brakes.

Fig. 9.

No. 1395 Name	Road Pennsylvania Rail Road	Type 4-4-0
Builder Pennsylvania R. R.	Boiler, type Conical	Wheelbase, Rigid 7' 9"
Works Juniata	" diam. 60" pressure 185 psi.	", Driving 7' 9"
Date built 1896 Bldr's. No.	Firebox, type Belpaire - narrow	", Engine 22' 9½"
Builder's Class	" length 119-5/8" width 40"	", Eng. & Tender 55' 0¼"
R.R. Class, Old L New D16a	Combustion Chamber, length	Weight in Working Order, lbs.:
Bldr's. Order No. Neg. No.	Grate Area, 33.2 sq. ft.	Front Truck 40,000
No. in Order Orig. Nos	No. of Tubes 310 No. of Flues	Driving Wheels 93,000
Orig. No. this Engine 1395	Diam. " 1-7/8" Diam "	Trailing
Gauge of Track 4' 8½"	Length, Tubes & Flues 11' 4-3/4"	Engine, total 133,000
Service Passenger	Heating Surface, sq ft.:	Tender 134,000
Cylinder diam. H.P. 18½" L.P.	" Tubes 1734 Flues Total 1734	Eng. & Tender 267,000
Stroke of Piston 26" No. of Cyls. 2	" Firebox 166 Arch Tubes	Tender, type Rectangular
Driving Wheels diam. 80"	" Syphons Total 1900	" No. of Wheels 8
Valves, type, H.P. Slide diam.	Superheater, type H.S.	Water, gals. 5,500 Coal, tons 12½
" " L.P. diam.	Feedwater Heater	Fuel Oil, gals.
Valve Gear Stephenson	Stoker Brakes WAB A-1	Max. Tractive Effort (a) 17,500 lbs.
Reverse Gear, Lever X Power	Throttle, type Dome	" " Booster (b) lbs.
Designer		Factor of Adhesion (a) 5.32 (b)
Source of Photo Frederick Westing Collection.		Notes on back of this sheet
		Retired or
Disposition: Sold to		scrapped

THE PENNSYLVANIA SPECIAL, with Engineer Martin H. Lee at the throttle, westbound, running through Morrisville, Pa., at 85 miles per hour, on June 16, 1902, on the second trip of this famous train.

Fig. 10.

No. 955 Name	Road Pennsylvania Rail Road	Type 4-4-0
Builder Pennsylvania R. R.	Boiler, type Conical	Wheelbase, Rigid 7' 9"
Works Juniata	" diam. 60" pressure 185 psi.	", Driving 7' 9"
Date built 1896 Bldr's. No.	Firebox, type Belpaire - narrow	", Engine 22' 9½"
Builder's Class	" length 119-5/8" width 40"	", Eng. & Tender 55' 0¼"
R.R. Class, Old L New D16a	Combustion Chamber, length	Weight in Working Order, lbs.:
Bldr's. Order No. Neg. No.	Grate Area, 33.2 sq. ft.	Front Truck 40,000
No. in Order Orig. Nos	No. of Tubes 310 No. of Flues	Driving Wheels 93,000
Orig. No. this Engine 955	Diam. " 1-7/8" Diam "	Trailing
Gauge of Track 4' 8½"	Length, Tubes & Flues 11' 4-3/4"	Engine, total 133,000
Service Passenger	Heating Surface, sq ft.:	Tender 134,000
Cylinder diam. H.P. 18½" L.P.	" Tubes 1734 Flues Total 1734	Eng. & Tender 267,000
Stroke of Piston 26" No. of Cyls. 2	" Firebox 166 Arch Tubes	Tender, type Rectangular
Driving Wheels diam. 80"	" Syphons Total 1900	" No. of Wheels 8
Valves, type, H.P. Slide diam.	Superheater, type H.S.	Water, gals. 5,500 Coal, tons 12½
" " L.P. diam.	Feedwater Heater	Fuel Oil, gals.
Valve Gear Stephenson	Stoker Brakes WAB A-1	Max. Tractive Effort (a) 17,500 lbs.
Reverse Gear, Lever X Power	Throttle, type Dome	" " Booster (b) lbs.
Designer		Factor of Adhesion (a) 5.32 (b)
Source of Photo Harold C. Zieber Collection.		Notes on back of this sheet
		Retired or
Disposition: Sold to		scrapped

An interesting action shot.

LA-4.500. 3-70

Fig. 11.

No. 7002 **Name**	**Road** Pennsylvania Rail Road	**Type** 4-4-2
Builder Pennsylvania R. R.	**Boiler, type** Extended wagon top	**Wheelbase, Rigid** 19' 1"
Works Juniata	" **diam.** 65½" **pressure** 205 **psi.**	" , **Driving** 7' 5"
Date built 1902 **Bldr's. No.** 929	**Firebox, type** Belpaire - wide	" , **Engine** 30' 9½"
Builder's Class	" **length** 111" **width** 72"	" , **Eng. & Tender** 63' 6-9/16"
R.R. Class, Old E2a **New** E7s	**Combustion Chamber, length**	**Weight in Working Order, lbs.:**
Bldr's. Order No. **Neg. No.**	**Grate Area,** 55.19 **sq. ft.**	**Front Truck** 35,000
No. in Order 19 **Orig. Nos** Assorted	**No. of Tubes** 170 **No. of Flues** 24	**Driving Wheels** 121,000
Orig. No. this Engine 8063	**Diam.** " 2" **Diam** " 5½"	**Trailing** 35,000
Gauge of Track 4' 8½"	**Length, Tubes & Flues** 15' 0"	**Engine, total** 191,000
Service Passenger	**Heating Surface, sq. ft.:**	**Tender** 162,650
Cylinder diam. H.P. 22½" **L.P.**	" **Tubes** 1335 **Flues** 528 **Total** 1863	**Eng. & Tender** 353,650
Stroke of Piston 26" **No. of Cyls.** 2	" **Firebox** 187 **Arch Tubes**	**Tender, type** Rectangular 70P 58F
Driving Wheels diam. 80"	" **Syphons** **Total** 2050	" **No. of Wheels** 8
Valves, type, H.P. Piston **diam.** 12"	**Superheater, type** "A" **H.S.** 412	**Water, gals.** 7,050 **Coal, tons** 13
" " **L.P.** **diam.**	**Feedwater Heater**	**Fuel Oil, gals.**
Valve Gear Stephenson	**Stoker** **Brakes** #6 ET	**Max. Tractive Effort (a)** 28,670 **lbs.**
Reverse Gear, Lever X **Power**	**Throttle, type** Dome	" " **Booster (b)** **lbs.**
Designer	**Factor of Adhesion (a)** 4.22 **(b)**	
Source of Photo Howard G. Hill Photo, Northumberland, Pa., 10-20-1957.		**Notes on back of this sheet**
Disposition: Sold **to**		**Retired or scrapped**

#8063 built 1902 as Class E2a with Belpaire firebox, Stephenson valve gear, slide valves, 20½" x 26" cylinders. Converted to Class E7s in 1916 with superheater, piston valves, Stephenson valve gear. Renumbered 7002 in 1947 for preservation in place of original #7002, which had been scrapped before her historical value had been recognized. The original #7002 ran 127.1 miles per hour on June 11, 1905 with THE PENNSYLVANIA SPECIAL between Crestline and Fort Wayne.

Fig. 12.

No. 1968 **Name**	**Road** Pennsylvania Rail Road	**Type** 4-4-2
Builder Pennsylvania R. R.	**Boiler, type** Extended wagon top	**Wheelbase, Rigid** 19' 1"
Works Juniata	" **diam** 65-5/8" **pressure** 205 **psi.**	" , **Driving** 7' 5"
Date built 1901 **Bldr's. No.** 829	**Firebox, type** Radial stay - wide	" , **Engine** 30' 9½"
Builder's Class	" **length** 111" **width** 72"	" , **Eng. & Tender** 60' 6-1/16"
R.R. Class, Old **New** E2	**Combustion Chamber, length**	**Weight in Working Order, lbs.:**
Bldr's. Order No. **Neg. No.** ME3168A	**Grate Area,** 55.5 **sq. ft.**	**Front Truck**
No. in Order 34 **Orig. Nos** Assorted	**No. of Tubes** 315 **No. of Flues**	**Driving Wheels** 118,280
Orig. No. this Engine 1968	**Diam.** " 2" **Diam** "	**Trailing**
Gauge of Track 4' 8½"	**Length, Tubes & Flues** 15' 0"	**Engine, total** 186,480
Service Passenger	**Heating Surface, sq ft.:**	**Tender** 134,020
Cylinder diam. H.P. 20½" **L.P.**	" **Tubes** 2471 **Flues** **Total** 2471	**Eng. & Tender** 320,500
Stroke of Piston 26" **No. of Cyls.** 2	" **Firebox** 157 **Arch Tubes**	**Tender, type** Rectangular
Driving Wheels diam. 80"	" **Syphons** **Total** 2628	" **No. of Wheels** 8
Valves, type, H.P. Balanced slide	**Superheater, type** **H.S.**	**Water, gals.** 5,500 **Coal, tons** 12½
" " **L.P.** **diam.**	**Feedwater Heater**	**Fuel Oil, gals.**
Valve Gear Stephenson	**Stoker** **Brakes** WAB A-1	**Max. Tractive Effort (a)** 23,800 **lbs.**
Reverse Gear, Lever X **Power**	**Throttle, type** Dome	" " **Booster (b)** **lbs.**
Designer	**Factor of Adhesion (a)** 4.98 **(b)**	
Source of Photo Pennsylvania Rail Road		**Notes on back of this sheet**
Disposition: Sold **to**		**Retired or scrapped**

One of 81 early Atlantic type locomotives built for Lines East and Lines West in 1901 and 1902. The first engine was No. 65, West Jersey & Seashore R. R. 15 Lines West engines were converted to Class E7sa. All Class E2 engines were off the roster by 1918.

Fig. 13.

No. 2024 Name	Road Pennsylvania Rail Road	Type 4-4-2.
Builder Pennsylvania R. R.	Boiler, type Extended wagon top	Wheelbase, Rigid 19' 1"
Works Juniata	" diam. 65-5/8" pressure 205 psi	", Driving 7' 5"
Date built 7-1902 Bldr's. No. 907	Firebox, type Belpaire – wide	", Engine 30' 9½"
Builder's Class	" length 111" width 72"	", Eng. & Tender 60' 6-11/16"
R.R. Class, Old New E3a	Combustion Chamber, length	Weight in Working Order, lbs.:
Bldr's. Order No. Neg. No. ME4441	Grate Area, 55.5 sq. ft.	Front Truck
No. in Order 8 Orig. Nos 2024-2031	No. of Tubes 315 No. of Flues	Driving Wheels 118,400
Orig. No. this Engine 2024	Diam. " 2" Diam "	Trailing
Gauge of Track 4' 8½"	Length, Tubes & Flues 15' 0"	Engine, total 190,600
Service Passenger	Heating Surface, sq ft.:	Tender
Cylinder diam. H.P. 20½" L.P.	" Tubes 2474 Flues Total 2474	Eng. & Tender
Stroke of Piston 26" No. of Cyls. 2	" Firebox 166 Arch Tubes	Tender, type Rectangular
Driving Wheels diam. 80"	" Syphons Total 2640	" No. of Wheels 8
Valves, type. H.P. Balanced slide diam.	Superheater, type H.S.	Water, gals. Coal, tons
" " L.P. diam.	Feedwater Heater	Fuel Oil, gals.
Valve Gear Stephenson	Stoker Brakes WAB A-1	Max. Tractive Effort (a) 27,410 lbs.
Reverse Gear, Lever X Power	Throttle, type Dome	" " Booster (b) lbs.
Designer		Factor of Adhesion (a) 4.32 (b)
Source of Photo Pennsylvania Rail Road. Howard G. Hill Collection.		Notes on back of this sheet Retired or scrapped
Disposition : Sold to		

LA-4.500. 3-70

Fig. 14.

No. 7374 Name	Road Pennsylvania Rail Road	Type 4-4-2
Builder American Locomotive Co.	Boiler, type Extended wagon top	Wheelbase, Rigid 19' 1"
Works Schenectady	" diam. 65-5/8" pressure 205 psi	", Driving 7' 5"
Date built 2-1903 Bldr's. No. 26780	Firebox, type Belpaire – wide	", Engine 30' 9½"
Builder's Class 442-186	" length 111" width 72"	", Eng. & Tender 60' 6-11/16"
R.R. Class, Old E2a New E2b	Combustion Chamber, length	Weight in Working Order, lbs.:
Bldr's. Order No. Neg. No. 7371-7375 8478-8482	Grate Area, 55.5 sq. ft.	Front Truck
No. in Order 10 Orig. Nos	No. of Tubes 315 No. of Flues	Driving Wheels 118,280
Orig. No. this Engine 7374	Diam. " 2" Diam "	Trailing
Gauge of Track 4' 8½"	Length, Tubes & Flues 15' 0"	Engine, total 186,480
Service Passenger	Heating Surface, sq ft.:	Tender 134,020
Cylinder diam. H.P. 20½" L.P.	" Tubes 2474 Flues Total 2474	Eng. & Tender 320,500
Stroke of Piston 26" No. of Cyls. 2	" Firebox 166 Arch Tubes	Tender, type Rectangular
Driving Wheels diam. 80"	" Syphons Total 2640	" No. of Wheels 8
Valves, type. H.P. Piston diam. 12"	Superheater, type H.S.	Water, gals. 5,500 Coal, tons 12½
" " L.P. diam.	Feedwater Heater	Fuel Oil, gals.
Valve Gear Stephenson	Stoker Brakes WAB A-1	Max. Tractive Effort (a) 23,800 lbs.
Reverse Gear, Lever X Power	Throttle, type Dome	" " Booster (b) lbs.
Designer		Factor of Adhesion (a) 4.98 (b)
Source of Photo Harold C. Zieber Collection.		Notes on back of this sheet Retired or scrapped
Disposition : Sold to		

LA-4.500. 3-70

Built as Class E2a with Belpaire firebox, Stephenson valve gear and slide valves. Converted in 1904 to Class E2b with inside piston valves for Stephenson valve gear. Converted in 1916 to Class E7s with outside piston valves, Walschaert valve gear and superheater. Renumbered 9716. Builder's Nos. 26777-26786. Photographed as Class E2b.

Fig. 16.

No. 7067 Name	Road Pennsylvania Rail Road	Type 4-6-2
Builder American Locomotive Co.	Boiler, type Straight top	Wheelbase, Rigid 13' 10"
Works Pittsburgh	" diam. 78" pressure 205 psi.	", Driving 13' 10"
Date built 5-1907 Bldr's. No. 41525	Firebox, type Radial stay - wide	", Engine
Builder's Class 462-273	" length width	", Eng. & Tender
R.R. Class, Old New K28	Combustion Chamber, length	Weight in Working Order, lbs.:
Bldr's. Order No. P-508 Neg. No. P-508	Grate Area, 61.86 sq. ft.	Front Truck 44,600
No. in Order 1 Orig. Nos 7067	No. of Tubes No. of Flues	Driving Wheels 183,900
Orig. No. this Engine 7067	Diam. " Diam "	Trailing 44,000
Gauge of Track 4' 8½"	Length, Tubes & Flues	Engine, total 272,500
Service Passenger	Heating Surface, sq ft.:	Tender 157,250
Cylinder diam. H.P. 24" L.P.	" Tubes Flues Total	Eng. & Tender 429,750
Stroke of Piston 26" No. of Cyls. 2	" Firebox Arch Tubes	Tender, type Rectangular
Driving Wheels diam. 80"	" Syphons Total 4427	" No. of Wheels 8
Valves, type, H.P. Piston diam. 16"	Superheater, type H.S.	Water, gals. 7,300 Coal, tons 15
" " L.P. diam.	Feedwater Heater	Fuel Oil, gals.
Valve Gear Walschaert	Stoker Brakes #6 ET	Max. Tractive Effort (a) 32,620 lbs.
Reverse Gear, Lever X Power	Throttle, type Dome	" " Booster (b) lbs.
Designer		Factor of Adhesion (a) 5.63 (b)
Source of Photo American Locomotive Co. Howard G. Hill Collection.		Notes on back of this sheet
Disposition: Sold to		Retired or scrapped

This was the first Pacific type locomotive on the Pennsylvania R. R. It was built for experimental purposes. It was very successful, and formed the basis for later designs of 4-6-2 type locomotives developed by the Pennsylvania. When superheated later, it became Class K28s.

Fig. 17.

No. 3337 Name	Road Pennsylvania Rail Road	Type 4-6-2
Builder Pennsylvania R. R.	Boiler, type Straight top	Wheelbase, Rigid 13' 10"
Works Juniata	" diam. 78" pressure 205 psi	", Driving 13' 10"
Date built 1910 Bldr's. No.	Firebox, type Belpaire - wide	", Engine 35' 2½"
Builder's Class	" length 110-3/4" width 72"	", Eng. & Tender 70' 3"
R.R. Class, Old New K2	Combustion Chamber, length	Weight in Working Order, lbs.:
Bldr's. Order No. Neg. No.	Grate Area, 55.38 sq. ft.	Front Truck
No. in Order Orig. Nos	No. of Tubes No. of Flues	Driving Wheels 185,900
Orig. No. this Engine 3337	Diam. " Diam "	Trailing
Gauge of Track 4' 8½"	Length, Tubes & Flues 21' 0-5/16"	Engine, total 278,800
Service Passenger	Heating Surface, sq ft.:	Tender 167,650
Cylinder diam. H.P. 24" L.P.	" Tubes 4409 Flues Total 4409	Eng. & Tender 446,450
Stroke of Piston 26" No. of Cyls. 2	" Firebox 220 Arch Tubes	Tender, type Rectangular 70-P-66
Driving Wheels diam. 80"	" Syphons Total 4629	" No. of Wheels 8
Valves, type, H.P. Piston diam. 16"	Superheater, type H.S.	Water, gals. 7,150 Coal, tons 15.8
" " L.P. diam.	Feedwater Heater	Fuel Oil, gals.
Valve Gear Walschaert	Stoker Brakes #6 ET	Max. Tractive Effort (a) 32,620 lbs.
Reverse Gear, Lever X Power	Throttle, type Dome	" " Booster (b) lbs.
Designer		Factor of Adhesion (a) 5.69 (b)
Source of Photo Frederick Westing Collection.		Notes on back of this sheet
Disposition: Sold to		Retired or scrapped

Fig. 18.

No. 3379 Name	Road Pennsylvania Rail Road	Type 4-6-2
Builder Pennsylvania R. R.	Boiler, type Straight top	Wheelbase, Rigid 13' 10"
Works Juniata	" diam. 78" pressure 205 psi.	" , Driving 13' 10"
Date built 1911 Bldr's. No.	Firebox, type Belpaire - wide	" , Engine 35' 2½"
Builder's Class	" length 110-3/4" width 72"	" , Eng. & Tender 70' 3"
R.R. Class, Old New K2	Combustion Chamber, length	Weight in Working Order, lbs.:
Bldr's. Order No. Neg. No.	Grate Area, 55.38 sq. ft.	Front Truck
No. in Order 153 Orig. Nos Assorted	No. of Tubes No. of Flues	Driving Wheels 185,900
Orig. No. this Engine 3379	Diam. " Diam "	Trailing
Gauge of Track 4' 8½"	Length, Tubes & Flues 21' 0-5/16"	Engine, total 278,800
Service Passenger	Heating Surface, sq ft.:	Tender 167,650
Cylinder diam. H.P. 24" L.P.	" Tubes 4409 Flues Total 4409	Eng. & Tender 446,450
Stroke of Piston 26" No. of Cyls. 2	" Firebox 220 Arch Tubes	Tender, type Rectangular 70-P-66
Driving Wheels diam. 80"	" Syphons Total 4629	" No. of Wheels 8
Valves, type, H.P. Piston diam. 16"	Superheater, type H.S.	Water, gals. 7,150 Coal, tons 15.8
" " L.P. diam.	Feedwater Heater	Fuel Oil, gals.
Valve Gear Walschaert	Stoker Brakes #6 ET	Max. Tractive Effort (a) 32,620 lbs.
Reverse Gear, Lever X Power	Throttle, type Dome	" " Booster (b) lbs.
Designer		Factor of Adhesion (a) 5.69 (b)
Source of Photo BALDWIN LOCOMOTIVES		Notes on back of this sheet
Disposition : Sold to		Retired or scrapped

Fig. 19.

No. 7049 Name	Road Pennsylvania Rail Road	Type 4-6-2
Builder American Locomotive Co.	Boiler, type Straight top	Wheelbase, Rigid 13' 10"
Works Schenectady	" diam. 78" pressure 205 psi.	" , Driving 13' 10"
Date built 1912 Bldr's. No.	Firebox, type Belpaire - wide	" , Engine 35' 2½"
Builder's Class 462-272	" length 110-3/4" width 72"	" , Eng. & Tender 70' 5"
R.R. Class, Old New K2a	Combustion Chamber, length	Weight in Working Order, lbs.:
Bldr's. Order No. S-847 Neg. No. S-847	Grate Area, 55.38 sq. ft.	Front Truck
No. in Order 10 Orig. Nos Assorted	No. of Tubes No. of Flues	Driving Wheels 178,500
Orig. No. this Engine 7049	Diam. " Diam "	Trailing
Gauge of Track 4' 8½"	Length, Tubes & Flues 21' 0-5/16"	Engine, total 272,000
Service Passenger	Heating Surface, sq ft.:	Tender 170,200
Cylinder diam. H.P. 24" L.P.	" Tubes 4409 Flues Total 4409	Eng. & Tender 442,200
Stroke of Piston 26" No. of Cyls. 2	" Firebox 220 Arch Tubes	Tender, type Rectangular 70-P-77
Driving Wheels diam. 80"	" Syphons Total 4629	" No. of Wheels 8
Valves, type, H.P. Piston diam. 16"	Superheater, type H.S.	Water, gals. 6,800 Coal, tons 16.15
" " L.P. diam.	Feedwater Heater	Fuel Oil, gals.
Valve Gear Walschaert	Stoker Brakes #6 ET	Max. Tractive Effort (a) 32,620 lbs.
Reverse Gear, Lever X Power	Throttle, type Dome	" " Booster (b) lbs.
Designer		Factor of Adhesion (a) 5.48 (b)
Source of Photo American Locomotive Co. Howard G. Hill Collection.		Notes on back of this sheet
Disposition : Sold to		Retired or scrapped

Juniata Shops also built 62 between 1911 and 1913 for Lines East and Lines West.
No. 86 was the first one, built in 1911 for Lines East. They were identical with
Class K2 except for higher firing decks. When superheated, they became Class K2sa.

LA-4.500. 3-70

Fig. 20.

No. 8704 Name	Road Pennsylvania Rail Road	Type 4-6-2
Builder American Locomotive Co.	Boiler, type Straight top	Wheelbase, Rigid 13' 10"
Works Schenectady	" diam. 76½" pressure 200 psi.	" , Driving 13' 10"
Date built 10-1911 Bldr's. No. 47740	Firebox, type Radial stay - wide	" , Engine 34' 8½"
Builder's Class 462-S-260	" length 108-1/8" width 75¼"	" , Eng. & Tender 66' 10¼"
R.R. Class, Old New K21s	Combustion Chamber, length	Weight in Working Order, lbs.:
Bldr's. Order No. S-853 Neg. No. EE8164	Grate Area, 56.6 sq. ft.	Front Truck 49,500
No. in Order 12 Orig. Nos 1-12	No. of Tubes 233 No. of Flues 30	Driving Wheels 165,000
Orig. No. this Engine 4	Diam. " 2" Diam. " 5-3/8".	Trailing 45,500
Gauge of Track 4' 8½"	Length, Tubes & Flues 21' 0"	Engine, total 260,000
Service Passenger	Heating Surface, sq ft.:	Tender 147,400
Cylinder diam. H.P. 24" L.P.	" Tubes 2562 Flues 871 Total 3433	Eng. & Tender 407,400
Stroke of Piston 26" No. of Cyls. 2	" Firebox 195 Arch Tubes	Tender, type Rectangular
Driving Wheels diam. 80"	" Syphons Total 3654	" No. of Wheels 8
Valves, type. H.P. Piston diam.	Superheater, type "A" H.S. 752	Water, gals. 7,500 Coal, tons 12
" " L.P. diam.	Feedwater Heater	Fuel Oil, gals.
Valve Gear Walschaert	Stoker Brakes #6 ET	Max. Tractive Effort (a) 31,800 lbs.
Reverse Gear, Lever X Power	Throttle, type Dome	" " Booster (b) lbs.
Designer		Factor of Adhesion (a) 5.19 (b)
Source of Photo Pennsylvania R. R. Howard G. Hill Collection.		Notes on back of this sheet Retired or scrapped
Disposition : Sold to		

Built for St. Louis, Vandalia & Terre Haute Railroad Co., "The Vandalia Line", as
Nos. 1 to 12, Inclusive. Renumbered 8701-8712, inclusive, when Vandalia Line was
absorbed by Pennsylvania R. R. in 1916. Never a standard class on Pennsylvania R. R.

Fig. 21.

No. 3375 Name	Road Pennsylvania Rail Road	Type 4-6-2
Builder Pennsylvania R. R.	Boiler, type Straight top	Wheelbase, Rigid 13' 10"
Works Juniata	" diam. 78" pressure 205 psi.	" , Driving 13' 10"
Date built 11-1911 Bldr's. No. 2333	Firebox, type Belpaire - wide	" , Engine 35' 4½"
Builder's Class	" length 110-3/4" width 72"	" , Eng. & Tender 70' 5"
R.R. Class, Old K2b New K2sb	Combustion Chamber, length	Weight in Working Order, lbs.:
Bldr's. Order No. Neg. No. E8476	Grate Area, 55.38 sq. ft.	Front Truck 46,200
No. in Order 2 Orig. Nos 3371, 3375	No. of Tubes 202 No. of Flues 32	Driving Wheels 192,500
Orig. No. this Engine 3375	Diam. " 2¼" Diam. " 5½"	Trailing 47,900
Gauge of Track 4' 8½"	Length, Tubes & Flues 21' 0-5/16"	Engine, total 286,000
Service Passenger	Heating Surface, sq ft.:	Tender 167,650
Cylinder diam. H.P. 24" L.P.	" Tubes 2498 Flues 973 Total 3471	Eng. & Tender 454,250
Stroke of Piston 26" No. of Cyls. 2	" Firebox 220 Arch Tubes	Tender, type Rectangular 70-P-66
Driving Wheels diam. 72"	" Syphons Total 3691	" No. of Wheels 8
Valves, type. H.P. Piston diam. 12"	Superheater, type "A" H.S. 791	Water, gals. 7,150 Coal, tons 15.8
" " L.P. diam.	Feedwater Heater	Fuel Oil, gals.
Valve Gear Walschaert	Stoker Brakes #6 ET	Max. Tractive Effort (a) 36,244 lbs.
Reverse Gear, Lever X Power	Throttle, type Dome	" " Booster (b) lbs.
Designer		Factor of Adhesion (a) 5.31 (b)
Source of Photo C. B. Cheney Photo. Smithsonian Institution Collection.		Notes on back of this sheet Retired or scrapped
Disposition : Sold to		

Similar to Class K2 except for 72" drivers. Built with KW style trailing truck,
later changed to Commonwealth Delta type trailing truck. Built saturated as Class
K2b; superheated later as Class K2sb. Built for Lines East.

Fig. 22.

No. 150 Name	Road Pennsylvania Rail Rpad...	Type ....
Builder Pennsylvania R. R.	Boiler, type Straight top	Wheelbase, Rigid 13' 10"
Works Juniata	" diam. 78" pressure 205 psi.	" , Driving 13' 10"
Date built 3-1910 Bldr's. No. 2001	Firebox, type Belpaire - wide	" , Engine 35' 2½"
Builder's Class	" length 110-3/4" width 72"	" , Eng. & Tender 70' 3"
R.R. Class, Old New K2s	Combustion Chamber, length	Weight in Working Order, lbs.:
Bldr's. Order No. Neg. No.	Grate Area, 53.72 sq. ft.	Front Truck 42,500
No. in Order 153 Orig. Nos Assorted	No. of Tubes 202 No. of Flues 32	Driving Wheels 188,000
Orig. No. this Engine 150	Diam. " 2¼" Diam " 5½"	Trailing 52,500
Gauge of Track 4' 8½"	Length, Tubes & Flues 21' 0-5/16"	Engine, total 283,000
Service Passenger	Heating Surface, sq ft.:	Tender 167,650
Cylinder diam. H.P. 24" L.P.	" Tubes 2502 Flues 934 Total 3436	Eng. & Tender 450,650
Stroke of Piston 26" No. of Cyls. 2	" Firebox 208 Arch Tubes	Tender, type Rectangular 70-P-66
Driving Wheels diam. 80"	" Syphons Total 3644	" No. of Wheels 8
Valves, type, H.P. Piston diam. 16"	Superheater, type "A" H.S. 989	Water, gals. 7,150 Coal, tons 15.8
" " L.P. diam.	Feedwater Heater	Fuel Oil, gals.
Valve Gear Walschaert	Stoker Brakes #6 ET	Max. Tractive Effort (a) 32,620 lbs.
Reverse Gear, Lever Power X	Throttle, type Dome	" " Booster (b) lbs.
Designer		Factor of Adhesion (a) 5.76 (b)
Source of Photo Lt. Col. T. Martin Flattley, Jr., Logansport, Ind.		Notes on back of this sheet
Disposition: Sold to		Retired or scrapped

Similar to Class K28 except for Belpaire firebox. Juniata Shops built 153 Classes K2 and K2s in 1910 and 1911; all were eventually superheated. For Lines East and Lines West. First engine was No. 7510, built in 1910 for Pittsburgh, Fort Wayne & Chicago R. R.

Fig. 23.

No. 9999 Name	Road Pennsylvania Rail Road...	Type 4-6-2
Builder Pennsylvania R. R.	Boiler, type Straight top	Wheelbase, Rigid 13' 10"
Works Juniata	" diam. 78" pressure 205 psi.	" , Driving 13' 10"
Date built 1-1911 Bldr's. No. 2179	Firebox, type Belpaire - wide	" , Engine 35' 2½"
Builder's Class	" length 110-3/4" width 72"	" , Eng. & Tender 70' 3"
R.R. Class, Old New K2s	Combustion Chamber, length	Weight in Working Order, lbs.:
Bldr's. Order No. Neg. No.	Grate Area, 53.72 sq. ft.	Front Truck 42,500
No. in Order 153 Orig. Nos Assorted	No. of Tubes 202 No. of Flues 32	Driving Wheels 188,000
Orig. No. this Engine 9999	Diam. " 2¼" Diam " 5½"	Trailing 52,500
Gauge of Track 4' 8½"	Length, Tubes & Flues 21' 0-5/16"	Engine, total 283,000
Service Passenger	Heating Surface, sq ft.:	Tender 167,650
Cylinder diam. H.P. 24" L.P.	" Tubes 2502 Flues 934 Total 3436	Eng. & Tender 450,650
Stroke of Piston 26" No. of Cyls. 2	" Firebox 208 Arch Tubes	Tender, type Rectangular 70-P-66
Driving Wheels diam. 80"	" Syphons Total 3644	" No. of Wheels 8
Valves, type, H.P. Piston diam. 16*	Superheater, type "A" H.S. 989	Water, gals. 7,150 Coal, tons 15.8
" " L.P. diam.	Feedwater Heater	Fuel Oil, gals.
Valve Gear Walschaert	Stoker Brakes #6 ET	Max. Tractive Effort (a) 32,620 lbs.
Reverse Gear, Lever Power X	Throttle, type Dome	" " Booster (b) lbs.
Designer		Factor of Adhesion (a) 5.76 (b)
Source of Photo Lt. Col. T. Martin Flattley, Jr., E. St. Louis, Ill., 5-16-1937		Notes on back of this sheet
Disposition: Sold to		Retired or scrapped

*Valves later changed to 12" piston valves. Similar to Class K28 except for Belpaire firebox. No. 9999 carried the highest regular number assigned to a P. R. R. locomotive.

Fig. 24.

No. 8661 Name	Road Pennsylvania Rail Road	Type 4-6-2
Builder Baldwin Locomotive Works	Boiler, type Straight top	Wheelbase, Rigid 13' 10"
Works Eddystone	" diam. 78" pressure 205 psi.	" , Driving 13' 10"
Date built 7-1913 Bldr's. No. 40,000	Firebox, type Belpaire - wide	" , Engine 35' 2½"
Builder's Class 12-46-¼-D,	" length 110-3/4" width 72"	" , Eng. & Tender 60' 2¼"
R.R. Class, Old New K3s	Combustion Chamber, length	Weight in Working Order, lbs.:
Bldr's. Order No. Neg. No. 4560	Grate Area, 55.4 sq. ft.	Front Truck 43,000
No. in Order 30 Orig. Nos Assorted	No. of Tubes 202 No. of Flues 32	Driving Wheels 196,300
Orig. No. this Engine 8661	Diam. " 2¼" Diam " 5½"	Trailing 54,300
Gauge of Track 4' 8½"	Length, Tubes & Flues 21' 0"	Engine, total 293,600
Service Passenger	Heating Surface, sq ft.:	Tender 178,550
Cylinder diam. H.P. 26" L.P.	" Tubes 2498 Flues 955 Total 3453	Eng. & Tender 472,150
Stroke of Piston 26" No. of Cyls. 2	" Firebox 204 Arch Tubes 23	Tender, type Rectangular 80-P-79
Driving Wheels diam. 80"	" Syphons Total 3680	" No. of Wheels 8
Valves, type. H.P. Piston diam. 16"*	Superheater, type "A: H.S. 845	Water, gals. 8,100 Coal, tons 17.3
" " L.P. diam.	Feedwater Heater	Fuel Oil, gals.
Valve Gear Walschaert	Stoker Crawford uf Brakes #6 ET	Max. Tractive Effort (a) 38,300 lbs.
Reverse Gear, Lever X Power	Throttle, type Dome	" " Booster (b) lbs.
Designer		Factor of Adhesion (a) 4.95 (b)
Source of Photo Baldwin Locomotive Works, Howard G. Hill Collection.		Notes on back of this sheet
Disposition: Sold to		Retired or scrapped

Security Sectional Arch in firebox. Cast steel frames 6" wide. *Valves later changed to 12" piston valves.

Fig. 25.

No. 8662 Name	Road Pennsylvania Rail Road	Type 4-6-2
Builder Baldwin Locomotive Works	Boiler, type Straight top	Wheelbase, Rigid 13' 10"
Works Eddystone	" diam 78" pressure 205 psi.	" , Driving 13' 10"
Date built 7-1913 Bldr's. No. 39995	Firebox, type Belpaire - wide	" , Engine 35' 2½"
Builder's Class 12-46-¼-D,	" length 110-3/4" width 72"	" , Eng. & Tender 60' 2¼"
R.R. Class, Old New K3s	Combustion Chamber, length	Weight in Working Order, lbs.:
Bldr's. Order No. Neg. No.	Grate Area, 55.4 sq. ft.	Front Truck 43,000
No. in Order 30 Orig. Nos Assorted	No. of Tubes 202 No. of Flues 32	Driving Wheels 196,300
Orig. No. this Engine 8662	Diam. " 2¼" Diam " 5½"	Trailing 54,300
Gauge of Track 4' 8½"	Length, Tubes & Flues 21' 0"	Engine, total 293,600
Service Passenger	Heating Surface, sq ft.:	Tender 178,550
Cylinder diam. H.P. 26" L.P.	" Tubes 2498 Flues 955 Total 3453	Eng. & Tender 472,150
Stroke of Piston 26" No. of Cyls. 2	" Firebox 204 Arch Tubes 23	Tender, type Rectangular 80-P-79
Driving Wheels diam. 80"	" Syphons Total 3680	" No. of Wheels 8
Valves, type. H.P. Piston diam. 16"*	Superheater, type "A" H.S. 845	Water, gals. 8,100 Coal, tons 17.3
" " L.P. diam.	Feedwater Heater	Fuel Oil, gals.
Valve Gear Walschaert	Stoker Crawford uf Brakes #6 ET	Max. Tractive Effort (a) 38,300 lbs.
Reverse Gear, Lever X Power	Throttle, type Dome	" " Booster (b) lbs.
Designer		Factor of Adhesion (a) 4.95 (b)
Source of Photo Lt. Col. T. Martin Flattley, Jr. Pittsburgh, Pa.	9-27-1936	Notes on back of this sheet
Disposition: Sold to		Retired or scrapped

Security Sectional Arch in firebox. Cast steel frames 6" wide. *Valves later changed to 12" piston valves.

Fig. 26.

No. 3395 Name	Road Pennsylvania Rail Road	Type 4-6-2
Builder American Locomotive Co.	Boiler, type Extended wagon top	Wheelbase, Rigid 13' 10"
Works Schenectady	" diam 80" pressure 200 psi.	" , Driving 13' 10"
Date built 11-1911 Bldr's. No. 50186	Firebox, type Radial stay - wide	" , Engine 36' 5"
Builder's Class 462-S-317	" length 120-1/8" width 79¼"	" , Eng. & Tender 71' 5-3/4"
R.R. Class, Old New K29s	Combustion Chamber, length	Weight in Working Order, lbs.:
Bldr's. Order No. S-820 Neg. No. ME738A	Grate Area, 70.73 sq. ft.	Front Truck 50,500
No. in Order 1 Orig. Nos 3395	No. of Tubes 241 No. of Flues 40	Driving Wheels 197,800
Orig. No. this Engine 3395	Diam. " 2¼" Diam " 5½"	Trailing 68,700
Gauge of Track 4' 8½"	Length, Tubes & Flues 22' 0"	Engine, total 317,000
Service Passenger	Heating Surface, sq ft.:	Tender 175,700
Cylinder diam. H.P. 27" L.P.	" Tubes 3123 Flues 1250 Total 4373	Eng. & Tender 492,700
Stroke of Piston 28" No. of Cyls. 2	" Firebox plus Arch Tubes 232	Tender, type Rectangular 80-P-83
Driving Wheels diam. 80"	" Syphons Total 4606	" No. of Wheels 8
Valves, type. H.P. Piston diam. 16"	Superheater, type "A" H.S. 1301	Water, gals. 8,280 Coal, tons 13.75
" " L.P. diam.	Feedwater Heater	Fuel Oil, gals.
Valve Gear Walschaert	Stoker Crawford uf Brakes #6 ET	Max. Tractive Effort (a) 40,824 / @80% MEP lbs.
Reverse Gear, Lever Power Screw	Throttle, type Dome	" " Booster (b) lbs.
Designer		Factor of Adhesion (a) 4.85 (b)
Source of Photo Pennsylvania R. R. Howard G. Hill Collection.		Notes on back of this sheet
Disposition: Sold to		Retired or scrapped

A very successful experimental locomotive, equipped with a brick arch. Tested
thoroughly on Altoona Locomotive Test Plant prior to use in road service. Results
of those tests formed the basis for the design of the Class K4s Pacific type locomotive
No. 1737 built May 1914 at Juniata Shops, P. R. R. See P. R. R. Test Plant Bulletin
No. 19, Tests of a Class K29 Locomotive, 1912.

Fig. 27.   THIS WAS THE FIRST CLASS K4s PACIFIC TYPE LOCOMOTIVE.

No. 1737 Name	Road Pennsylvania Rail Road	Type 4-6-2
Builder Pennsylvania R. R.	Boiler, type Extended wagon top	Wheelbase, Rigid 13' 10"
Works Juniata	" diam 78½" pressure 205 psi.	" , Driving 13' 10"
Date built 5-1914 Bldr's. No. 2825	Firebox, type Belpaire - wide	" , Engine 36' 2"
Builder's Class	" length 126" width 80"	" , Eng. & Tender
R.R. Class, Old New K4s	Combustion Chamber, length 36"	Weight in Working Order, lbs.:
Bldr's. Order No. Neg. No.	Grate Area, 69.26 sq. ft.	Front Truck
No. in Order 1 Orig. Nos 1737	No. of Tubes 237 No. of Flues 40	Driving Wheels 202,880
Orig. No. this Engine 1737	Diam. " 2¼" Diam " 5½"	Trailing
Gauge of Track 4' 8½"	Length, Tubes & Flues 19' 0"	Engine, total 309,140
Service Passenger	Heating Surface, sq ft.:	Tender
Cylinder diam. H.P. 27" L.P.	" Tubes 2652 Flues 1076 Total 3728	Eng. & Tender
Stroke of Piston 28" No. of Cyls. 2	" Firebox plus Arch Tubes 307	Tender, type Rectangular
Driving Wheels diam. 80"	" Syphons Total 4035	" No. of Wheels 8
Valves, type. H.P. Piston diam. 12"	Superheater, type "A" H.S. 1172	Water, gals. Coal, tons
" " L.P. diam.	Feedwater Heater	Fuel Oil, gals.
Valve Gear Walschaert	Stoker Brakes #6 ET	Max. Tractive Effort (a) 41,845 / @80% MEP lbs.
Reverse Gear, Lever Power Screw	Throttle, type Dome Altoona, Pa.	" " Booster (b) lbs.
Designer Wm. F. Kiesel, Jr., Mech. Engr., P. R. R.,		Factor of Adhesion (a) 4.85 (b)
Source of Photo Pennsylvania R. R. Howard G. Hill Collection,		Notes on back of this sheet
Disposition: Sold to		Retired or scrapped

In main line service three months prior to tests on Altoona Test Plant. See P. R. R.
Test Plant Bulletin No. 29, Tests of a Class K4s Locomotive, December 1, 1915.
424 duplicates of this locomotive had been built by or for Pennsylvania R. R. by
1928, with only minor changes in details. Fig. 28 shows this locomotive shortly
before she was scrapped.

LA-4.500. 3-70

Fig. 29.

No. 5453 Name	Road Pennsylvania Rail Road	Type 4-6-2
Builder Baldwin Locomotive Works	Boiler, type Extended wagon top	Wheelbase, Rigid 13' 10"
Works Eddystone	" diam. 78½" pressure 205 psi	" , Driving 13' 10"
Date built 1927 Bldr's. No.	Firebox, type Belpaire - wide	" , Engine 36' 2"
Builder's Class 12-48-¼-D,	" length 126" width 80"	" , Eng. & Tender 90' 7⅓"
R.R. Class, Old K4s New K4	Combustion Chamber, length 36"	Weight in Working Order, lbs.:
Bldr's. Order No. Neg. No.	Grate Area, 69.89 sq. ft.	Front Truck 53,640
No. in Order 75 Orig. Nos 5400-5474	No. of Tubes 236 No. of Flues 40	Driving Wheels 202,030
Orig. No. this Engine 5453	Diam. " 2¼" Diam " 5½"	Trailing 57,420
Gauge of Track 4' 8½"	Length, Tubes & Flues 19' 0"	Engine, total 313,000
Service Passenger	Heating Surface, sq ft.:	Tender 395,835
Cylinder diam. H.P. 27" L.P.	" Tubes 2641 Flues 1095 Total 3736	Eng. & Tender 708,925
Stroke of Piston 28" No. of Cyls. 2	" Firebox plus Arch Tubes 305	Tender, type Rectangular 250-P-75
Driving Wheels diam. 80	" Syphons Total 4041	" No. of Wheels 12
Valves, type. H.P. Piston diam. 12"	Superheater, type "A" H.S. 943	Water, gals. 24,410 Coal, tons 25 a 12
" " L.P. diam.	Feedwater Heater	Fuel Oil, gals.
Valve Gear Walschaert	Stoker Brakes #6 ET	Max. Tractive Effort (a) 44,460 lbs.
Reverse Gear, Lever Power X	Throttle, type Dome	" " Booster (b) lbs.
Designer		Factor of Adhesion (a) 4.55 (b)
Source of Photo Howard G. Hill Collection		Notes on back of this sheet
Disposition : Sold to		Retired or scrapped

This "Coast-to-Coast" tender was tested on the Eastern Region. Several more were used for a few years, but their use was finally discontinued.

Fig. 30.

No. 5698 Name	Road Pensylvania Rail Road	Type 4-6-2
Builder Pennsylvania R. R.	Boiler, type Extended wagon top	Wheelbase, Rigid 13' 10"
Works Juniata	" diam. 82-7/8" pressure 250 psi	" , Driving 13' 10"
Date built 3-1929 Bldr's. No. 4205	Firebox, type Belpaire - wide	" , Engine 36' 10½"
Builder's Class	" length 126" width 79-7/8"	" , Eng. & Tender 79' 5"
R.R. Class, Old New K5	Combustion Chamber, length	Weight in Working Order, lbs.:
Bldr's. Order No. Neg. No. EE8335	Grate Area, 69.89 sq. ft.	Front Truck 54,200
No. in Order 1 Orig. Nos 5698	No. of Tubes 90 No. of Flues 170	Driving Wheels 207,600
Orig. No. this Engine 5698	Diam. " 2¼" Diam " 3½"	Trailing 56,900
Gauge of Track 4' 8½"	Length, Tubes & Flues 19' 0"	Engine, total 318,700
Service Passenger	Heating Surface, sq ft.:	Tender 254,450
Cylinder diam. H.P. 27" L.P.	" Tubes 1007 Flues 2973 Total 3980	Eng. & Tender 573,150
Stroke of Piston 30" No. of Cyls. 2	" Firebox plus Arch Tubes 305	Tender, type Rectangular 130-P-75
Driving Wheels diam. 80"	" Syphons Total 4285	" No. of Wheels 8
Valves, type. H.P. Piston diam. 12"	Superheater, type "E" H.S. 1634	Water, gals. 13,475 Coal, tons 21 a 8
" " L.P. diam.	Feedwater Heater Worthington "S"	Fuel Oil, gals.
Valve Gear Walschaert	Stoker Standard HT Brakes #8 ET	Max. Tractive Effort (a) 54,675 / @80% MEP lbs.
Reverse Gear, Lever Power X	Throttle, type Dome	" " Booster (b) lbs.
Designer		Factor of Adhesion (a) 3.8 (b)
Source of Photo Pennsylvania R. R. Howard G. Hill Collection.		Notes on back of this sheet
Disposition : Sold to		Retired or scrapped

An experimental locomotive. Only two were built. The design was not duplicated.
They were larger than the Class K4 in almost every detail except their grate area
and diameter of driving wheels. Built as hand-fired engines - stokers applied later.

LA-4.500. 3-70

Fig. 31.

No. 5699 Name	Road Pennsylvania Rail Road	Type 4-6-2
Builder Baldwin Locomotive Works	Boiler, type Extended wagon top	Wheelbase, Rigid 13' 10"
Works Eddystone	" diam. 82-7/8" pressure 250 psi.	", Driving 13' 10"
Date built 9-1929 Bldr's. No. 60660	Firebox, type Belpaire - wide	", Engine 36' 10½"
Builder's Class 12-48-¼-D,	" length 126" width 79-7/8"	", Eng. & Tender 79' 5"
R.R. Class, Old New K5	Combustion Chamber, length	Weight in Working Order, lbs.:
Bldr's. Order No. Neg. No. 10443	Grate Area, 69.89 sq. ft.	Front Truck 66,240
No. in Order 1 Orig. Nos 5699	No. of Tubes 90 No. of Flues 170	Driving Wheels 209,410
Orig. No. this Engine 5699	Diam. " 2¼" Diam " 3½"	Trailing 59,700
Gauge of Track 4' 8½"	Length, Tubes & Flues 19' 0"	Engine, total 335,350
Service Passenger	Heating Surface, sq ft.:	Tender 254,450
Cylinder diam. H.P. 27" L.P.	" Tubes 1007 Flues 2973 Total 3980	Eng. & Tender 589,800
Stroke of Piston 30" No. of Cyls. 2	" Firebox plus Arch Tubes 305	Tender, type Rectangular 130-P-75
Driving Wheels diam. 80"	" Syphons Total 4285	" No. of Wheels 8
Valves, type. H.P. Poppet diam.	Superheater, type "E" H.S. 1634	Water, gals. 13,475 Coal, tons 21.8
" " L.P. diam.	Feedwater Heater Worthington "S"	Fuel Oil, gals.
Valve Gear Caprotti	Stoker Standard HT Brakes #6 ET	Max. Tractive Effort (a) 54,765/ @80% MEP lbs.
Reverse Gear, Lever Power X	Throttle, type Dome	" " Booster (b) lbs.
Designer		Factor of Adhesion (a) 3.83 (b)
Source of Photo Baldwin Locomotive Works, H. L. Broadbelt Collection.		Notes on back of this sheet
Disposition: Sold to		Retired or scrapped

Similar to No. 5698. Caprotti valve gear and poppet valves were later removed and engine was equipped with new 12" piston valve cylinders and Walschaert valve gear, in 1937. Built as hand-fired engines - stokers applied later.

Fig. 32.

No. 4700 Name	Road Pennsylvania Rail Road	Type 4-8-2
Builder Pennsylvania R. R.	Boiler, type Conical	Wheelbase, Rigid 18' 10"
Works Juniata	" diam. 84½" pressure 250 psi.	", Driving 18' 10"
Date built 1923 Bldr's. No. 3819	Firebox, type Belpaire - wide	", Engine 41' 0½"
Builder's Class	" length 126" width 79-7/8"	", Eng. & Tender 79' 3-7/8"
R.R. Class, Old New M1	Combustion Chamber, length	Weight in Working Order, lbs.:
Bldr's. Order No. Neg. No.	Grate Area, 70 sq. ft.	Front Truck 60,000
No. in Order 1 Orig. Nos 4700	No. of Tubes 114 No. of Flues 200	Driving Wheels 267,000
Orig. No. this Engine 4700	Diam. " 2¼" Diam " 3¼"	Trailing 58,000
Gauge of Track 4' 8½"	Length, Tubes & Flues 19' 0"	Engine, total 385,000
Service Freight & Passenger	Heating Surface, sq ft.:	Tender 221,050
Cylinder diam. H.P. 27" L.P.	" Tubes 1275 Flues 3028 Total 4303	Eng. & Tender 606,050
Stroke of Piston 30" No. of Cyls. 2	" Firebox plus Arch Tubes 395	Tender, type Rectangular 110-P-75
Driving Wheels diam. 72"	" Syphons Total 4698	" No. of Wheels 8
Valves, type. H.P. Piston diam. 12"	Superheater, type "E" H.S. 1634	Water, gals. 11,980 Coal, tons 18½
" " L.P. diam.	Feedwater Heater	Fuel Oil, gals.
Valve Gear Walschaert	Stoker Brakes #6 ET	Max. Tractive Effort (a) 64,550 lbs.
Reverse Gear, Lever Power X	Throttle, type Dome	" " Booster (b) lbs.
Designer		Factor of Adhesion (a) 4.14 (b)
Source of Photo BALDWIN LOCOMOTIVES		Notes on back of this sheet
Disposition: Sold to		Retired or scrapped

This was the first Mountain (4-8-2) type locomotive on the Pennsylvania R. R.
Tested exhaustively on the road and on the Altoona Test Plant; the results were
the basis for the design of the Class M1a locomotives, 300 of which were built
between 1926 and 1930.

LA-4.500. 3-70

Fig. 33.

No. 6703 Name	Road Pennsylvania Rail Road	Type 4-8-2
Builder Baldwin Locomotive Works	Boiler, type Extended wagon top	Wheelbase, Rigid 18' 10"
Works Eddystone	" diam. 82¼" pressure 250 psi.	" , Driving 18' 10"
Date built 1930 Bldr's. No.	Firebox, type Belpaire - wide	" , Engine 41' 9½"
Builder's Class 14-48-¼-E,	" length 125-15/16" width 79-7/8"	" , Eng. & Tender 96' 6-3/8"
R.R. Class, Old New M1a	Combustion Chamber, length	Weight in Working Order, lbs.:
Bldr's. Order No. Neg. No. 10567	Grate Area 69.86 sq. ft.	Front Truck 59,000
No. in Order Orig. Nos	No. of Tubes 120 No. of Flues 170	Driving Wheels 271,000
Orig. No. this Engine 6703	Diam. " 2¼" Diam " 3½"	Trailing 60,000
Gauge of Track 4' 8½"	Length, Tubes & Flues 19' 0"	Engine, total 390,000
Service Freight & Passenger	Heating Surface, sq ft.:	Tender 378,360
Cylinder diam. H.P. 27" L.P.	" Tubes 1343 Flues 2960 Total 4303	Eng. & Tender 768,360
Stroke of Piston 30" No. of Cyls. 2	" Firebox plus Arch Tubes 395	Tender, type Rectangular 210-F-75
Driving Wheels diam. 72"	" Syphons Total 4698	" No. of Wheels 12
Valves, type, H.P. Piston diam. 12"	Superheater, type "E" H.S. 1634	Water, gals. 22,090 Coal, tons 31½
" " L.P. diam.	Feedwater Heater	Fuel Oil, gals.
Valve Gear Walschaert	Stoker Brakes #6 ET	Max. Tractive Effort (a) 64,550 lbs.
Reverse Gear, Lever Power X	Throttle, type Dome	" " Booster (b) lbs.
Designer		Factor of Adhesion (a) 4.19 (b)
Source of Photo Lt. Col. T. Martin Flattley, Jr. Photo, Ernest, Pa.	10-21-1948.	Notes on back of this sheet
Disposition: Sold to		Retired or scrapped

I rode in the cab of this locomotive from Pittsburgh to Altoona, 113 miles, on
March 15, 1931, hauling Train No. 66, THE AMERICAN. 300 Class M1a locomotives
were built between 1926 and 1930 by Baldwin, Juniata and Lima.

Fig. 34.

No. 5533 Name	Road Pennsylvania Rail Road	Type 4-4-4-4
Builder Baldwin Locomotive Works	Boiler, type Straight top	Wheelbase, Rigid 25' 4"
Works Eddystone	" diam. 91½" pressure 300 psi	" , Driving 25' 4"
Date built 1946 Bldr's. No.	Firebox, type Belpaire - wide	" , Engine 51' 11"
Builder's Class 16-33½/33½-¼-CC, 35	" length 138" width 96"	" , Eng. & Tender 107' 0"
R.R. Class, Old New T1	Combustion Chamber, length 96"	Weight in Working Order, lbs.:
Bldr's. Order No. Neg. No. 13165	Grate Area 92 sq. ft.	Front Truck 107,290
No. in Order 25 Orig. Nos 5525-5549	No. of Tubes 184 No. of Flues 69	Driving Wheels 272,365
Orig. No. this Engine 5533	Diam. " 2¼" Diam " 5½"	Trailing 131,215
Gauge of Track 4' 8½"	Length, Tubes & Flues 18' 0"	Engine, total 510,870
Service Passenger	Heating Surface, sq ft.:	Tender 442,500
Cylinder diam. H.P. 18-3/4" L.P.	" Tubes 1940 Flues 1779 Total 3719	Eng. & Tender 953,370
Stroke of Piston 26" No. of Cyls. 4	CC-150 " Firebox 269 Arch Tubes	Tender, type Rectangular 180-P-84
Driving Wheels diam. 80"	Circulators 71 " Syphons Total 4209	" No. of Wheels 16
Valves, type, H.P. Poppet diam.	Superheater, type "A" H.S. 1430	Water, gals. 19,200 Coal, tons 42.6
" " L.P. diam.	Feedwater Heater Turbo	Fuel Oil, gals.
Valve Gear Franklin Oscil. Cams	Stoker Standard HT Brakes #8 ET	Max. Tractive Effort (a) 58,300 lbs.
Reverse Gear, Lever Power X	Throttle, type American Multiple	" " Booster (b) lbs.
Designer Ralph P. Johnson, Chief Engr., Baldwin Locomotive Wks.		Factor of Adhesion (a) 4.68 (b)
Source of Photo Baldwin Locomotive Works. H. L. Broadbelt Collection.		Notes on back of this sheet
Disposition: Sold to		Retired or scrapped

The final attempt by the Pennsylvania R. R. to develop a modern steam locomotive.

LA-4.500. 3-70

Fig. 35.

Road: United States Railroad Administration (VGN) Type 2-8-8-2B

No. 900 Name _____

Builder American Locomotive Co.
Works Schenectady
Date built 3-1919 Bldr's. No. 59853
Builder's Class 2882-CS-531
R.R. Class, Old _____ New Y-3
Bldr's. Order No. S-1261 Neg. No. S-1261
No. in Order 5 Orig. Nos 900-904
Orig. No. this Engine 900
Gauge of Track 4' 8½"
Service Freight
Cylinder diam. H.P. 25" L.P. 39"
Stroke of Piston 32" No. of Cyls. 4
Driving Wheels diam. 57"
Valves, type, H.P. Piston diam. 14"
" " L.P. Piston diam. 14"
Valve Gear Baker
Reverse Gear, Lever _____ Power X
Designer _____
Source of Photo American Locomotive Co. Howard G. Hill Collection.
Disposition: Sold 1943 to Pennsylvania R. R. as No. 373.

Boiler, type Straight top
" diam. 95-15/16" pressure 240 psi.
Firebox, type Radial stay - wide
" length 170-1/8" width 96¼"
Combustion Chamber, length 37"
Grate Area, 96 sq. ft.
No. of Tubes 274 No. of Flues 53
Diam. " 2¼" Diam " 5½"
Length, Tubes & Flues 24' 0"
Heating Surface, sq ft.:
" Tubes 3860 Flues 1825 Total 5685
" CC & Firebox 386 Arch Tubes 49
" Syphons Total 6120
Superheater, type "A" H.S. 1475
Feedwater Heater _____
Stoker Duplex Brakes #6 ET
Throttle, type Dome

Wheelbase, Rigid 15' 9"
" , Driving 42' 4"
" , Engine 58' 0"
" , Eng. & Tender 94' 6"
Weight in Working Order, lbs.:
Front Truck 32,000
Driving Wheels 474,000
Trailing 25,000
Engine, total 531,000
Tender 209,100
Eng. & Tender 740,100
Tender, type Rectangular
" No. of Wheels 8
Water, gals. 12,000 Coal, tons 16
Fuel Oil, gals. _____
Max. Tractive Effort (a) S-121,600 C-101,300 lbs.
" " Booster (b) _____ lbs.
Factor of Adhesion (a) S-3.9 (b) C-4.67
Notes on back of this sheet
Retired or scrapped _____

Built for Virginian Railway but delivered to Norfolk and Western Railway as
No. 2000, (2000-2004, Builder's Nos. 59853-59857).

Fig. 36.

Road Norfolk and Western Railway. Type 2-8-8-2

No. 2056 Name _____

Builder American Locomotive Co.
Works Richmond
Date built 1923 Bldr's. No. _____
Builder's Class 2882-CS-531
R.R. Class, Old _____ New Y-3a
Bldr's. Order No. _____ Neg. No. _____
No. in Order 30 Orig. Nos 2050-2079
Orig. No. this Engine 2056
Gauge of Track 4' 8½"
Service Freight
Cylinder diam. H.P. 25" L.P. 39"
Stroke of Piston 32" No. of Cyls. 4
Driving Wheels diam. 57"
Valves, type, H.P. Piston diam. 14"
" " L.P. Piston diam. 14"
Valve Gear Baker
Reverse Gear, Lever _____ Power X
Designer _____
Source of Photo Harry Beichert Photo.
Disposition: Sold _____ to _____

Boiler, type Straight top
" diam. 98" pressure 240 psi.
Firebox, type Radial stay - wide
" length 170-1/8" width 96¼"
Combustion Chamber, length 37"
Grate Area, 96.3 sq. ft.
No. of Tubes 274 No. of Flues 53
Diam. " 2¼" Diam " 5½"
Length, Tubes & Flues 24' 0"
Heating Surface, sq ft.:
" Tubes 3860 Flues 1825 Total 5685
" CC & Firebox 386 Arch Tubes 49
" Syphons Total 6120
Superheater, type "A" H.S. 1475
Feedwater Heater Worthington "BL"
Stoker Duplex Brakes #6 ET
Throttle, type Dome

Wheelbase, Rigid 15' 9"
" , Driving 42' 4"
" , Engine 58' 0"
" , Eng. & Tender 94' 6"
Weight in Working Order, lbs.:
Front Truck 28,000
Driving Wheels 478,000
Trailing 25,000
Engine, total 531,000
Tender 271,200
Eng. & Tender 802,200
Tender, type Rectangular
" No. of Wheels 12
Water, gals. 15,000 Coal, tons 20
Fuel Oil, gals. _____
Max. Tractive Effort (a) S-121,600 C-107,373 lbs.
" " Booster (b) _____ lbs.
Factor of Adhesion (a) S-3.94 (b) C-4.45
Notes on back of this sheet
Retired or scrapped _____

LA-4.500. 3-70

Fig. 37.

No. 132 Name	Road Norfolk and Western Railway	Type 4-8-2
Builder Baldwin Locomotive Works	Boiler, type Conical	Wheelbase, Rigid 18' 3"
Works Eddystone	" diam. 86" pressure 200 psi.	" , Driving 18' 3"
Date built 1923 Bldr's. No.	Firebox, type Radial stay - wide	" , Engine 40' 0"
Builder's Class 14-50-¼-E,	" length 114-1/8" width 96¼"	" , Eng. & Tender 83' 8-3/4"
R.R. Class, Old New K-2a	Combustion Chamber, length 68"	Weight in Working Order, lbs.:
Bldr's. Order No. Neg. No. 8746	Grate Area, 76.3 sq. ft.	Front Truck 51,500
No. in Order 12 Orig. Nos 126-137	No. of Tubes 247 No. of Flues 45	Driving Wheels 243,000
Orig. No. this Engine 132	Diam. " 2¼" Diam " 5½"	Trailing 57,500
Gauge of Track 4' 8½"	Length, Tubes & Flues 20' 6"	Engine, total 352,000
Service Passenger	Heating Surface, sq ft.:	Tender 271,200
Cylinder diam. H.P. 28" L.P.	" Tubes 2972 Flues 1325 Total 4297	Eng. & Tender 623,200
Stroke of Piston 30" No. of Cyls. 2	" CC & Firebox 335 Arch Tubes 34	Tender, type Rectangular
Driving Wheels diam. 69"	" Syphons Total 4666	" No. of Wheels 12
Valves, type, H.P. Piston diam. 14"	Superheater, type "A" H.S. 1085	Water, gals. 15,000 Coal, tons 20
" " L.P. diam.	Feedwater Heater	Fuel Oil, gals.
Valve Gear Baker	Stoker Duplex Brakes #6 ET	Max. Tractive Effort (a) 58,000 lbs.
Reverse Gear, Lever Power X	Throttle, type Dome	" " Booster (b) lbs.
Designer Based on USRA 4-8-2R Heavy Mountain Type.		Factor of Adhesion (a) 4.19 (b)
Source of Photo Baldwin Locomotive Works. H. L. Broadbelt Collection.		Notes on back of this sheet
Disposition: Sold to		Retired or scrapped

LA-4.500. 3-70

Fig. 38.

No. 201 Name	Road Norfolk and Western Railway	Type 4-8-2
Builder Norfolk and Western Ry.	Boiler, type Extended wagon top	Wheelbase, Rigid 16' 9"
Works Roanoke	" diam 101-7/8" pressure 225 psi.	" , Driving 16' 9"
Date built 1926 Bldr's. No.	Firebox, type Radial stay - wide	" , Engine 39' 4"
Builder's Class	" length 126-1/16" width 96¼"	" , Eng. & Tender 83' 2-3/4"
R.R. Class, Old New K-3	Combustion Chamber, length	Weight in Working Order, lbs.:
Bldr's. Order No. Neg. No. 9261	Grate Area, 84.1 sq. ft.	Front Truck 56,000
No. in Order 10 Orig. Nos 200-209	No. of Tubes 245 No. of Flues 58	Driving Wheels 264,000
Orig. No. this Engine 201	Diam. " 2¼" Diam " 5½"	Trailing 62,000
Gauge of Track 4' 8½"	Length, Tubes & Flues 19' 5"	Engine, total 382,000
Service Freight	Heating Surface, sq ft.:	Tender 286,530
Cylinder diam. H.P. 28" L.P.	" Tubes 2802 Flues 1621 Total 4423	Eng. & Tender 668,530
Stroke of Piston 30" No. of Cyls. 2	" Firebox plus Arch Tubes 380	Tender, type Rectangular
Driving Wheels diam. 63"	" Syphons Total 4803	" No. of Wheels 12
Valves, type, H.P. Piston diam.	Superheater, type "A" H.S. 1380	Water, gals. 16,000 Coal, tons 23
" " L.P. diam.	Feedwater Heater Worthington "BL"	Fuel Oil, gals.
Valve Gear Baker	Stoker Duplex Brakes #6 ET	Max. Tractive Effort (a) 68,061 lbs.
Reverse Gear, Lever Power X	Throttle, type Dome	" " Booster (b) lbs.
Designer John Pilcher, Mech. Engr., N&WRy., and Staff.		Factor of Adhesion (a) 3.968 (b)
Source of Photo Norfolk and Western Railway. Howard G. Hill Collection.		Notes on back of this sheet
Disposition: Sold to		Retired or scrapped

LA-4.500. 3-70

Operated in time freight service between Roanoke and Norfolk, 258 miles, over
Blue Ridge Mountains between Roanoke and Lynchburg.

Fig. 39.

No. 2063 Name	Road Norfolk and Western Railway	Type 2-8-8-2
Builder American Locomotive Co.	Boiler, type Straight top	Wheelbase, Rigid 15' 9"
Works Richmond	" diam. 98" pressure 240 psi.	", Driving 42' 4"
Date built 4-1923 Bldr's. No.	Firebox, type Radial stay - wide	", Engine 58' 0"
Builder's Class 2882-CS-531	" length 170-1/8" width 96¼"	", Eng. & Tender 94' 6"
R.R. Class, Old New Y-3a	Combustion Chamber, length 37"	Weight in Working Order, lbs.:
Bldr's. Order No. R-315 Neg. No. R-315	Grate Area, 96.3 sq. ft.	Front Truck 28,000
No. in Order 30 Orig. Nos 2050-2079	No. of Tubes 274 No. of Flues 53	Driving Wheels 478,000
Orig. No. this Engine 2063	Diam. " 2¼" Diam " 5½"	Trailing 25,000
Gauge of Track 4' 8½"	Length, Tubes & Flues 24' 0"	Engine, total 531,000
Service Freight	Heating Surface, sq ft.:	Tender 271,200
Cylinder diam. H.P. 25" L.P. 39"	" Tubes 3860 Flues 1825 Total 5685	Eng. & Tender 802,200
Stroke of Piston 32" No. of Cyls. 4	CC & " Firebox plus Arch Tubes 435	Tender, type Rectangular
Driving Wheels diam. 57	" Syphons Total 6120	" No. of Wheels 12
Valves, type. H.P. Piston diam. 14"	Superheater, type "A" H.S. 1475	Water, gals. 15,000 Coal, tons 20
" " L.P. Piston diam. 14"	Feedwater Heater	Fuel Oil, gals.
Valve Gear Baker	Stoker Duplex Brakes #6 ET	Max. Tractive Effort (a) S-121,600 C-107,373 lbs.
Reverse Gear, Lever Power X	Throttle, type Dome	" " Booster (b) lbs.
Designer		Factor of Adhesion (a) S-3.94 (b) C-4.45
Source of Photo American Locomotive Co. Howard G. Hill Collection.		Notes on back of this sheet
Disposition : Sold to		Retired or scrapped

Fig. 41.

No. 5400 Name	Road Pennsylvania Rail Road	Type 4-6-2
Builder Baldwin Locomotive Works	Boiler, type Extended wagon top	Wheelbase, Rigid 13' 10"
Works Eddystone	" diam. 78½" pressure 205 psi.	", Driving 13' 10"
Date built 1-1927 Bldr's. No. 59761	Firebox, type Belpaire - wide	", Engine 36' 2"
Builder's Class 12-48-¼-D,	" length 126" width 80"	", Eng. & Tender 78' 8"
R.R. Class, Old K4s New K4	Combustion Chamber, length 36"	Weight in Working Order, lbs.:
Bldr's. Order No. Neg. No. EE7569	Grate Area, 69.89 sq. ft.	Front Truck 53,640
No. in Order 75 Orig. Nos 5400-5474	No. of Tubes 236 No. of Flues 40	Driving Wheels 201,830
Orig. No. this Engine 5400	Diam. " 2¼" Diam " 5½"	Trailing 53,420
Gauge of Track 4' 8½"	Length, Tubes & Flues 19' 0"	Engine, total 308,890
Service Passenger	Heating Surface, sq ft.:	Tender 221,050
Cylinder diam. H.P. 27" L.P.	" Tubes 2641 Flues 1095 Total 3736	Eng. & Tender 529,850
Stroke of Piston 28" No. of Cyls. 2	CC & " Firebox plus Arch Tubes 305	Tender, type Rectangular 110-P-75
Driving Wheels diam. 80"	" Syphons Total 4041	" No. of Wheels 8
Valves, type. H.P. Piston diam. 12"	Superheater, type "A" H.S. 943	Water, gals. 11,980 Coal, tons 18½
" " L.P. diam.	Feedwater Heater	Fuel Oil, gals.
Valve Gear Walschaert	Stoker Brakes #6 ET	Max. Tractive Effort (a) 44,460 lbs.
Reverse Gear, Lever Power X	Throttle, type Dome	" " Booster (b) lbs.
Designer		Factor of Adhesion (a) 4.54 (b)
Source of Photo Pennsylvania R. R. Howard G. Hill Collection.		Notes on back of this sheet
Disposition : Sold to		Retired or scrapped

LA-4.500. 3-70

Fig. 42.

No. 3768 Name	Road Pennsylvania Rail Road	Type 4-6-2
Builder Pennsylvania R. R.	Boiler, type Extended wagon top	Wheelbase, Rigid 13' 10"
Works Juniata	" diam. 78½" pressure 205 psi.	", Driving 13' 10"
Date built 5-1920 Bldr's. No. 3721	Firebox, type Belpaire - wide	", Engine 36' 2"
Builder's Class	" length 126" width 80"	", Eng. & Tender 87' 0"
R.R. Class, Old K4s New K4	Combustion Chamber, length 36"	Weight in Working Order, lbs.:
Bldr's. Order No. Neg. No. 11212	Grate Area, 69.89 sq. ft.	Front Truck 55,600
No. in Order 50 Orig. Nos 3726-3775	No. of Tubes 236 No. of Flues 40	Driving Wheels 223,000
Orig. No. this Engine 3768	Diam. " 2¼" Diam " 5½"	Trailing 59,400
Gauge of Track 4' 8½"	Length, Tubes & Flues 19' 0"	Engine, total 338,000
Service Passenger	Heating Surface, sq ft.:	Tender 292,000
Cylinder diam. H.P. 27" L.P.	" Tubes 2641 Flues 1095 Total 3736	Eng. & Tender 630,000
Stroke of Piston 28" No. of Cyls. 2	CC & Firebox plus Arch Tubes 305	Tender, type Rectangular 180-P-75
Driving Wheels diam. 80"	" Syphons Total 4041	" No. of Wheels 12
Valves, type. H.P. Piston diam. 12"	Superheater, type "A" H.S. 943	Water, gals. 18,500 Coal, tons 18.75
" " L.P. diam.	Feedwater Heater	Fuel Oil, gals.
Valve Gear Walschaert	Stoker Brakes #6 ET	Max. Tractive Effort (a) 44,460 lbs.
Reverse Gear, Lever Power Screw	Throttle, type Dome	" " Booster (b) lbs.
Designer		Factor of Adhesion (a) 5.02 (b)
Source of Photo Baldwin Locomotive Works, H. L. Broadbelt Collection.		Notes on back of this sheet
Disposition: Sold to		Retired or scrapped

Streamlining applied in 1936, removed later.

Fig. 43.

"A TYPICAL MODERN HEAVY HIGH SPEED PASSENGER LOCOMOTIVE"

No. 5400 Name	Road	Type 4-6-2
Builder Baldwin Locomotive Works	Boiler, type Extended wagon top	Wheelbase, Rigid 13' 10"
Works Eddystone	" diam. 78½" pressure 205 psi.	", Driving 13' 10"
Date built 1-1927 Bldr's. No. 59761	Firebox, type Belpaire - wide	", Engine 36' 2"
Builder's Class 12-48-¼-D,	" length 126" width 80"	", Eng. & Tender 78' 8"
R.R. Class, Old K4s New K4	Combustion Chamber, length 36	Weight in Working Order, lbs.:
Bldr's. Order No. Neg. No. 9912	Grate Area, 69.89 sq. ft.	Front Truck 53,640
No. in Order 75 Orig. Nos 5400-5474	No. of Tubes 236 No. of Flues 40	Driving Wheels 201,830
Orig. No. this Engine 5400	Diam. " 2¼" Diam " 5½"	Trailing 53,420
Gauge of Track 4' 8½"	Length, Tubes & Flues 19' 0"	Engine, total 308,890
Service Passenger	Heating Surface, sq ft.:	Tender
Cylinder diam. H.P. 27" L.P.	" Tubes 2641 Flues 1095 Total 3736	Eng. & Tender
Stroke of Piston 28" No. of Cyls. 2	CC & Firebox plus Arch Tubes 305	Tender, type
Driving Wheels diam. 80"	" Syphons Total 4041	" No. of Wheels
Valves, type. H.P. Piston diam. 12"	Superheater, type "A" H.S. 943	Water, gals. Coal, tons
" " L.P. diam.	Feedwater Heater	Fuel Oil, gals.
Valve Gear Walschaert	Stoker Brakes #6 ET	Max. Tractive Effort (a) 44,460 lbs.
Reverse Gear, Lever Power X	Throttle, type Dome	" " Booster (b) lbs.
Designer		Factor of Adhesion (a) 4.54 (b)
Source of Photo Baldwin Locomotive Works, H. L. Broadbelt Collection		Notes on back of this sheet
Disposition: Sold to		Retired or scrapped

This photograph, 10" x 24" size, was directly responsible for my trip from New York to Chicago in the cabs of the Class K4s locomotives hauling THE BROADWAY LIMITED on February 5-6, 1931.

LA-4.500. 3-70

Fig. 46.

No. 3930 Name	Road Pennsylvania Rail Road.	Type 2-4-4-2
Builder Pennsylvania R. R.	Boiler, type	Wheelbase, Rigid 22' 3"
Works Juniata	" diam. pressure psi.	", Driving 22' 3"
Date built 1924 Bldr's. No.	Firebox, type	", Engine 54' 11"
Builder's Class	" length width	", Eng. & Tender
R.R. Class, Old L5 New L5pdw	Combustion Chamber, length	Weight in Working Order, lbs.:
Bldr's. Order No. Neg. No.	Grate Area, sq. ft.	Front Truck 50,000
No. in Order 1 Orig. Nos 3930	No. of Tubes No. of Flues	Driving Wheels 308,600
Orig. No. this Engine 3930	Diam. " Diam "	Trailing 50,000
Gauge of Track 4' 8½"	Length, Tubes & Flues	Engine, total 408,600
Service Passenger & Freight	Heating Surface, sq ft.:	Tender
Cylinder diam. H.P. L.P.	" Tubes Flues Total	Eng. & Tender
Stroke of Piston No. of Cyls.	" Firebox Arch Tubes	Tender, type
Driving Wheels diam. 80"	" Syphons Total	" No. of Wheels
Valves, type. H.P. diam.	Superheater, type H.S.	Water, gals. Coal, tons
" " L.P. diam.	Feedwater Heater	3,340 HP
Valve Gear	Stoker Brakes #6 ET	Max. Tractive Effort (a) 100,000 lbs.
Reverse Gear, Lever Power	Throttle, type	" " Booster (b) lbs.
Designer		Factor of Adhesion (a) 3.086 (b)
Source of Photo BALDWIN LOCOMOTIVES.		Notes on back of this sheet
		Retired or scrapped
Disposition : Sold to		

I rode in the cab of Locomotive 3924 from Penn Station, New York City, to Manhattan Transfer, N.J., 9 miles, on February 5, 1931, hauling THE BROADWAY LIMITED.

Fig. 47.

No. 5439 Name	Road Pennsylvania Rail Road	Type 4-6-2
Builder Baldwin Locomotive Works	Boiler, type Extended wagon top	Wheelbase, Rigid 13' 10"
Works Eddystone	" diam. 78½" pressure 205	", Driving 13' 10"
Date built 1927 Bldr's. No.	Firebox, t. Belpaire - wide	", Engine 36' 2"
Builder's Class 12-48-¼-D,	" length 126" width 80"	", Eng. & Tender 78' 8"
R.R. Class, Old K4s New K4	Combustion Chamber, length 36"	Weight in Working Order, lbs.:
Bldr's. Order No. Neg. No.	Grate Area, 69.89 sq. ft.	Front Truck 53,640
No. in Order 75 Orig. Nos 5400-5474	No. of Tubes 236 No. of Flues 40	Driving Wheels 201,830
Orig. No. this Engine 5439	Diam. " 2¼" Diam " 5½"	Trailing 53,420
Gauge of Track 4' 8½"	Length, Tubes & Flues 19' 0"	Engine, total 308,890
Service Passenger	Heating Surface, sq ft.:	Tender 254,450
Cylinder diam. H.P. 27" L.P.	" Tubes 2641 Flues 1095 Total 3736	Eng. & Tender 563,340
Stroke of Piston 28" No. of Cyls. 2	CC & Firebox plus Arch Tubes 305	Tender, type Rectangular 130-P-75
Driving Wheels diam. 80"	" Syphons Total 4041	" No. of Wheels 8
Valves, type. H.P. Piston diam. 12"	Superheater, type "A" H.S. 943	Water, gals. 13,475 Coal, tons 21.8
" " L.P. diam.	Feedwater Heater	Fuel Oil, gals.
Valve Gear Walschaert	Stoker Brakes #6 ET	Max. Tractive Effort (a) 44,460 lbs.
Reverse Gear, Lever Power X	Throttle, type Dome	" " Booster (b) lbs.
Designer		Factor of Adhesion (a) 4.54 (b)
Source of Photo Clarence R. Weaver Photo.		Notes on back of this sheet
		Retired or scrapped
Disposition : Sold to		

Fig. 48, photo by the Author, shows No. 5439 at North Philadelphia, Pa., on Train No. 29, THE BROADWAY LIMITED, on February 5, 1931. Fireman Pratt in gangway, a Traveling Fireman, and Engineer Lighty next to engine. I rode in the cab of this engine from Manhattan Transfer, N. J., to Harrisburg, Pa., 186 miles, on this trip.

LA-4.500. 3-70

Fig. 49.

No. 5417 Name	Road Pennsylvania Rail Road	Type 4-6-2
Builder Baldwin Locomotive Works	Boiler, type Extended wagon top	Wheelbase, Rigid 13' 10"
Works Eddystone	" diam. 78½" pressure 205 psi.	" , Driving 13' 10"
Date built 1927 Bldr's. No.	Firebox, type Belpaire - wide	" , Engine 36' 2"
Builder's Class 12-48-¼-D,	" length 126" width 80"	" , Eng. & Tender 78' 8"
R.R. Class, Old K4s New K4	Combustion Chamber, length 36"	Weight in Working Order, lbs.:
Bldr's. Order No. Neg. No.	Grate Area, 69.89 sq. ft.	Front Truck 53,460
No. in Order 75 Orig. Nos 5400-5474	No. of Tubes 236 No. of Flues 40	Driving Wheels 201,830
Orig. No. this Engine 5417	Diam. " 2¼" Diam " 5½"	Trailing 53,420
Gauge of Track 4' 8½"	Length, Tubes & Flues 19' 0"	Engine, total 308,890
Service Passenger	Heating Surface, sq. ft.:	Tender 254,450
Cylinder diam. H.P. 27" L.P.	" Tubes 2641 Flues 1095 Total 3736	Eng. & Tender 563,340
Stroke of Piston 28" No. of Cyls. 2	CC & Firebox plus Arch Tubes 305	Tender, type Rectangular 130-P-75
Driving Wheels diam. 80"	" Syphons Total 4041	" No. of Wheels 8
Valves, type, H.P. Piston diam. 12"	Superheater, type "A" H.S. 943	Water, gals. 13,475 Coal, tons 21.8
" " L.P. diam.	Feedwater Heater	Fuel Oil, gals.
Valve Gear Walschaert	Stoker Brakes #6 ET	Max. Tractive Effort (a) 44,460 lbs.
Reverse Gear, Lever Power X	Throttle, type Dome	" " Booster (b) lbs.
Designer		Factor of Adhesion (a) 4.54 (b)
Source of Photo Clarence R. Weaver Photo, Sunbury, Pa., 6-21-1946, PRR Tr. RJ10		Notes on back of this sheet
Disposition : Sold to		Retired or scrapped

I rode in the cab of this locomotive from Harrisburg, Pa., to Pittsburgh, Pa., on
February 5-6, 1931, 220 miles, hauling THE BROADWAY LIMITED, PRR Train No. 29, not
including 12 miles in the cab of K4s helper No. 7116 from Altoona to Gallitzin,
including the famous Horseshoe Curve.

Fig. 51.

No. 5075 Name	Road Pennsylvania Rail Road	Type 4-4-2
Builder Pennsylvania R. R.	Boiler, type Extended wagon top	Wheelbase, Rigid 7' 5"
Works Juniata	" diam. 76-3/4" pressure 205 psi.	" , Driving 7' 5"
Date built 12-1910 Bldr's. No. 2159	Firebox, type Belpaire - wide	" , Engine 29' 9"
Builder's Class	" length 110-3/4" width 72"	" , Eng. & Tender 64' 0"
R.R. Class, Old New E6	Combustion Chamber, length 36"	Weight in Working Order, lbs.:
Bldr's. Order No. Neg. No.	Grate Area, 54.75 sq. ft.	Front Truck 50,000
No. in Order 1 Orig. Nos 5075	No. of Tubes 460 No. of Flues	Driving Wheels 133,300
Orig. No. this Engine 5075	Diam. " 2" Diam "	Trailing 48,200
Gauge of Track 4' 8½"	Length, Tubes & Flues 13' 8-5/8"	Engine, total 231,500
Service Passenger	Heating Surface, sq. ft.:	Tender 167,650
Cylinder diam. H.P. 22" L.P.	" Tubes 3582 Flues Total 3582	Eng. & Tender 399,150
Stroke of Piston 26" No. of Cyls. 2	" Firebox 218 Arch Tubes	Tender, type Rectangular 70-P-66
Driving Wheels diam. 80"	" Syphons Total 3800	" No. of Wheels 8
Valves, type, H.P. Piston diam. 14"	Superheater, type H.S.	Water, gals. 7,150 Coal, tons 15.8
" " L.P. diam.	Feedwater Heater	Fuel Oil, gals.
Valve Gear Walschaert	Stoker Brakes #6 ET	Max. Tractive Effort (a) 27,409 lbs.
Reverse Gear, Lever X Power	Throttle, type Dome	" " Booster (b) lbs.
Designer Alfred W. Gibbs, GSMP, PRR, Altoona, Pa.		Factor of Adhesion (a) 4.86 (b)
Source of Photo Frederick Westing Collection.		Notes on back of this sheet
Disposition : Sold to		Retired or scrapped

The first Class E6 locomotive, prototype of the famous Class E6s locomotives.
No. 5075 was later equipped with a superheater, and was renumbered 1067, a number
formerly carried by a Class E3d New York Division Atlantic.

150

LA-4.500. 3-70

Fig. 52.

No. 7116 Name	Road Pennsylvania Rail Road	Type 4-6-2
Builder Pennsylvania R. R.	Boiler, type Extended wagon top	Wheelbase, Rigid 13' 10"
Works Juniata	" diam. 78½" pressure 205 psi.	", Driving 13' 10"
Date built 7-1918 Bldr's. No. 3512	Firebox, type Belpaire - wide	", Engine 36' 2"
Builder's Class	" length 126" width 80"	", Eng. & Tender 72' 4"
R.R. Class, Old K4s New K4	Combustion Chamber, length 36"	Weight in Working Order, lbs.:
Bldr's. Order N Neg. No.	Grate Area, 69.89 sq. ft.	Front Truck 53,460
No. in Order 110 Orig. Nos Assorted	No. of Tubes 236 No. of Flues 40	Driving Wheels 201,830
Orig. No. this Engine 7116	Diam. " 2¼" Diam " 5½"	Trailing 53,420
Gauge of Track 4' 8½"	Length, Tubes & Flues 19' 0"	Engine, total 308,890
Service Passenger	Heating Surface, sq ft.:	Tender 178,550
Cylinder diam. H.P. 27" L.P.	" Tubes 2641 Flues 1095 Total 3736	Eng. & Tender 487,440
Stroke of Piston 28" No. of Cyls. 2	CC & Firebox plus Arch Tubes 305	Tender, type Rectangular 80-P-79
Driving Wheels diam. 80"	" Syphons Total 4041	" No. of Wheels 8
Valves, type, H.P. Piston diam. 12	Superheater, type "A" H.S. 943	Water, gals. 8,100 Coal, tons 17.2
" " L.P. diam.	Feedwater Heater	Fuel Oil, gals.
Valve Gear Walschaert	Stoker Brakes #6 ET	Max. Tractive Effort (a) 44,460 lbs.
Reverse Gear, Lever Power X	Throttle, type Dome	" " Booster (b) lbs.
Designer		Factor of Adhesion (a) 4.54 (b)
Source of Photo Lt. Col. T. Martin Flattley, Jr., Photo. Buffalo, N. Y. 8-1-1939		Notes on back of this sheet
Disposition: Sold to		Retired or scrapped

I rode in the cab of this locomotive from Altoona, Pa., to Gallitzin, Pa., 12 miles, as the helper engine doubleheading with K4 No. 5417 climbing the Allegheny Mts., on PRR Train No. 29, THE BROADWAY LIMITED, on February 5, 1931.

Fig. 55.

No. 1361 Name	Road Pennsylvania Rail Road	Type 4-6-2
Builder Pennsylvania R. R.	Boiler, type Extended wagon top	Wheelbase, Rigid 13' 10"
Works Juniata	" diam. 78½" pressure 205 psi.	", Driving 13' 10"
Date built 5-1918 Bldr's. No. 3475	Firebox, type Belpaire - wide	", Engine 36' 2"
Builder's Class	" length 126" width 80"	", Eng. & Tender 78' 8"
R.R. Class, Old K4s New K4	Combustion Chamber, length 36"	Weight in Working Order, lbs.:
Bldr's. Order No. Neg. No.	Grate Area, 69.89 sq. ft.	Front Truck 53,460
No. in Order 110 Orig. Nos Assorted	No. of Tubes 236 No. of Flues 40	Driving Wheels 201,830
Orig. No. this Engine 1361	Diam. " 2¼" Diam " 5½"	Trailing 53,420
Gauge of Track 4' 8½"	Length, Tubes & Flues 19' 0"	Engine, total 308,890
Service Passenger	Heating Surface, sq ft.:	Tender 254,450
Cylinder diam. H.P. 27" L.P.	" Tubes 2641 Flues 1095 Total 3736	Eng. & Tender 563,340
Stroke of Piston 28" No. of Cyls. 2	CC & Firebox plus Arch Tubes 305	Tender, type Rectangular
Driving Wheels diam. 80"	" Syphons Total 4041	" No. of Wheels 8
Valves, type, H.P. Piston diam. 12"	Superheater, type "A" H.S. 943	Water, gals. 13,475 Coal, tons 21.8
" " L.P. diam.	Feedwater Heater	Fuel Oil, gals.
Valve Gear Walschaert	Stoker Brakes #6 ET	Max. Tractive Effort (a) 44,460 lbs.
Reverse Gear, Lever Power Screw	Throttle, type Dome	" " Booster (b) lbs.
Designer		Factor of Adhesion (a) 4.54 (b)
Source of Photo Richard J. Dent Collection.		Notes on back of this sheet
Disposition: Sold to		Retired or scrapped

This engine is on permanent exhibition at Kittaning Point, Pa., mid-point on the famous Horseshoe Curve, between Altoona and Gallitzin, on the main line of the Pennsylvania Rail Road.

LA-4.500. 3-70

Fig. 56.

No. 5373 Name ....
Road Pennsylvania Rail Road .... Type 4-6-2

Builder Pennsylvania R. R.
Boiler, type Extended wagon top .... Wheelbase, Rigid 13' 10"

Works Juniata
" diam. 78½" pressure 205 psi .... ", Driving 13' 10"

Date built 1924 Bldr's. No. 3897
Firebox, type Belpaire - wide .... ", Engine 36' 2"

Builder's Class
" length 126" width 80" .... ", Eng. & Tender 78' 8"

R.R. Class, Old K4s New K4
Combustion Chamber, length 36" .... Weight in Working Order, lbs.:

Bldr's. Order No. Neg. No.
Grate Area, 69.89 sq. ft. .... Front Truck 53,460

No. in Order 50 Orig. Nos 5350-5399
No. of Tubes 236 No. of Flues 40 .... Driving Wheels 201,830

Orig. No. this Engine 5373
Diam. " 2¼" Diam " 5½" .... Trailing 53,420

Gauge of Track 4' 8½"
Length, Tubes & Flues 19' 0" .... Engine, total 308,890

Service Passenger
Heating Surface, sq. ft.: .... Tender 254,450

Cylinder diam. H.P. 27" L.P.
" Tubes 2641 Flues 1095 Total 3736 .... Eng. & Tender 563,340

Stroke of Piston 28" No. of Cyls. 2.
" CC & Firebox plus Arch Tubes 305 .... Tender, type Rectangular 130-P-75

Driving Wheels diam. 80"
" Syphons Total 4041 .... " No. of Wheels 8

Valves, type, H.P. Piston diam. 12"
Superheater, type "A" H.S. 943 .... Water, gals. 13,475 Coal, tons 21.8

" " L.P. diam.
Feedwater Heater .... Fuel Oil, gals.

Valve Gear Walschaert
Stoker Brakes #6 ET .... Max. Tractive Effort (a) 44,460 lbs.

Reverse Gear, Lever Power X
Throttle, type Dome .... " " Booster (b) lbs.

Designer .... Factor of Adhesion (a) 4.54 (b)

Source of Photo Lt. Col. T. Martin Flattley, Jr., Photo, Crestline, Ohio, 8-5-1939 Notes on back of this sheet

Disposition: Sold to .... Retired or scrapped

I rode in the cab of this locomotive from Pittsburgh, Pa., to Crestline, Ohio, 189 miles, on February 6, 1931, hauling PRR Train No. 29, THE BROADWAY LIMITED.

Fig. 57.

No. 3878 Name ....
Road Pennsylvania Rail Road .... Type 4-6-2

Builder Pennsylvania R. R.
Boiler, type Extended wagon top .... Wheelbase, Rigid 13' 10"

Works Juniata
" diam. 78½" pressure 205 psi .... ", Driving 13' 10"

Date built 6-1923 Bldr's. No. 3774
Firebox, type Belpaire - wide .... ", Engine 36' 2"

Builder's Class
" length 126" width 80" .... ", Eng. & Tender 74' 8"

R.R. Class, Old K4s New K4
Combustion Chamber, length 36" .... Weight in Working Order, lbs.:

Bldr's. Order No. Neg. No.
Grate Area, 69.89 sq. ft. .... Front Truck 53,460

No. in Order 57 Orig. Nos Assorted*
No. of Tubes 236 No. of Flues 40 .... Driving Wheels 201,830

Orig. No. this Engine 3878
Diam. " 2¼" Diam " 5½" .... Trailing 53,420

Gauge of Track 4' 8½"
Length, Tubes & Flues 19' 0" .... Engine, total 308,890

Service Passenger
Heating Surface, sq. ft.: .... Tender 221,050

Cylinder diam. H.P. 27" L.P.
" Tubes 2641 Flues 1095 Total 3736 .... Eng. & Tender 529,940

Stroke of Piston 28" No. of Cyls. 2.
" CC & Firebox plus Arch Tubes 305 .... Tender, type Rectangular 110-P-75

Driving Wheels diam. 80"
" Syphons Total 4041 .... " No. of Wheels 8

Valves, type, H.P. Piston diam. 12"
Superheater, type "A" H.S. 943 .... Water, gals. 11,980 Coal, tons 18.5

" " L.P. diam.
Feedwater Heater .... Fuel Oil, gals.

Valve Gear Walschaert
Stoker Brakes #6 ET .... Max. Tractive Effort (a) 44,460 lbs.

Reverse Gear, Lever Power X
Throttle, type Dome .... " " Booster (b) lbs.

Designer .... Factor of Adhesion (a) 4.54 (b)

Source of Photo Lt. Col. T. Martin Flattley, Jr., Photo, Englewood, Ill., 4-1-1938 Notes on back of this sheet

Disposition: Sold to .... Retired or scrapped

I rode in the cab of this locomotive from Crestline, Ohio, to Chicago, Illinois, 280 miles, on February 6, 1931, hauling PRR Train No. 29, THE BROADWAY LIMITED, thus completing a continuous trip of 908 miles in the locomotive cabs from New York to Chicago on the 20-hour schedule.

*This group numbered 3800, 3801, 3805-3807, 3838-3889.

Fig. 59.　　　　　　　　　　　　　　　　　　　　　　　(NYC)

No. 567　Name	Road New York Central & Hudson River Rail Road	Type 4-4-0
Builder Schenectady Locomotive Wks.	Boiler, type Wagon top	Wheelbase, Rigid 8' 6"
Works Schenectady	" diam. 50"　pressure 145 psi.	" , Driving 8' 6"
Date built 1877　Bldr's. No. 1055	Firebox, type Crown bar - narrow	" , Engine 22' 6½"
Builder's Class 440-85	" length　width	" , Eng. & Tender 43' 6-3/4"
R.R. Class, Old A　New C-4	Combustion Chamber, length	Weight in Working Order, lbs.:
Bldr's. Order No.　Neg. No.	Grate Area, 18 sq. ft.	Front Truck 31,250
No. in Order 4　Orig. Nos 564-567	No. of Tubes 198　No. of Flues	Driving Wheels 53,450
Orig. No. this Engine 567	Diam. " 2"　Diam "	Trailing
Gauge of Track 4' 8½"	Length, Tubes & Flues	Engine, total 84,700
Service Passenger	Heating Surface, sq ft.:	Tender 62,220
Cylinder diam. H.P. 17"　L.P.	" Tubes　Flues　Total	Eng. & Tender 146,920
Stroke of Piston 24"　No. of Cyls. 2	" Firebox　Arch Tubes	Tender, type Rectangular
Driving Wheels diam. 70"	" Syphons　Total 1353	" No. of Wheels 8
Valves, type, H.P. Balanced slide　diam.	Superheater, type　H.S.	Water, gals. 3,500　Coal, tons 6
" " L.P.　diam.	Feedwater Heater	Fuel Oil, gals.
Valve Gear Stephenson	Stoker　Brakes WAB A-1	Max. Tractive Effort (a) 12,600 lbs.
Reverse Gear, Lever X　Power	Throttle, type Dome	" " Booster (b) lbs.
Designer		Factor of Adhesion (a) 4.24 (b)
Source of Photo New York Central Lines. W. D. Edson Collection.		Notes on back of this sheet　Retired or scrapped 1899
Disposition: Sold　to		

Renumbered 781 in 1890; 1100 in 1892. Builder's Nos. 1052-1055.

Fig. 60.

No. 317　Name	Road Lake Shore & Michigan Southern Railway (NYC)	Type 4-4-0
Builder LS&MS Ry.	Boiler, type Straight top	Wheelbase, Rigid
Works	" diam.　pressure psi.	" , Driving
Date built 1871　Bldr's. No.	Firebox, type Crown bar - narrow	" , Engine
Builder's Class	" length　width	" , Eng. & Tender
R.R. Class, Old　New	Combustion Chamber, length	Weight in Working Order, lbs.:
Bldr's. Order No.　Neg. No.	Grate Area,　sq. ft.	Front Truck
No. in Order 1　Orig. Nos 317	No. of Tubes　No. of Flues	Driving Wheels
Orig. No. this Engine 317	Diam. "　Diam "	Trailing
Gauge of Track 4' 8½"	Length, Tubes & Flues	Engine, total 64,000
Service Passenger	Heating Surface, sq ft.:	Tender
Cylinder diam. H.P. 16"　L.P.	" Tubes　Flues　Total	Eng. & Tender
Stroke of Piston 24"　No. of Cyls. 2	" Firebox　Arch Tubes	Tender, type Rectangular
Driving Wheels diam. 66"	" Syphons　Total	" No. of Wheels 8
Valves, type, H.P. Slide　diam.	Superheater, type　H.S.	Water, gals.　Coal, tons
" " L.P.　diam.	Feedwater Heater	Fuel Oil, gals.
Valve Gear Stephenson	Stoker　Brakes	Max. Tractive Effort (a) lbs.
Reverse Gear, Lever X　Power	Throttle, type Dome	" " Booster (b) lbs.
Designer		Factor of Adhesion (a) (b)
Source of Photo Penn Central Rail Road, Howard G. Hill Collection.		Notes on back of this sheet　Retired or scrapped
Disposition: Sold　to		

An artist's conception of THE FAST MAIL, which began operation between New York and Chicago on September 14, 1875, on a schedule of 27 hours 12 minutes, the first regular, fast, through service in both directions between New York and Chicago.

Fig. 61.

No. 160 Name	Road Lake Shore & Michigan Southern Railway (NYC) Type 4-4-0	
Builder Brooks Locomotive Works	Boiler, type Wagon top	Wheelbase, Rigid 9' 0"
Works Dunkirk	" diam. 52" pressure 150 psi.	", Driving 9' 0"
Date built 1893 Bldr's. No. 2257	Firebox, type Belpaire - narrow	", Engine 23' 9"
Builder's Class	" length width	", Eng. & Tender 46' 9"
R.R. Class, Old Q New C-53	Combustion Chamber, length	Weight in Working Order, lbs.:
Bldr's. Order No. 94, 160, 597-599	Grate Area, sq. ft.	Front Truck 42,600
No. in Order 5 Orig. Nos	No. of Tubes 202 No. of Flues	Driving Wheels 63,400
Orig. No. this Engine 160	Diam. " 2" Diam "	Trailing
Gauge of Track 4' 8½"	Length, Tubes & Flues 12' 1"	Engine, total 116,000
Service Passenger	Heating Surface, sq. ft.:	Tender
Cylinder diam. H.P. 17" L.P.	" Tubes 1269 Flues Total 1269	Eng. & Tender
Stroke of Piston 24" No. of Cyls. 2	" Firebox Arch Tubes	Tender, type Rectangular
Driving Wheels diam. 73"	" Syphons Total	" No. of Wheels 8
Valves, type, H.P. Slide diam.	Superheater, type H.S.	Water, gals. Coal, tons
" " L.P. diam.	Feedwater Heater	Fuel Oil, gals.
Valve Gear Stephenson	Stoker Brakes WAB A-1	Max. Tractive Effort (a) 14,900 lbs.
Reverse Gear, Lever X Power	Throttle, type Dome	" " Booster (b) lbs.
Designer		Factor of Adhesion (a) 4.26 (b)
Source of Photo Penn Central Rail Road, Howard G. Hill Collection.		Notes on back of this sheet
Disposition: Sold to		Retired or scrapped

An artist's conception of THE EXPOSITION FLYER which operated from May 29 to November 19, 1893, making the run between New York and Chicago, 980 miles, in 20 hours, the fastest regular train for the distance in the world.
Renumbered 4107 in 1905; 4177 in 1915.

Fig. 62.   (NYC)

No. 862 Name	Road New York Central & Hudson River Rail Road Type 4-4-0	
Builder Schenectady Loco. Wks.	Boiler, type Wagon top	Wheelbase, Rigid 8' 6"
Works Schenectady	" diam. 58" pressure 180 psi.	", Driving 8' 6"
Date built 1890 Bldr's. No. 3057	Firebox, type Crown bar - narrow	", Engine 23' 11"
Builder's Class 440-120	" length 96" width 40-7/8"	", Eng. & Tender 46' 8½"
R.R. Class, Old I New C	Combustion Chamber, length	Weight in Working Order, lbs.:
Bldr's. Order No. Neg. No.	Grate Area, 27.3 sq. ft.	Front Truck 40,000
No. in Order 10 Orig. Nos 860-869	No. of Tubes 268 No. of Flues	Driving Wheels 80,000
Orig. No. this Engine 862	Diam. " 2" Diam "	Trailing
Gauge of Track 4' 8½"	Length, Tubes & Flues 12' 0"	Engine, total 120,000
Service Passenger	Heating Surface, sq. ft.:	Tender 80,000
Cylinder diam. H.P. 19" L.P.	" Tubes 1684 Flues Total 1684	Eng. & Tender 200,000
Stroke of Piston 24" No. of Cyls. 2	" Firebox 138 Arch Tubes	Tender, type Rectangular
Driving Wheels diam. 70"	" Syphons Total 1822	" No. of Wheels 8
Valves, type, H.P. Slide diam.	Superheater, type H.S.	Water, gals. 3,587 Coal, tons 6.75
" " L.P. diam.	Feedwater Heater	Fuel Oil, gals.
Valve Gear Stephenson	Stoker Brakes WAB A-1	Max. Tractive Effort (a) 18,800 lbs.
Reverse Gear, Lever X Power	Throttle, type Dome	" " Booster (b) lbs.
Designer William Buchanan, SMP&RS, NYC&HR RR, Albany, New York		Factor of Adhesion (a) 4.26 (b)
Source of Photo Howard G. Hill Collection.		Notes on back of this sheet
Disposition: Sold to		Retired or scrapped

Hauled the LIMITED trains between New York and Buffalo.

LA-4.500. 3-70

Fig. 63.

No. 871 Name	Road New York Central & Hudson River Rail Road Type 4-4-0	
Builder Schenectady Loco. Wks.	Boiler, type Wagon top	Wheelbase, Rigid 8' 6"
Works Schenectady	" diam. 58" pressure 180 psi.	" , Driving 8' 6"
Date built 1890 Bldr's. No. 3066	Firebox, type Crown bar - narrow	" , Engine 23' 11"
Builder's Class 440-120	" length 96" width 40-7/8"	" , Eng. & Tender 46' 8½"
R.R. Class, Old I New Ca	Combustion Chamber, length	Weight in Working Order, lbs.:
Bldr's. Order No. Neg. No.	Grate Area, 27.3 sq. ft.	Front Truck 40,000
No. in Order 2 Orig. Nos 871-872	No. of Tubes 268 No. of Flues	Driving Wheels 80,000
Orig. No. this Engine 871	Diam. " 2" Diam "	Trailing
Gauge of Track 4' 8½"	Length, Tubes & Flues 12' 0"	Engine, total 120,000
Service Passenger	Heating Surface, sq ft.:	Tender 80,000
Cylinder diam. H.P. 19" L.P.	" Tubes Flues Total	Eng. & Tender 200,000
Stroke of Piston 24" No. of Cyls. 2	" Firebox Arch Tubes	Tender, type Rectangular
Driving Wheels diam. 78"	" Syphons Total 1821.5	" No. of Wheels 8
Valves, type. H.P. Slide diam.	Superheater, type H.S.	Water, gals. 3,587 Coal, tons 6.75
" " L.P. diam.	Feedwater Heater	Fuel Oil, gals.
Valve Gear Stephenson	Stoker Brakes WAB A-1	Max. Tractive Effort (a) 18,800 lbs.
Reverse Gear, Lever X Power	Throttle, type Dome	" " Booster (b) lbs.
Designer Wm. Buchanan, SMP&RS, NYC&HR RR., Albany, NY		Factor of Adhesion (a) 4.25 (b)
Source of Photo New York Central Lines.		Notes on back of this sheet
Disposition : Sold to		Retired or scrapped 1924

Rebuilt in 1904. Hauled the Limited trains between New York City and Buffalo.

LA-4.500. 3-70

Fig. 65.

No. 2960 Name	Road New York Central & Hudson River Rail Road Type 4-4-2	
Builder American Locomotive Co.	Boiler, type Straight top	Wheelbase, Rigid 16' 6"
Works Schenectady	" diam. 70-5/8" pressure 200 psi.	" , Driving 7' 0"
Date built 5-1902 Bldr's. No. 25028	Firebox, type Crown bar - wide	" , Engine 27' 7"
Builder's Class 442-186	" length 96-1/8" width 75¼"	" , Eng. & Tender 59' 0½"
R.R. Class, Old New I	Combustion Chamber, length	Weight in Working Order, lbs.:
Bldr's. Order No. S-22 Neg. No. 4152	Grate Area, 50.2 sq. ft.	Front Truck
No. in Order 15 Orig. Nos 2954-2968	No. of Tubes 390 No. of Flues	Driving Wheels 108,000
Orig. No. this Engine 2960	Diam. " 2" Diam "	Trailing
Gauge of Track 4' 8½"	Length, Tubes & Flues 16' 0"	Engine, total 176,000
Service Passenger	Heating Surface, sq ft.:	Tender 130,000
Cylinder diam. H.P. 20½" L.P.	" Tubes 3248 Flues Total 3248	Eng. & Tender 306,000
Stroke of Piston 26" No. of Cyls. 2	" Firebox plus Arch Tubes 198	Tender, type Rectangular
Driving Wheels diam. 79"	" Syphons Total 3446	" No. of Wheels 8
Valves, type. H.P. Piston diam. 12"	Superheater, type H.S.	Water, gals. 6,000 Coal, tons 10
" " L.P. diam.	Feedwater Heater	Fuel Oil, gals.
Valve Gear Stephenson	Stoker Brakes WAB A-1	Max. Tractive Effort (a) 23,520 lbs.
Reverse Gear, Lever X Power	Throttle, type Dome	" " Booster (b) lbs.
Designer		Factor of Adhesion (a) 4.6 (b)
Source of Photo New York Central Lines. Howard G. Hill Collection.		Notes on back of this sheet
Disposition : Sold to		Retired or scrapped

Builder's Nos. 25022-25036. Renumbered 3960 in 1905; 960 in 1913.
Shown hauling THE TWENTIETH CENTURY between Albany and New York City on the first eastbound trip of Train No. 26, June 16, 1902.

LA-4.500. 3-70

Fig. 66.

No. 107 Name	Road Lake Shore & Michigan Southern Railway (NYC) Type 4-6-0	Wheelbase, Rigid 15' 0"
Builder Schenectady Loco. Wks.	Boiler, type Extended wagon top	", Driving 15' 0"
Works Schenectady	" diam. 56" pressure 190 psi	", Engine 24' 9"
Date built 1896 Bldr's. No. 4512	Firebox, type Crown bar – narrow	", Eng. & Tender 47' 8"
Builder's Class 460-118	" length 95" width 41½"	Weight in Working Order, lbs.:
R.R. Class, Old F New F-45	Combustion Chamber, length	Front Truck 30,000
Bldr's. Order No. S-33 Neg. No. S-33	Grate Area, 27.4 sq. ft.	Driving Wheels 88,000
No. in Order 10 Orig. Nos Assorted	No. of Tubes 249 No. of Flues	Trailing
Orig. No. this Engine 107	Diam. " 2" Diam "	Engine, total 118,000
Gauge of Track 4' 8½"	Length, Tubes & Flues 13' 3"	Tender 87,000
Service Passenger	Heating Surface, sq ft.:	Eng. & Tender 205,000
Cylinder diam. H.P. 18" L.P.	" Tubes 1717 Flues Total 1717	Tender, type Rectangular
Stroke of Piston 24" No. of Cyls. 2	" Firebox 135 Arch Tubes 15	" No. of Wheels 8
Driving Wheels diam. 69"	" Syphons Total 1867	Water, gals. 4,000 Coal, tons 6½
Valves, type. H.P. Slide diam.	Superheater, type H.S.	Fuel Oil, gals.
" " L.P. diam.	Feedwater Heater	Max. Tractive Effort (a) 18,200 lbs.
Valve Gear Stephenson	Stoker Brakes WAB A-1	" " Booster (b) lbs.
Reverse Gear, Lever X Power	Throttle, type Dome	Factor of Adhesion (a) 4.83 (b)
Designer		Notes on back of this sheet
Source of Photo Howard G. Hill Collection		Retired or scrapped
Disposition: Sold to		

Builder's Nos. 4509-4518. Original numbers 10, 20, 90, 107, 116, 128, 146, 148, 149, 212. 212 renumbered 147. Renumbered in 1905 to 5020-5026, 5028, 5029, 5027. 107 renumbered 5023 in 1905.

Fig. 67.

No. 660 Name	Road Lake Shore & Michigan Southern Railway (NYC) Type 2-6-2	Wheelbase, Rigid 22' 10"
Builder Brooks Locomotive Works	Boiler, type Conical wagon top	", Driving 14' 0"
Works Dunkirk	" diam 64-3/4" pressure 180 psi	", Engine 31' 10"
Date built 6-1901 Bldr's. No. 3817	Firebox, type Radial stay – wide	", Eng. & Tender 57' 4½"
Builder's Class 262-186	" length 84-1/8" width 83¼"	Weight in Working Order, lbs.:
R.R. Class, Old Jb, J40b New J40f	Combustion Chamber, length	Front Truck 22,000
Bldr's. Order No. B-806 Neg. No. B-806	Grate Area, 48.6 sq. ft.	Driving Wheels 134,000
No. in Order 1 Orig. Nos 660	No. of Tubes 344 No. of Flues	Trailing 30,000
Orig. No. this Engine 660	Diam. " 2" Diam "	Engine, total 186,000
Gauge of Track 4' 8½"	Length, Tubes & Flues 19' 0"	Tender 126,600
Service Passenger	Heating Surface, sq ft.:	Eng. & Tender 312,600
Cylinder diam. H.P. 20½" L.P.	" Tubes 3406 Flues Total 3406	Tender, type Rectangular
Stroke of Piston 28" No. of Cyls. 2	" Firebox plus Arch Tubes 190	" No. of Wheels 8
Driving Wheels diam. 80"	" Syphons Total 3596	Water, gals. 6,000 Coal, tons 13
Valves, type. H.P. Piston diam. 11"	Superheater, type H.S.	Fuel Oil, gals.
" " L.P. diam.	Feedwater Heater	Max. Tractive Effort (a) 22,500 lbs.
Valve Gear Stephenson	Stoker Brakes WAB A-1	" " Booster (b) lbs.
Reverse Gear, Lever X Power	Throttle, type Dome	Factor of Adhesion (a) 5.96 (b)
Designer		Notes on back of this sheet
Source of Photo Howard G. Hill Collection		Retired or scrapped
Disposition: Sold to		

Renumbered 4660 in 1905. Rebuilt 7-1909. See "Locomotive Exhibits", from ENGINEERING, Louisiana Purchase Exposition, 1904, for details of locomotive No. 695, 2-6-2 type, developed from tests of above locomotive.

LA-4.500. 3-70

Fig. 68.

No. 4670   Name

Builder American Locomotive Co.

Works Brooks

Date built 11-1902   Bldr's. No. 26442

Builder's Class 262-186

R.R. Class, Old JC, J40c   New J-40g

Bldr's. Order No. B-878   Neg. No. B-878

No. in Order 12   Orig. Nos 663-674

Orig. No. this Engine 670

Gauge of Track 4' 8½"

Service Passenger

Cylinder diam. H.P. 20½"   L.P.

Stroke of Piston 28"   No. of Cyls. 2

Driving Wheels diam. 80"

Valves type H.P. Piston   diam. 11"

  "   " L.P.   diam.

Valve Gear Stephenson

Reverse Gear, Lever X   Power

Designer

Source of Photo Brooks Locomotive Works, Howard G. Hill Collection.

Disposition: Sold   to

Road Lake Shore & Michigan Southern Railway (NYC)   Type 2-6-2.

Boiler, type Extended wagon top

" diam. 64-3/4" pressure 200 psi

Firebox, type Crown bar – wide

" length 84-1/8" width 83¼"

Combustion Chamber, length

Grate Area 48.6 sq. ft.

No. of Tubes 344   No. of Flues

Diam. 2"   Diam "

Length, Tubes & Flues 19' 0"

Heating Surface, sq ft.:

  " Tubes 3406 Flues   Total 3406

  " Firebox plus Arch Tubes 190

  " Syphons   Total 3596

Superheater, type H.S.

Feedwater Heater

Stoker   Brakes WAB A-1

Throttle, type Dome

Wheelbase, Rigid 22' 10"

" , Driving 14' 0"

" , Engine 31' 10"

" , Eng. & Tender 57' 4½"

Weight in Working Order, lbs.:

Front Truck 22,000

Driving Wheels 134,000

Trailing 30,000

Engine, total 186,000

Tender 126,600

Eng. & Tender 312,600

Tender, type Rectangular

" No. of Wheels 8

Water, gals. 6,000   Coal, tons 13

Fuel Oil, gals.

Max. Tractive Effort (a) 23,800 lbs.

" " Booster (b) lbs.

Factor of Adhesion (a) 5.68 (b)

Notes on back of this sheet

Retired or scrapped 9-1925

Renumbered 4670 (4663-4674) in 1905. Four of the class, not including 4670, were renumbered twice later. Builder's Nos. 26435-26446.
Shown hauling THE TWENTIETH CENTURY LIMITED on the Lake Shore & Michigan Southern Railway about 1905, after the number was changed.

Fig. 69.

No. 613   Name

Builder Brooks Locomotive Works

Works Dunkirk

Date built 1900   Bldr's. No. 3606

Builder's Class 460-172

R.R. Class, Old I-1   New F-52

Bldr's. Order No. B-764   Neg. No. B-764

No. in Order 5   Orig. Nos 611-615

Orig. No. this Engine 613

Gauge of Track 4' 8½"

Service Passenger

Cylinder diam. H.P. 20"   L.P.

Stroke of Piston 28"   No. of Cyls. 2

Driving Wheels diam. 80"

Valves type H.P. Piston   diam.

  "   " L.P.   diam.

Valve Gear Stephenson

Reverse Gear, Lever X   Power

Designer

Source of Photo Brooks Locomotive Works, Howard G. Hill Collection.

Disposition: Sold   to

Road Lake Shore & Michigan Southern Railway (NYC)   Type 4-6-0

Boiler, type Extended wagon top

" diam. 66"   pressure 200 psi

Firebox, type Crown bar – narrow

" length 121" width 44-3/4"

Combustion Chamber, length

Grate Area 33.6 sq. ft.

No. of Tubes 343   No. of Flues

Diam. 2"   Diam "

Length, Tubes & Flues 15' 0"

Heating Surface, sq ft.:

  " Tubes 2675 Flues   Total 2675

  " Firebox 190   Arch Tubes 25

  " Syphons   Total 2890

Superheater, type H.S.

Feedwater Heater

Stoker   Brakes WAB A-1

Throttle, type Dome

Wheelbase, Rigid 16' 6"

" , Driving 16' 6"

" , Engine 27' 4"

" , Eng. & Tender 55' 2"

Weight in Working Order, lbs.:

Front Truck 37,500

Driving Wheels 135,000

Trailing

Engine, total 172,500

Tender 128,000

Eng. & Tender 300,500

Tender, type Rectangular

" No. of Wheels 8

Water, gals. 6,000   Coal, tons 12

Fuel Oil, gals.

Max. Tractive Effort (a) 23,800 lbs.

" " Booster (b) lbs.

Factor of Adhesion (a) 5.68 (b)

Notes on back of this sheet

Retired or scrapped by 1920

Builder's Nos. 3604-3608. Renumbered 5013 (5011-5015) in 1905.
Driving wheel diameter later increased to 81".

LA-4.500. 3-70

Fig. 70.

No. 604 Name	Road Lake Shore & Michigan Southern Railway (NYC)	Type 4-6-0
Builder Brooks Locomotive Works	Boiler, type Extended wagon top	Wheelbase, Rigid 16' 6"
Works Dunkirk	" diam. 64-3/4" pressure 200 psi	" , Driving 16' 6"
Date built 10-1899 Bldr's. No. 3335	Firebox, type Crown bar - narrow	" , Engine 27' 4"
Builder's Class 460-172	" length 120-1/8" width 40¼"	" , Eng. & Tender 55' 3⅓"
R.R. Class, Old I New F-51	Combustion Chamber, length	Weight in Working Order, lbs.:
Bldr's. Order No. B-720 Neg. No. 371	Grate Area, 33.5 sq. ft.	Front Truck 38,600
No. in Order 11 Orig. Nos 600-610	No. of Tubes 343 No. of Flues	Driving Wheels 133,000
Orig. No. this Engine 604	Diam. " 2" Diam "	Trailing
Gauge of Track 4' 8½"	Length, Tubes & Flues 15' 0½"	Engine, total 171,600
Service Passenger	Heating Surface, sq ft.:	Tender 126,600
Cylinder diam. H.P. 20" L.P.	" Tubes 2660 Flues Total 2660	Eng. & Tender 298,200
Stroke of Piston 28" No. of Cyls. 2	" Firebox plus Arch Tubes 202	Tender, type Rectangular
Driving Wheels diam. 80"	" Syphons Total 2862	" No. of Wheels 8
Valves, type, H.P. Slide* diam.	Superheater, type H.S.	Water, gals. 6,000 Coal, tons 13
" " L.P. diam.	Feedwater Heater	Fuel Oil, gals.
Valve Gear Stephenson	Stoker Brakes WAB A-1	Max. Tractive Effort (a) 23,940 lbs.
Reverse Gear, Lever X Power	Throttle, type Dome	" " Booster (b) lbs.
Designer Waldo H. Marshall, SMP, LS&MS Ry.		Factor of Adhesion (a) 5.56 (b)
Source of Photo New York Central Lines. Howard G. Hill Collection.		Notes on back of this sheet
Disposition: Sold to		Retired or scrapped 10-1919

*Allen-Richardson Balanced Slide Valves. Renumbered 5004 (5000-5010) in 1905.
Builder's Nos. 3331-3341. Driving wheels later increased to 81". Shown hauling
Train No. 25, THE TWENTIETH CENTURY LIMITED, westbound on the Lake Shore & Michigan
Southern Railway about 1904. These Brooks 10-wheelers superceded the Class J-40
Prairie (2-6-2) type locomotives because of their greater safety at high speed with
4-wheeled engine trucks.

Fig. 71. (NYC)

No. 2701 Name	Road New York Central & Hudson River Rail Road	Type 4-6-2
Builder American Locomotive Co.	Boiler, type Straight top	Wheelbase, Rigid 13' 0"
Works Schenectady	" diam. 70½" pressure 200 psi	" , Driving 13' 0"
Date built 1903 Bldr's. No. 28961	Firebox, type Crown bar - wide	" , Engine 33' 7½"
Builder's Class 462-207	" length 96" width 75¼"	" , Eng. & Tender 58' 7"
R.R. Class, Old K-1 New A-1a	Combustion Chamber, length	Weight in Working Order, lbs.:
Bldr's. Order No. Neg. No.	Grate Area, 50.2 sq. ft.	Front Truck 39,000
No. in Order 4 Orig. Nos 2700-2703	No. of Tubes 285 No. of Flues	Driving Wheels 131,200
Orig. No. this Engine 2701	Diam. " 2¼" Diam "	Trailing 36,800
Gauge of Track 4' 8½"	Length, Tubes & Flues 19' 6"	Engine, total 207,000
Service Passenger	Heating Surface, sq ft.:	Tender 113,900
Cylinder diam. H.P. 21" L.P.	" Tubes 3258 Flues Total 3258	Eng. & Tender 320,900
Stroke of Piston 28" No. of Cyls. 2	" Firebox 175 Arch Tubes	Tender, type Rectangular
Driving Wheels diam. 75"	" Syphons Total 3457	" No. of Wheels 8
Valves, type, H.P. Piston diam.	Superheater, type H.S.	Water, gals. 6,000 Coal, tons 8
" " L.P. diam.	Feedwater Heater	Fuel Oil, gals.
Valve Gear Stephenson	Stoker Brakes WAB A-1	Max. Tractive Effort (a) 28,800 lbs.
Reverse Gear, Lever X Power	Throttle, type Dome	" " Booster (b) lbs.
Designer		Factor of Adhesion (a) 4.69 (b)
Source of Photo Frederick Westing Collection.		Notes on back of this sheet
Disposition: Sold to		Retired or scrapped by 1929

Builder's Nos. 28960-28963. Operated on Boston & Albany R. R. only under No. 3501
(3500-3503). Renumbered B&A 501 (500-503) in 1912. This was the first group of
Pacific (4-6-2) type locomotives on the New York Central System.

Fig. 72.

No. 8452 Name	Road Michigan Central Rail Road. (NYC)	Type 4-6-2
Builder American Locomotive Co.	Boiler, type Straight top	Wheelbase, Rigid 13' 0"
Works Schenectady	" diam. 70-5/8" pressure 200 psi.	", Driving 13' 0"
Date built 1905 Bldr's. No. 30778	Firebox, type Crown bar - wide	", Engine 33' 7½"
Builder's Class 462-221	" length 96" width 75¼"	", Eng. & Tender 61' 2½"
R.R. Class, Old K-80 New K-80b	Combustion Chamber, length	Weight in Working Order, lbs.:
Bldr's. Order No. Neg. No.	Grate Area, 50.23 sq. ft.	Front Truck 42,000
No. in Order 1 Orig. Nos 8452	No. of Tubes 354 No. of Flues	Driving Wheels 140,500
Orig. No. this Engine 8452	Diam. " 2" Diam "	Trailing 38,500
Gauge of Track 4' 8½"	Length, Tubes & Flues 20' 0"	Engine, total 221,000
Service Passenger	Heating Surface, sq ft.:	Tender 122,600
Cylinder diam. H.P. 22" L.P.	" Tubes 3691 Flues Total 3691	Eng. & Tender 343,600
Stroke of Piston 26" No. of Cyls. 2	" Firebox 180 Arch Tubes 23	Tender, type Rectangular
Driving Wheels diam. 75"	" Syphons Total 3894	" No. of Wheels 8
Valves, type, H.P. Piston diam.	Superheater, type H.S.	Water, gals. 6,000 Coal, tons 10
" " L.P. diam.	Feedwater Heater	Fuel Oil, gals.
Valve Gear Stephenson	Stoker Brakes WAB HS	Max. Tractive Effort (a) 28,500 lbs.
Reverse Gear, Lever X Power	Throttle, type Dome	" " Booster (b) lbs.
Designer		Factor of Adhesion (a) 4.93 (b)
Source of Photo C. B. Cheney Photo. Wm. D. Edson Collection.		Notes on back of this sheet
Disposition : Sold to		Retired or scrapped 1932

Fig. 73.

		(NYC)
No. 3565 Name	Road New York Central & Hudson River Rail Road.	Type 4-6-2
Builder American Locomotive Co.	Boiler, type Extended wagon top	Wheelbase, Rigid 14' 0"
Works Schenectady	" diam. 70-5/8" pressure 200 psi.	", Driving 14' 0"
Date built 1908 Bldr's. No. 45254	Firebox, type Radial stay - wide	", Engine 36' 6"
Builder's Class 462-262	" length 108-5/8" width 75¼"	", Eng. & Tender 67' 10"
R.R. Class, Old New K-2e	Combustion Chamber, length	Weight in Working Order, lbs.:
Bldr's. Order No. S-547 Neg. No. S-547	Grate Area, 56.8 sq. ft.	Front Truck 46,000
No. in Order 40 Orig. Nos 3555-3594	No. of Tubes 380 No. of Flues	Driving Wheels 172,000
Orig. No. this Engine 3565	Diam. " 2" Diam "	Trailing 44,000
Gauge of Track 4' 8½"	Length, Tubes & Flues 20' 0"	Engine, total 262,000
Service Passenger	Heating Surface, sq ft.:	Tender 162,200
Cylinder diam. H.P. 22" L.P.	" Tubes 3960 Flues Total 3960	Eng. & Tender 424,200
Stroke of Piston 28" No. of Cyls. 2	" Firebox plus Arch Tubes 231	Tender, type Rectangular
Driving Wheels diam. 79"	" Syphons Total 4191	" No. of Wheels 8
Valves, type, H.P. Piston diam. 14"	Superheater, type H.S.	Water, gals. 8,000 Coal, tons 14
" " L.P. diam.	Feedwater Heater	Fuel Oil, gals.
Valve Gear Walschaert	Stoker Brakes #6 ET	Max. Tractive Effort (a) 29,160 lbs.
Reverse Gear, Lever X Power	Throttle, type Dome	" " Booster (b) lbs.
Designer		Factor of Adhesion (a) 5.9 (b)
Source of Photo American Locomotive Co. Howard G. Hill Collection.		Notes on back of this sheet
Disposition : Sold to		Retired or scrapped by 1938

Builder's Nos. 45244-45283. Nos. 3564, 3578 renumbered 4652, 4653 in 1936.

Fig. 74. 4854, 4863, 4858, 4871, 4868.

No. (LtoR) Name	Road Lake Shore & Michigan Southern Railway (NYC) Type 4-6-2	
Builder American Locomotive Co.	Boiler, type Conical	Wheelbase, Rigid 14' 0"
Works Schenectady	" diam 70-5/8" pressure 200 psi.	" , Driving 14' 0"
Date built 1910 Bldr's. No. Note	Firebox, type Radial stay - wide	" , Engine 36' 6"
Builder's Class 462-262	" length 108-5/8" width 75¼"	" , Eng. & Tender 67' 10"
R.R. Class, Old New K-21	Combustion Chamber, length	Weight in Working Order, lbs.:
Bldr's. Order No. S-685 Neg. No. S-685	Grate Area. 56.8 sq. ft.	Front Truck 46,000
No. in Order 50 Orig. Nos 4845-4894	No. of Tubes 380 No. of Flues	Driving Wheels 172,000
Orig. No. this Engine See above	Diam. " 2" Diam "	Trailing 44,000
Gauge of Track 4' 8½"	Length, Tubes & Flues 20' 0"	Engine, total 262,000
Service Passenger	Heating Surface, sq ft.:	Tender 162,200
Cylinder diam. H.P. 22" L.P.	" Tubes 3961 Flues Total 3961	Eng. & Tender 424,200
Stroke of Piston 28" No. of Cyls. 2	" Firebox plus Arch Tubes 231	Tender, type Rectangular
Driving Wheels diam. 79"	" Syphons Total 4192	" No. of Wheels 8
Valves, type, H.P. Piston diam. 14"	Superheater, type H.S.	Water, gals. 8,000 Coal, tons 14
" " L.P. diam.	Feedwater Heater	Fuel Oil, gals.
Valve Gear Walschaert	Stoker Brakes #6 ET	Max. Tractive Effort (a) 29,160 lbs.
Reverse Gear, Lever Power X	Throttle, type Dome	" " Booster (b) lbs.
Designer		Factor of Adhesion (a) 5.89 (b)
Source of Photo Penn Central Rail Road, Howard G. Hill Collection.		Notes on back of this sheet
Disposition: Sold to		Retired or scrapped by 1936

Builder's Nos: 4854 - 47187; 4863 - 47196; 4858 - 47191; 4871 - 47204; 4868 - 47201.
Five sections of Train No. 26, THE TWENTIETH CENTURY LIMITED, lined up for departure from La Salle Street Depot, Chicago, to New York. No. 4863 will run as the fifth section of No. 26. These locomotives were not renumbered. Photographed in 1927.

Fig. 75.

(NYC)

No. 3426 Name	Road New York Central & Hudson River Rail Road Type 4-6-2	
Builder American Locomotive Co.	Boiler, type Conical	Wheelbase, Rigid 14' 0"
Works Schenectady	" diam. 70-5/8" pressure 200 psi	" , Driving 14' 0"
Date built 1911 Bldr's. No. 49457	Firebox, type Radial stay - wide	" , Engine 36' 6"
Builder's Class 462-S-269	" length 108-1/8" width 75¼"	" , Eng. & Tender 68' 0"
R.R. Class, Old New K-3a	Combustion Chamber, length	Weight in Working Order, lbs.:
Bldr's. Order No. Neg. No.	Grate Area. 56.5 sq. ft.	Front Truck 50,000
No. in Order 20 Orig. Nos 3418-3437	No. of Tubes 175 No. of Flues 32	Driving Wheels 171,500
Orig. No. this Engine 3426	Diam. " 2¼" Diam " 5½"	Trailing 47,500
Gauge of Track 4' 8½"	Length, Tubes & Flues 21' 6"	Engine, total 269,000
Service Passenger	Heating Surface, sq ft.:	Tender 167,000
Cylinder diam. H.P. 23½" L.P.	" Tubes 2216 Flues 977 Total 3193	Eng. & Tender 436,000
Stroke of Piston 26" No. of Cyls. 2	" Firebox plus Arch Tubes 231	Tender, type Rectangular
Driving Wheels diam. 79"	" Syphons Total 3424	" No. of Wheels 8
Valves, type, H.P. Piston diam. 14"	Superheater, type "A" H.S. 839	Water, gals. 7,500 Coal, tons 12
" " L.P. diam.	Feedwater Heater	Fuel Oil, gals.
Valve Gear Walschaert	Stoker Brakes #6 ET	Max. Tractive Effort (a) 30,900 lbs.
Reverse Gear, Lever X Power	Throttle, type Dome	" " Booster (b) lbs.
Designer		Factor of Adhesion (a) 5.56 (b)
Source of Photo Railway Age Gazette, 3-31-1911. Howard G. Hill Collection.		Notes on back of this sheet
Disposition: Sold to		Retired or scrapped by 1939

Builder's Nos. 49449-49468.

Fig. 76.

No. 4723 Name	Road New York Central Lines	Type 4-6-2
Builder American Locomotive Co.	Boiler, type Extended wagon top	Wheelbase, Rigid 14' 0"
Works Brooks	" diam. 68-5/8" pressure 200 psi	", Driving 14' 0"
Date built 1905 Bldr's. No. 37719	Firebox, type Radial stay - wide	", Engine 36' 6"
Builder's Class	" length 108-1/8" width 73¼"	", Eng. & Tender 68' 1-5/8"
R.R. Class, Old J-41a New K-41a	Combustion Chamber, length	Weight in Working Order, lbs.:
Bldr's. Order No. Neg. No.	Grate Area, 55 sq. ft.	Front Truck 47,300
No. in Order 9 Orig. Nos 4715-4723	No. of Tubes 221 No. of Flues 30	Driving Wheels 170,500
Orig. No. this Engine 4723	Diam. " 2" Diam " 5-3/8"	Trailing 47,200
Gauge of Track 4' 8½"	Length, Tubes & Flues 21' 6"	Engine, total 265,000
Service Passenger	Heating Surface, sq ft.:	Tender 156,500
Cylinder diam. H.P. 22" L.P.	" Tubes 2488 Flues 893 Total 3381	Eng. & Tender 421,500
Stroke of Piston 28" No. of Cyls. 2	" Firebox plus Arch Tubes 222	Tender, type Rectangular
Driving Wheels diam. 79"	" Syphons Total 3603	" No. of Wheels 8
Valves, type, H.P. Piston diam. 14"	Superheater, type "A" H.S. 766	Water, gals. 7,500 Coal, tons 12
" " L.P. diam.	Feedwater Heater	Fuel Oil, gals.
Valve Gear Walschaert	Stoker Brakes #6 ET	Max. Tractive Effort (a) 29,160 lbs.
Reverse Gear, Lever X Power	Throttle, type Dome	" " Booster (b) lbs.
Designer		Factor of Adhesion (a) 5.86 (b)
Source of Photo William D. Edson Collection.		Notes on back of this sheet Retired or scrapped by 1932.
Disposition: Sold to		

Built as Class J-41a Prairie (2-6-2) type locomotives for the Lake Shore & Michigan
Southern Railway. Rebuilt in Company shops between 1915-1919 as Class K-41a Pacific
(4-6-2) type locomotives under the same numbers, for service on various divisions.

Fig. 77. (NYC)

No. 3406 Name	Road New York Central & Hudson River Rail Road	Type 4-6-2
Builder Baldwin Locomotive Works	Boiler, type Extended wagon top	Wheelbase, Rigid 14' 0"
Works Eddystone	" diam. 72" pressure 200 psi	", Driving 14' 0"
Date built 1-1912 Bldr's. No. 37431	Firebox, type Radial stay - wide	", Engine 36' 6"
Builder's Class 12-40-¼-D, 23	" length 108-1/8" width 75¼"	", Eng. & Tender 67' 10"
R.R. Class, Old New K-3c	Combustion Chamber, length	Weight in Working Order, lbs.:
Bldr's. Order No. Neg. No. 3792	Grate Area, 56.5 sq. ft.	Front Truck 50,150
No. in Order 20 Orig. Nos 3398-3417	No. of Tubes 175 No. of Flues 32	Driving Wheels 171,300
Orig. No. this Engine 3406	Diam. " 2¼" Diam " 5½"	Trailing 47,900
Gauge of Track 4' 8½"	Length, Tubes & Flues 21' 6"	Engine, total 269,350
Service Passenger	Heating Surface, sq ft.:	Tender 148,650
Cylinder diam. H.P. 23½" L.P.	" Tubes 2216 Flues 977 Total 3193	Eng. & Tender 418,000
Stroke of Piston 26" No. of Cyls. 2	" Firebox 204 Arch Tubes 30	Tender, type Rectangular
Driving Wheels diam. 79"	" Syphons Total 3427	" No. of Wheels 8
Valves, type, H.P. Piston diam. 14"	Superheater, type "A" H.S. 803	Water, gals. 7,500 Coal, tons 12
" " L.P. diam.	Feedwater Heater	Fuel Oil, gals.
Valve Gear Walschaert	Stoker Brakes #6 ET	Max. Tractive Effort (a) 30,900 lbs.
Reverse Gear, Lever X Power	Throttle, type Dome	" " Booster (b) lbs.
Designer		Factor of Adhesion (a) 5.55 (b)
Source of Photo Baldwin Locomotive Works. H. L. Broadbelt Collection.		Notes on back of this sheet Retired or scrapped by 1950
Disposition: Sold to		

3398, 3400, 3402, 3403, 3404, 3407, 3408, 3415, 3416, 3417 renumbered in 1936 to
4821-4830. 4826 renumbered in 1938 to P&E 60.
Builder's Nos.: 3398-3407, 37423-37432; 3408-3412, 37468-37472; 3413-3417, 37491-
37495. One of the very few Baldwin locomotives on the New York Central System.

Fig. 78.

No. 3359 Name ....

Road New York Central & Hudson River Rail Road   Type 4-6-2
14' 0"

Builder American Locomotive Co.

Boiler, type Conical ....

Wheelbase, Rigid .... 14' 0"

Works Schenectady

" diam. 70-5/8" pressure 200 psi.

", Driving .... 14' 0"

Date built 9-1913 Bldr's. No. 54045

Firebox, type Radial stay - wide

", Engine .... 36' 6"

Builder's Class 462-S-271

" length 108-1/8" width 75¼"

", Eng. & Tender .... 68' 1"

R.R. Class, Old   New K-3g

Combustion Chamber, length

Weight in Working Order, lbs.:

Bldr's. Order No. S-987 Neg. No. S-987

Grate Area, 56.5 sq. ft.

Front Truck 50,000

No. in Order 20 Orig. Nos 3358-3377

No. of Tubes 175 No. of Flues 32

Driving Wheels 172,000

Orig. No. this Engine 3359

Diam. " 2¼" Diam " 5½"

Trailing 49,000

Gauge of Track 4' 8½"

Length, Tubes & Flues 21' 6"

Engine, total 271,000

Service Passenger

Heating Surface, sq ft.:

Tender 157,100

Cylinder diam. H.P. 23½" L.P.

" Tubes 2216 Flues 976 Total 3192

Eng. & Tender 428,100

Stroke of Piston 26" No. of Cyls. 2

" Firebox plus Arch Tubes 230

Tender, type Rectangular

Driving Wheels diam. 79"

" Syphons Total 3422

" No. of Wheels 8

Valves, type. H.P. Piston diam. 14"

Superheater, type "A" H.S. 823

Water, gals. 10,000 Coal, tons 17

" " L.P. diam.

Feedwater Heater

Fuel Oil, gals.

Valve Gear Walschaert

Stoker Brakes #6 ET

Max. Tractive Effort (a) 30,900 lbs.

Reverse Gear, Lever X Power

Throttle, type Dome

" " Booster (b) .... lbs.

Designer

Factor of Adhesion (a) 5.58 (b) ....

Source of Photo Howard G. Hill Collection

Notes on back of this sheet

Disposition: Sold   to

Retired or scrapped 2-1951

Booster applied later. Renumbered 4848 in 1936, P&E 61 in 1938.
Builder's Nos. 54044-54063.

Fig. 79.

Cleveland, Cincinnati, Chicago & St. Louis R. R.

No. 6510 Name

Road (NYC) Type 4-6-2

Builder American Locomotive Co.

Boiler, type Straight top

Wheelbase, Rigid .... 13' 8"

Works Schenectady

" diam. 79½" pressure 205 psi.

", Driving .... 13' 8"

Date built 11-1926 Bldr's. No. 67114

Firebox, type Radial stay - wide

", Engine .... 36' 11"

Builder's Class 462-S-298

" length 108-1/8" width 90¼"

", Eng. & Tender .... 79' 5½"

R.R. Class, Old   New K-5b

Combustion Chamber, length

Weight in Working Order, lbs.:

Bldr's. Order No. S-1569 Neg. No. S-1569

Grate Area, 67.8 sq. ft.

Front Truck 54,500

No. in Order 10 Orig. Nos 6505-6514

No. of Tubes 190 No. of Flues 45

Driving Wheels 184,500

Orig. No. this Engine 6510

Diam. " 2¼" Diam " 5½"

Trailing 58,500

Gauge of Track 4' 8½"

Length, Tubes & Flues 21' 0"

Engine, total 297,500

Service Passenger

Heating Surface, sq ft.:

Tender 274,500

Cylinder diam. H.P. 25" L.P.

" Tubes 2350 Flues 1345 Total 3695

Eng. & Tender 572,000

Stroke of Piston 28" No. of Cyls. 2

" Firebox plus Arch Tubes 257

Tender, type Rectangular

Driving Wheels diam. 79"

" Syphons Total 3952

" No. of Wheels 12

Valves, type. H.P. Piston diam. 14"

Superheater, type "A" H.S. 1150

Water, gals. 15,000 Coal, tons 16

" " L.P. diam.

Feedwater Heater

Fuel Oil, gals.

Valve Gear Walschaert

Stoker Standard HT Brakes #6 ET

Max. Tractive Effort (a) 38,600 lbs.

Reverse Gear, Lever Power Precision

Throttle, type American Multiple

" " Booster (b) .... lbs.

Designer

Factor of Adhesion (a) 4.78 (b) ....

Source of Photo Howard G. Hill Collection

Notes on back of this sheet

Disposition: Sold   to

Retired or scrapped 6-1952

Renumbered 4910 (4905-4914) in 1936. Builder's Nos. 67109-67118.

LA-4.500. 3-70

Fig. 80.

No. 5241 Name	Road New York Central Lines	Type 4-6-4
Builder American Locomotive Co.	Boiler, type Straight top	Wheelbase, Rigid 14' 0"
Works Schenectady	" diam.82-7/16" pressure 225 psi.	", Driving 14" 0"
Date built 10-1927 Bldr's. No. 67472	Firebox, type Radial stay - wide	", Engine 40' 4"
Builder's Class 464-S-360	" length 130" width 90¼"	", Eng. & Tender 83' 7½"
R.R. Class, Old New J-1b	Combustion Chamber, length	Weight in Working Order, lbs.:
Bldr's. Order No. S-1597 Neg. No. S-1597	Grate Area. 81.5 sq. ft.	Front Truck 66,200
No. in Order 10 Orig. Nos 5240-5249	No. of Tubes 37 No. of Flues 201	Driving Wheels 192,400
Orig. No. this Engine 5241	Diam. " 2¼" Diam " 3½"	Trailing f-46,100 b- 55,600
Gauge of Track 4' 8½"	Length, Tubes & Flues 20' 6"	Engine, total 360,300
Service Passenger	Heating Surface, sq ft.:	Tender 280,700
Cylinder diam. H.P. 25" L.P.	" Tubes 447 Flues 3756 Total 4203	Eng. & Tender 641,000
Stroke of Piston 28" No. of Cyls. 2	" Firebox plus Arch Tubes 281	Tender, type Rectangular
Driving Wheels diam. 79"	" Syphons Total 4484	" No. of Wheels 12
Valves, type. H.P. Piston diam. 14"	Superheater, type "E" H.S. 1951	Water, gals. 12,500 Coal, tons 24
" " L.P. diam.	Feedwater Heater Coffin	Fuel Oil, gals.
Valve Gear Baker	Stoker Standard HT Brakes #8 ET	Max. Tractive Effort (a) 42,360 lbs.
Reverse Gear, Lever Power Precision	Throttle, type American Multiple	" " Booster (b) 10,900 lbs.
Designer Paul W. Kiefer, Ch. Engr., MP&RS., NYC. Lines.		Factor of Adhesion (a) 4.55 (b) 5.11
Source of Photo Arnold Haas Photo.		Notes on back of this sheet
Disposition : Sold to		Retired or scrapped by 1956

One of 59 Class J-1b locomotives built in 1927 and 1928. They were essentially duplicates of Class J-1a locomotive No. 5200, the first 4-6-4 type locomotive built in the United States, with minor improvements.

Fig. 81.

No. 5442 Name	Road New York Central Lines	Type 4-6-4
Builder American Locomotive Co.	Boiler, type Conical	Wheelbase, Rigid 14' 0"
Works Schenectady	" diam 80-5/8" pressure 265 psi	", Driving 14' 0"
Date built 11-1937 Bldr's. No. 68876	Firebox, type Radial stay - wide	", Engine 40' 4"
Builder's Class 464-S-360	" length 130-13/16" width 90¼"	", Eng. & Tender 88' 5-7/8"
R.R. Class, Old New J-3a	Combustion Chamber, length 60"	Weight in Working Order, lbs.:
Bldr's. Order No. S-1772 Neg. No. S-1772	Grate Area. 82 sq. ft.	Front Truck 63,500
No. in Order 50 Orig. Nos 5405-5454	No. of Tubes 59 No. of Flues 183	Driving Wheels 201,500
Orig. No. this Engine 5442	Diam. " 2¼" Diam " 3½"	Trailing f-41,200 b-53,800
Gauge of Track 4' 8½"	Length, Tubes & Flues 19' 0"	Engine, total 360,000
Service Passenger	Heating Surface, sq ft.:	Tender 420,000
Cylinder diam. H.P. 22½" L.P.	" Tubes 660 Flues 3167 Total 3827	Eng. & Tender 780,000
Stroke of Piston 29" No. of Cyls. 2	" CC & Firebox plus Arch Tubes 360	Tender, type Rectangular PT
Driving Wheels diam. 79"	" Syphons Total 4187	" No. of Wheels 14
Valves, type. H.P. Piston diam. 14"	Superheater, type "E" H.S. 1745	Water, gals. 18,000 Coal, tons 46
" " L.P. diam.	Feedwater Heater Elesco	Fuel Oil, gals.
Valve Gear Baker	Stoker Standard HT Brakes #8 ET	Max. Tractive Effort (a) 41,860 lbs.
Reverse Gear, Lever Power Y	Throttle, type American Multiple	" " Booster (b) 12,100 lbs.
Designer		Factor of Adhesion (a) 4.82 (b) 4.84
Source of Photo Arnold Haas Photo, Collinwood, Ohio, 11-27-1955		Notes on back of this sheet
Disposition : Sold to		Retired or scrapped 1956

LA-4.500. 3-70

Fig. 82.

No. 5445 Name _____ Road New York Central Lines _____ Type 4-6-4

Builder American Locomotive Co. Boiler, type Conical wagon top Wheelbase, Rigid 14' 0"

Works Schenectady " diam 80-5/8" pressure 265 psi. ", Driving 14' 0"

Date built 3-1938 Bldr's. No. 68879 Firebox, type Radial stay - wide ", Engine 40' 4"

Builder's Class 464-S-366 " length 130-13/16" width 90¼" ", Eng. & Tender 83' 7½"

R.R. Class, Old _____ New J-3a Combustion Chamber, length 60"

Bldr's. Order No. S-1772 Neg. No. S-1772 Grate Area, 82 sq. ft. Weight in Working Order, lbs.:

No. in Order 50 Orig. Nos 5405-5454 No. of Tubes 59 No. of Flues 183 Front Truck 67,100

Orig. No. this Engine 5445 Diam. " 2¼" Diam " 3½" Driving Wheels 201,800

Gauge of Track 4' 8½" Length, Tubes & Flues 19' 0" Trailing f-41,900 b-54,700

Service Passenger Heating Surface, sq ft.: Engine, total 365,500

Cylinder diam. H.P. 22½" L.P. " Tubes 657 Flues 3170 Total 3827 Tender 316,400

Stroke of Piston 29" No. of Cyls. 2 " Firebox 323 Arch Tubes 37 Eng. & Tender 681,900

Driving Wheels diam. 79" " Syphons Total 4187 Tender, type Rectangular

Valves, type. H.P. Piston diam. 14" Superheater, type "E" H.S. 1745 " No. of Wheels 12

" " L.P. diam. Feedwater Heater Elesco Water, gals. 13,600 Coal, tons 28

Valve Gear Baker Stoker Standard HT Brakes #8 ET Fuel Oil, gals.

Reverse Gear, Lever Power Precision Throttle, type American Multiple Max. Tractive Effort (a) 41,860 lbs.

Designer _____ " " Booster (b) 12,100 lbs.

Source of Photo American Locomotive Co. Howard G. Hill Collection. Factor of Adhesion (a) 4.82 (b) 4.52

Notes on back of this sheet

Disposition: Sold _____ to _____ Retired or scrapped by 1956

2 8½" cross-compound air pumps on front end. Bethlehem type B Booster. Water scoop. Automatic train control. Roller bearings on engine truck, driving journals, trailer truck and tender trucks. 5445-5454 were streamlined until 1947 and were used on THE TWENTIETH CENTURY LIMITED and other limited trains. 5426 and 5429 were streamlined from 1941 until 1950.

Fig. 83.

No. 6001 Name _____ Road New York Central Lines. Type 4-8-4

Builder American Locomotive Co. Boiler, type Conical Wheelbase, Rigid _____

Works Schenectady " diam 90" pressure 275 psi. ", Driving 20' 6"

Date built 1945 Bldr's. No. 73779 Firebox, type Radial stay - wide ", Engine 48' 5"

Builder's Class 484-S-471 " length 151-1/16" width 96¼" ", Eng. & Tender 97' 2½"

R.R. Class, Old _____ New S-1b Combustion Chamber, length _____

Bldr's. Order No. S-1980 Neg. No. S-1980 Grate Area, 101 sq. ft. Weight in Working Order, lbs.:

No. in Order 25 Orig. Nos 6001-6025 No. of Tubes 55 No. of Flues 177 Front Truck 91,400

Orig. No. this Engine 6001 Diam. " 2¼" Diam " 4" Driving Wheels 275,000

Gauge of Track 4' 8½" Length, Tubes & Flues 19' 11¼" Trailing fp52,300 b-52,300

Service Passenger & Freight Heating Surface, sq ft.: Engine, total 471,000

Cylinder diam. H.P. 25½" L.P. " Tubes 646 Flues 3674 Total 4320 Tender 420,000

Stroke of Piston 32" No. of Cyls. 2 " Firebox plus Arch Tubes 499 Eng. & Tender 891,000

Driving Wheels diam. 79" " Syphons Total 4819 Tender, type PT-5

Valves, type. H.P. Piston diam. Superheater, type "E" H.S. 2073 " No. of Wheels 14

" " L.P. diam. Feedwater Heater Worthington Water, gals. 18,000 Coal, tons 46

Valve Gear Baker Stoker Standard HT Brakes #8 ET Fuel Oil, gals.

Reverse Gear, Lever Power Precision Throttle, type American Multiple Max. Tractive Effort (a) 62,400 lbs.

Designer _____ " " Booster (b) lbs.

Source of Photo Charles M. Smith Collection. Factor of Adhesion (a) 4.42 (b)

Notes on back of this sheet

Disposition: Sold _____ to _____ Retired or scrapped

Fig. 87.

No. 1174 Name	Road New York Central Lines	Type B+B+B+B
Builder American Locomotive Co.	Boiler, type Vertical (Heater)	Wheelbase, Rigid 6' 6" 5' 0"
General Electric Co.	" diam. pressure 220 psi.	" , Driving 46' 5"
Works Schenectady — Erie	Firebox, type	" , Engine 46' 5"
Date built 12-1926 Bldr's. No. 66706	" length width	" , Eng. & Tender
Builder's Class BBBB265/265E8GE91A	Combustion Chamber, length	Weight in Working Order, lbs.:
R.R. Class, Old S-1534 New T-3a	Grate Area, sq. ft.	Front Truck
Bldr's. Order No. N-52640 Neg. No.	No. of Tubes No. of Flues	Driving Wheels 292,600
No. in Order 10 Orig. Nos 1173-1182	Diam. " Diam ".	Trailing
Orig. No. this Engine 1174	Length, Tubes & Flues	Engine, total 292,600
Gauge of Track 4' 8½"	Heating Surface, sq ft.:	Tender
Service Passenger	" Tubes Flues Total	Eng. & Tender
Cylinder diam. H.P. L.P.	" Firebox Arch Tubes	Tender, type None
Stroke of Piston No. of Cyls.	" Syphons Total	" No. of Wheels
Driving Wheels diam. 36"	Superheater, type H.S.	Water, gals. 912 Coal, tons
Valves, type, H.P. diam.	Feedwater Heater	Fuel Oil, gals. 172 2,488 HP.
" L.P. diam.	Stoker Brakes #14 EL	Max. Tractive Effort (a) 73,150 (25%) lbs.
Valve Gear	Throttle, type	" " Booster (b) lbs.
Reverse Gear, Lever Power		Factor of Adhesion (a) 4.0 (b)
Designer		
Source of Photo New York Central Lines. Howard G. Hill Collection.		Notes on back of this sheet
Disposition: Sold to		Retired or scrapped 1959

Renumbered 274 (273-282) in 1936. Builder's Nos. 66705-66714. All axles are motor-driven by gearless motors. Hauls passenger trains between New York (Grand Central Terminal) and Harmon, 32.7 miles. On February 17, 1931, I rode in the cab of engine 1176 from Grand Central Terminal to Harmon, hauling THE TWENTIETH CENTURY LIMITED.

Fig.88.

No. 1153 Name	Road New York Central Lines.	Type B+B+B+B
Builder American Locomotive Co.	Boiler, type Vertical (Heater)	Wheelbase, Rigid 6' 6" 5' 0"
General Electric Co.	" diam. pressure 115 psi.	" , Driving 45' 7"
Works Schenectady — Erie	Firebox, type	" , Engine 45' 7"
Date built 8-1913 Bldr's. No. 53785	" length width	" , Eng. & Tender
Builder's Class	Combustion Chamber, length	Weight in Working Order, lbs.:
R.R. Class, Old New T-1b	Grate Area, sq. ft.	Front Truck
Bldr's. Order No. S-967 Neg. No. 1134	No. of Tubes No. of Flues	Driving Wheels 252,200
No. in Order 9 Orig. Nos 3248-3256	Diam. " Diam ".	Trailing
Orig. No. this Engine 3253	Length, Tubes & Flues	Engine, total 252,200
Gauge of Track 4' 8½"	Heating Surface, sq ft.:	Tender None
Service Passenger	" Tubes Flues Total	Eng. & Tender
Cylinder diam. H.P. L.P.	" Firebox Arch Tubes	Tender, type
Stroke of Piston No. of Cyls.	" Syphons Total	" No. of Wheels
Driving Wheels diam. 36"	Superheater, type H.S.	Water, gals. 671 Coal, tons
Valves, type, H.P. diam.	Feedwater Heater	Fuel Oil, gals. 102 2,475 HP
" L.P. diam.	Stoker Brakes	Max. Tractive Effort (a) 63,050 lbs.
Valve Gear	Throttle, type	" " Booster (b) lbs.
Reverse Gear, Lever Power		Factor of Adhesion (a) 4.0 (b)
Designer		
Source of Photo New York Central Lines. Howard G. Hill Collection.		Notes on back of this sheet
Disposition: Sold to		Retired or scrapped 1959

THE TWENTIETH CENTURY LIMITED leaving Grand Central Terminal, New York City, behind Class T-1b electric locomotive No. 1153 on June 10, 1914. Renumbered 1153 (1148-1156) in 1913. Renumbered 253 (248-256) in 1936.

LA-4.500. 3-70

Fig. 89.

No. **1166** Name	Road **New York Central Lines.**	Type **B+B+B+B**
Builder **General Electric Co.**	Boiler, type **Vertical (Heater)**	Wheelbase, Rigid **6' 6" 5' 0"**
Works **Erie**	" diam. pressure **115** psi.	", Driving **46' 5"**
Date built **6-1917** Bldr's. No. **5863**	Firebox, type	", Engine **46' 5"**
Builder's Class	" length width	", Eng. & Tender
R.R. Class, Old New **T-2b**	Combustion Chamber, length	Weight in Working Order, lbs.:
Bldr's. Order No. **GE31031** Neg. No.	Grate Area, sq. ft.	Front Truck
No. in Order **10** Orig. Nos **1163-1172**	No. of Tubes No. of Flues	Driving Wheels **280,500**
Orig. No. this Engine **1166**	Diam. " Diam "	Trailing
Gauge of Track **4' 8½"**	Length, Tubes & Flues	Engine, total **280,500**
Service **Passenger**	Heating Surface, sq ft.:	Tender
Cylinder diam. H.P. L.P.	" Tubes Flues Total	Eng. & Tender
Stroke of Piston No. of Cyls.	" Firebox Arch Tubes	Tender, type **None**
Driving Wheels diam. **36"**	" Syphons Total	" No. of Wheels
Valves, type, H.P. diam.	Superheater, type **H.S.**	Water, gals. **671** Coal, tons
" " L.P. diam.	Feedwater Heater	Fuel Oil, gals. **102**
Valve Gear	Stoker Brakes **#12 EL**	Max. Tractive Effort (a) **70,125** lbs.
Reverse Gear, Lever **Power**	Throttle, type	" " Booster (b) lbs.
Designer		Factor of Adhesion (a) **4.0** (b)
Source of Photo **New York Central Lines. Howard G. Hill Collection.**		Notes on back of this sheet
Disposition: **Sold** to		Retired or scrapped **2-1967**

Renumbered 266 (263-272) in 1936. 265, 268 and 270 retired between 1955 and 1962.
Others in class still active in 1966. Builder's Nos. 5860-5869.
No. 1166 shown hauling THE TWENTIETH CENTURY LIMITED on the Hudson River Division.

Fig. 90.

No. **5302** Name	Road **New York Central Lines.**	Type **4-6-4**
Builder **American Locomotive Co.**	Boiler, type **Straight top**	Wheelbase, Rigid **14' 0"**
Works **Schenectady**	" diam **87-5/8"** pressure **225** psi.	", Driving **14' 0"**
Date built **1-1930** Bldr's. No. **68180**	Firebox, type **Radial stay - wide**	", Engine **40' 4"**
Builder's Class **464-S-363**	" length **130"** width **90¼"**	", Eng. & Tender **83' 7½"**
R.R. Class, Old New **J-1d**	Combustion Chamber, length	Weight in Working Order, lbs.:
Bldr's. Order No. **S-1669** Neg. No. **S-1669**	Grate Area, **81.5** sq. ft.	Front Truck **66,000**
No. in Order **40** Orig. Nos **5275-5314**	No. of Tubes **37** No. of Flues **201**	Driving Wheels **193,200**
Orig. No. this Engine **5302**	Diam. " **2¼"** Diam " **3½"**	Trailing f-**46,000** b-**56,700**
Gauge of Track **4' 8½"**	Length, Tubes & Flues **20' 6"**	Engine, total **362,500**
Service **Passenger**	Heating Surface, sq ft.:	Tender **307,800**
Cylinder diam. H.P. **25"** L.P.	" Tubes **447** Flues **3756** Total **4203**	Eng. & Tender **670,300**
Stroke of Piston **28"** No. of Cyls. **2**	" Firebox **plus** Arch Tubes **281**	Tender, type **Rectangular**
Driving Wheels diam. **79"**	" Syphons Total **4484**	" No. of Wheels **12**
Valves, type, H.P. **Piston** diam. **14"**	Superheater, type **"E"** H.S. **1951**	Water, gals. **14,000** Coal, tons **28**
" " L.P. diam.	Feedwater Heater **Elesco**	Fuel Oil, gals.
Valve Gear **Baker**	Stoker **Standard HT** Brakes No. **8 ET**	Max. Tractive Effort (a) **42,360** lbs.
Reverse Gear, Lever Power **Precision**	Throttle, type **American Multiple**	" " Booster (b) **10,900** lbs.
Designer **Paul W. Kiefer, Ch. Engr., MP&RS, NYC. Lines.**		Factor of Adhesion (a) **4.57** (b) **5.15**
Source of Photo **Edward L. May. Photo. Harmon, N. Y., 8-3-1946.**		Notes on back of this sheet
Disposition: **Sold** to		Retired or scrapped **1953**

Cost $90,256.00. 2 8½" cross-compound air pumps on front end. Franklin trailer
booster. Water scoop. Automatic train control. Roller bearings on engine truck.
Coal pusher. I rode in the cab of this engine from Harmon, N. Y., to Collinwood,
Ohio, 581.3 miles, on February 17, 1931, hauling THE TWENTIETH CENTURY LIMITED,
with Bob Butterfield at the throttle from Harmon to Albany, ON TIME.

Fig. 94.

No. 5215 Name	Road New York Central Lines.	Type 4-6-4
Builder American Locomotive Co.	Boiler, type Straight top	Wheelbase, Rigid 14' 0"
Works Schenectady	" diam. 82-7/16" pressure 225 psi.	" , Driving 14' 0"
Date built 9-1927 Bldr's. No. 67446	Firebox, type Radial stay - wide	" , Engine 40' 4"
Builder's Class 464-S-360	" length 130" width 90¼"	" , Eng. & Tender 83' 7½"
R.R. Class, Old New J-1b	Combustion Chamber, length	Weight in Working Order, lbs.:
Bldr's. Order No. S-1595 Neg. No. S-1595	Grate Area, 81.5 sq. ft.	Front Truck 66,200
No. in Order 39 Orig. Nos 5201-5239	No. of Tubes 37 No. of Flues 201	Driving Wheels 192,400
Orig. No. this Engine 5215	Diam. " 2¼" Diam " 3½"	Trailing f-46,100 b-55,600
Gauge of Track 4' 8½"	Length, Tubes & Flues 20' 6"	Engine, total 360,300
Service Passenger	Heating Surface, sq ft.:	Tender 280,700
Cylinder diam. H.P. 25" L.P.	" Tubes 447 Flues 3756 Total 4203	Eng. & Tender 641,000
Stroke of Piston 28" No. of Cyls. 2	" Firebox plus Arch Tubes 281	Tender, type Rectangular
Driving Wheels diam. 79"	" Syphons Total 4484	" No. of Wheels 12
Valves, type. H.P. Piston diam. 14"	Superheater, type "E" H.S. 1951	Water, gals. 12,500 Coal, tons 24
" " L.P. diam.	Feedwater Heater Coffin	Fuel Oil, gals.
Valve Gear Walschaert	Stoker Standard HT Brakes #8 ET	Max. Tractive Effort (a) 42,360 lbs.
Reverse Gear, Lever Power Precision	Throttle, type American Multiple	" " Booster (b) 10,900 lbs.
Designer Paul W. Kiefer, Ch. Engr., MP&RS, NYC Lines		Factor of Adhesion (a) 4.55 (b) 5.1
Source of Photo New York Central Lines. Howard G. Hill Collection.		Notes on back of this sheet
Disposition: Sold to		Retired or scrapped 7-1953

Class J-1b Hudson type locomotive ready to leave Harmon westbound with THE TWENTIETH CENTURY LIMITED.

Fig. 96.

No. 5271 Name	Road New York Central Lines.	Type 4-6-4
Builder American Locomotive Co.	Boiler, type Straight top	Wheelbase, Rigid 14' 0"
Works Schenectady	" diam. 82-7/16" pressure 225 psi.	" , Driving 14' 0"
Date built 1-1929 Bldr's. No. 67733	Firebox, type Radial stay - wide	" , Engine 40' 4"
Builder's Class 464-S-359	" length 130" width 90¼"	" , Eng. & Tender 83' 7½"
R.R. Class, Old New J-1c	Combustion Chamber, length	Weight in Working Order, lbs.:
Bldr's. Order No. S-1636 Neg. No. S-1636	Grate Area, 81.5 sq. ft.	Front Truck 63,600
No. in Order 25 Orig. Nos 5250-5274	No. of Tubes 37 No. of Flues 201	Driving Wheels 193,100
Orig. No. this Engine 5271	Diam. " 2¼" Diam " 3½"	Trailing f-46,100 b-56,100
Gauge of Track 4' 8½"	Length, Tubes & Flues 20' 6"	Engine, total 358,900
Service Passenger	Heating Surfaces, sq. ft.:	Tender 280,700
Cylinder diam. H.P. 25" L.P.	" Tubes 447 Flues 3756 Total 4203	Eng. & Tender 639,600
Stroke of Piston 28" No. of Cyls. 2	" Firebox plus Arch Tubes 262	Tender, type Rectangular
Driving Wheels diam. 79"	" Syphons 90 Total 4555	" No. of Wheels 12
Valves, type. H.P. Piston diam. 14"	Superheater, type "E" H.S. 1951	Water, gals. 12,500 Coal, tons 24
" " L.P. diam.	Feedwater Heater Coffin	Fuel Oil, gals.
Valve Gear Walschaert	Stoker Standard HT Brakes #8 ET	Max. Tractive Effort (a) 42,360 lbs.
Reverse Gear, Lever Power Precision	Throttle, type American Multiple	" " Booster (b) 10,900 lbs.
Designer Paul W. Kiefer, Ch. Engr., MP&RS, NYC Lines		Factor of Adhesion (a) 4.57 (b) 5.14
Source of Photo Arnold Haas Collection.		Notes on back of this sheet
Disposition: Sold to		Retired or scrapped 3-1955

Photographed with THE TWENTIETH CENTURY LIMITED near Cold Spring, N. Y., in 1929 when locomotive and train were brand new.
Fig. 100 shows No. 5271 rolling THE TWENTIETH CENTURY LIMITED along the Hudson River Division.

LA-4.500. 3-70

Fig. 98.

No. 5240 Name	Road New York Central Lines	Type 4-6-4
Builder American Locomotive Co.	Boiler, type Straight top	Wheelbase, Rigid 14' 0"
Works Schenectady	" diam. 82-7/16" pressure 225 psi.	", Driving 14' 0"
Date built 10-1927 Bldr's. No. 67471	Firebox, type Radial stay - wide	", Engine 40' 4"
Builder's Class 464-S-360	" length 130" width 90¼"	", Eng. & Tender 83' 7½"
R.R. Class, Old New J-1b	Combustion Chamber, length	Weight in Working Order, lbs.:
Bldr's. Order No. S-1597 Neg. No. S-1597	Grate Area, 81.5 sq. ft.	Front Truck 66,200
No. in Order 10 Orig. Nos 5240-5249	No. of Tubes 37 No. of Flues 201	Driving Wheels 192,400
Orig. No. this Engine 5240	Diam. " 2¼" Diam " 3½"	Trailing f-46,100 b-55,600
Gauge of Track 4' 8½"	Length, Tubes & Flues 20' 6"	Engine, total 360,300
Service Passenger	Heating Surface, sq ft.:	Tender 280,700
Cylinder diam. H.P. 25" L.P.	" Tubes 447 Flues 3756 Total 4203	Eng. & Tender 641,000
Stroke of Piston 28" No. of Cyls. 2	" Firebox plus Arch Tubes 281	Tender, type Rectangular
Driving Wheels diam. 79"	" Syphons Total 4484	" No. of Wheels 12
Valves, type, H.P. Piston diam. 14"	Superheater, type "E" H.S. 1951	Water, gals. 12,500 Coal, tons 2½
" " L.P. diam.	Feedwater Heater Coffin	Fuel Oil, gals.
Valve Gear Walschaert	Stoker Standard HT Brakes #8 ET	Max. Tractive Effort (a) 42,360 lbs.
Reverse Gear, Lever Power Precision	Throttle, type American Multiple	" " Booster (b) 10,900 lbs.
Designer Paul W. Kiefer, Ch. Engr., MP&RS, NYC Lines		Factor of Adhesion (a) 4.54 (b) 5.1
Source of Photo New York Central Lines, Howard G. Hill Collection		Notes on back of this sheet
Disposition: Sold to		Retired or scrapped 6-1953

No. 5240 scooping water from a track pan while running 45 miles per hour along the Hudson River Division.

Fig. 99.

No. 5214 Name	Road New York Central Lines	Type 4-6-4
Builder American Locomotive Co.	Boiler, type Straight top	Wheelbase, Rigid 14' 0"
Works Schenectady	" diam. 82-7/16" pressure 225 psi.	", Driving 14' 0"
Date built 9-1927 Bldr's. No. 67445	Firebox, type Radial stay - wide	", Engine 40' 4"
Builder's Class 464-S-360	" length 130" width 90¼"	", Eng. & Tender 83' 7½"
R.R. Class, Old New J-1b	Combustion Chamber, length	Weight in Working Order, lbs.:
Bldr's. Order No. S-1595 Neg. No. S-1595	Grate Area, 81.5 sq. ft.	Front Truck 66,200
No. in Order 39 Orig. Nos 5201-5239	No. of Tubes 37 No. of Flues 201	Driving Wheels 192,400
Orig. No. this Engine 5214	Diam. " 2¼" Diam " 3½"	Trailing f-46,100 b-55,600
Gauge of Track 4' 8½"	Length, Tubes & Flues 20' 6"	Engine, total 360,300
Service Passenger	Heating Surface, sq ft.:	Tender 280,700
Cylinder diam. H.P. 25" L.P.	" Tubes 447 Flues 3756 Total 4203	Eng. & Tender 642,000
Stroke of Piston 28" No. of Cyls. 2	" Firebox plus Arch Tubes 281	Tender, type Rectangular
Driving Wheels diam. 79"	" Syphons Total 4484	" No. of Wheels 12
Valves, type, H.P. Piston diam. 14"	Superheater, type "E" H.S. 1951	Water, gals. 12,500 Coal, tons 24
" " L.P. diam.	Feedwater Heater Coffin	Fuel Oil, gals.
Valve Gear Walschaert	Stoker Standard HT Brakes #8 ET	Max. Tractive Effort (a) 42,360 lbs.
Reverse Gear, Lever Power Precision	Throttle, type American Multiple	" " Booster (b) 10,900 lbs.
Designer Paul W. Kiefer, Ch. Engr., MP&RS, NYC Lines		Factor of Adhesion (a) 4.55 (b) 5.1
Source of Photo New York Central Lines, Howard G. Hill Collection		Notes on back of this sheet
Disposition: Sold to		Retired or scrapped 7-1953

The 5214 looms up large and impressive at the head end of THE TWENTIETH CENTURY LIMITED as she dashes along the Hudson River Division at 65 miles per hour.

Fig. 101.

No. 1050 Name	Road Cleveland Union Terminals Co. (NYC)	Type 2-C+C-2
Builder American Locomotive Co. General Electric Co.	Boiler, type Train heating	Wheelbase, Rigid 15' 0"
Works Schenectady - Erie	" diam. pressure 155 psi.	" , Driving 39' 0"
Date built 11-1929 Bldr's. No. 67679	Firebox, type	" , Engine 69' 0"
Builder's Class 4664-419	" length width	" , Eng. & Tender
R.R. Class, Old New P-1a	Combustion Chamber, length	Weight in Working Order, lbs.:
Bldr's. Order No. Neg. No.	Grate Area, sq. ft.	Front Truck 53,600
No. in Order 22 Orig. Nos 1050-1071	No. of Tubes No. of Flues	Driving Wheels 311,700
Orig. No. this Engine 1050	Diam. " Diam "	Trailing 53,600
Gauge of Track 4' 8½"	Length, Tubes & Flues	Engine, total 418,900
Service Passenger	Heating Surface, sq ft.:	Tender
Cylinder diam. H.P. L.P.	" Tubes Flues Total	Eng. & Tender
Stroke of Piston No. of Cyls.	" Firebox Arch Tubes	Tender, type None
Driving Wheels diam. 48"	" Syphons Total	" No. of Wheels
Valves type. H.P. diam.	Superheater, type H.S.	Water, gals. 671 Coal, tons
" " L.P. diam.	Feedwater Heater	Fuel Oil, gals. 102 2,635 H.P.
Valve Gear	Stoker Brakes #14 EL	Max. Tractive Effort (a) 77,925 lbs.
Reverse Gear, Lever Power	Throttle, type	" " Booster (b) lbs.
Designer		Factor of Adhesion (a) 4.02 (b)
Source of Photo Railway Age. Howard G. Hill Collection.		Notes on back of this sheet
Disposition: Sold to		Retired or scrapped

Renumbered 200 (200-221) in 1936. Retired 1953. Rebuilt by GECo in 1955 to Class P-2b
No. 240. No. 1061 built 12-1929, renumbered 211 in 1936, Builder's No. 67690, retired
1953, rebuilt as Class P-2b No. 235 in 1955 by GECo. On February 18, 1931, I rode in
the cab of No. 1061 from Collinwood, Ohio, to Linndale, Ohio, 13.2 miles, through
Cleveland Union Terminal Station, hauling THE TWENTIETH CENTURY LIMITED.

Fig. 102.

No. 5246 Name	Road New York Central Lines	Type 4-6-4
Builder American Locomotive Co.	Boiler, type Straight top	Wheelbase, Rigid 14' 0"
Works Schenectady	" diam. 82-7/16" pressure 225 psi.	" , Driving 14' 0"
Date built 11-1927 Bldr's. No. 67477	Firebox, type Radial stay - wide	" , Engine 40' 4"
Builder's Class 464-S-360	" length 130" width 90¼"	" , Eng. & Tender 83' 7½"
R.R. Class, Old New J-1b	Combustion Chamber, length	Weight in Working Order, lbs.:
Bldr's. Order No. S-1597 Neg. No S-1597	Grate Area, 81.5 sq. ft.	Front Truck 66,200
No. in Order 10 Orig. Nos 5240-5249	No. of Tubes 37 No. of Flues 201	Driving Wheels 192,400
Orig. No. this Engine 5246	Diam. " 2¼" Diam " 3½"	Trailing f-46,100 b-55,600
Gauge of Track 4' 8½"	Length, Tubes & Flues 20' 6"	Engine, total 360,300
Service Passenger	Heating Surface, sq ft.:	Tender 280,700
Cylinder diam. H.P. 25" L.P.	" Tubes 447 Flues 3756 Total 4203	Eng. & Tender 641,000
Stroke of Piston 28" No. of Cyls. 2	" Firebox plus Arch Tubes 262	Tender, type Rectangular
Driving Wheels diam. 79"	" Syphons 90 Total 4555	" No. of Wheels 12
Valves type. H.P. Piston diam. 14"	Superheater, type "E" H.S. 1951	Water, gals. 12,500 Coal, tons 24
" " L.P. diam.	Feedwater Heater Elesco	Fuel Oil, gals.
Valve Gear Baker	Stoker Standard HT Brakes #8 ET	Max. Tractive Effort (a) 42,360 lbs.
Reverse Gear, Lever Power Precision	Throttle, type American Multiple	" " Booster (b) 10,900 lbs.
Designer Paul W. Kiefer, Ch. Engr., MP&RS, NYC Lines.		Factor of Adhesion (a) 4.55 (b) 5.1
Source of Photo Arnold Haas Photo, Chicago, Ill., 11-27-1946.		Notes on back of this sheet
Disposition: Sold to		Retired or scrapped 7-1953

I rode in the cab of this locomotive from Linndale, Ohio, to Chicago, Illinois,
334 miles, hauling Train No. 25, THE TWENTIETH CENTURY LIMITED, on February 18, 1931,
thus completing a continuous trip of 961.2 miles in the locomotive cabs on the
20-hour schedule.

LA-4.500. 3-70

INDEX

Acceleration, 52, 54, 56, 99
Acknowledgements, 8
A. H. Smith Memorial Bridge, 98
Albany, NY, 17, 97, 98, 99, 100, 101
Albany Hill, NY, 99
Alexander, E. P., 8
Allegheny River, 54
Allegrippus, PA, 54
Allen, Horatio, 18
Alliance, OH, 54
Altoona, PA, 53, 54
Altoona Machine Shops, 24
Altoona Locomotive Test Plant, 26
Altoona Locomotive Test Plant *Bulletins*, 8, 48, 52
American Locomotive Co., 8
  Brooks Works, 78
  Pittsburgh Works, 25
  Schenectady Works, 25, 26, 78, 79, 96, 97, 100
American Magazine, 8
American Railway, The, 8
American Society of Mechanical Engineers, 8, 17
Annulment of *The Twentieth Century Limited*, 117
Anthony's Nose, NY, 98
Apex of the Atlantics, 8
Appendix, 119
Appleton, J. A., 56
Argosy Magazine, 8
Army Corps of Engineers, Railway Branch, 6
Atkinson, Charles, 50
Atmospheric conditions, 55, 99
Author's first cab ride, 16
Author's initial locomotive studies, 16
AY Tower, OH, 25
Bacon, Lord, 19
Baldwin-Lima-Hamilton Corporation, 8

Baldwin Locomotive Works, 8, 26, 50, 51, 53
Baldwin Locomotives, 8
Basso profundo, 118
Beacon, NY, 98
Bear Mountain, NY, 118
Bear Mountain Bridge, NY, 98
Bearings, driving journal, 48, 49
Beaver Falls, PA, 54
Beebe, Lucius, 8, 117
Beech Grove Shops, 78
Beichert, Harry, 8
Bentfield, Bob, Locomotive Engineer, 17
Belpaire boilers, 24, 50
Bergen Hill, NJ, 51
Big Four, 78, 79
Boehm, Miss Joan H., 8
Boiler pressure, 52, 78, 79, 98, 101
Booster, 78
Boston, MA, 5, 98, 99
Boston & Albany R. R., 78, 79, 98
Boston & Lowell R. R., 16
Boston & Maine R. R., 16
Brake valve, 99
Braking, 56, 98, 99, 100
Brazen diesel throat, 118
Break-in-two, 100
Breakneck, NY, 98
Breakneck Tunnel, 98
Bristol, PA, 52
Broadbelt, H. Lee, 8
Broadway Limited, The, 8, 16, 17, 25, 26, 48, 50, 51, 53, 55, 96, 101, 118, 119, 123, 124, 127
Brooks, Bert B., 8
Brown, Clement R., Sr., 8, 17
Bruce, Alfred W., 8
Bryn Mawr, PA, 52, 53
Buffalo, NY, 78, 100, 101

Butterfield, Bob, Locomotive Engineer, 17, 97, 98, 99
Button, Hon. Daniel E., M. C., 8
Cab controls, Hudson type locomotives, 112
Cab rides, 56
Cab ride permit, Train No. 25, 96
Cab ride permit, Train No. 29, 50
Cab ride request, 50, 56, 96
Cab signals, 51, 55
Cab rides, New York to Chicago, 6, 17, 50, 96, 97, 99, 101, 117, 119
Canada, 16
Canada Southern R. R., 78
Car miles, 79
Casey Jones, Locomotive Engineer, 53
Catholic University, 17
Castleton-on-Hudson, NY, 98
Catskill nights, 118
Centuries at Harmon, 109, 110
Century's last run, 117
Chaney, C. B., 8
Chat Moss, England, 14
Chicago, IL, 6, 24, 26, 48, 49, 55, 56, 77, 78, 96, 99, 100, 101, 117, 119
Chicago Limited, The, 77
Chicago Terminals, 55, 101
Chicago Union Station, 55, 119
Chief, The, 118
Civil War, 20
Classification and Diagrams of Locomotives, 8
Clearance limits, 79
Cleveland, Cincinnati, Chicago & St. Louis R. R., 78, 79
Cleveland, OH, 101
Cleveland Union Terminals, 100
Clinton Point, NY, 98

Coal trains, 48
Coatesville, PA, 53
Cold-set grease, 48, 50, 56
   Composition, 48
   Failures, 48, 56
   Processing, 48
Collinwood, OH, 100, 101
Competition, 6, 24, 77
Conditions in tunnel, 54
Conductor, 51, 55, 56, 101
Contents, 9
Continuous locomotive runs, 79, 80
Controls in cab, Hudson type locomotive, 112
Cooley, Thomas M., 8
Copyright, 17
Counterbalancing, 52, 100
Court decision, 56
Crater Compound, 48, 49
Crescent Limited, The, 118
Crestline, OH, 25, 54, 55, 119
Crewe, VA, 57
Cutoff, 52, 54
Cylinder horsepower, 79
Daily Advance, The, 117
Dedication, 5
Dehydrated Driving Journal Compound "M",
   Characteristics, 48, 49
   Development of competitive products, 49
   Elimination of shop repairs, 49
   Evidence illustrating locomotive growth, 49
   Increased locomotive availability, 49
   Increased locomotive mileage, 49
   Initial road tests, 49
   Litigation, 49
   Processing, 48
   Rapid extension of use, 49
   Reduced engine failures and train delays, 49
   U. S. Patent Specification, 48, 56
Dent, Richard J., 8
Denver & Rio Grande Railway, 17
Design improvements, 78

Development and Performance, Hudson Type Locomotives, 8
Development of Steam Power — New York Central Lines, 77
Development of Steam Power — Pennsylvania R. R., 24
Diesels, 26, 118
Dining cars, 51, 53, 54, 79, 96, 99, 118
Dining car courtesy, 52, 119
Discontinuance of *The Twentieth Century Limited*, 117
Dispatcher, 100
Double-heading, 25
Dover, NH, 16
Drawbar horsepower, 52
Drawbar pull, 52, 78
Dredge, James, 8
Driving journal bearings, 48, 50, 53
Driving journal compound, 48, 50, 56
Driving wheels —
   68-inch diameter, 24, 25
   72-inch diameter, 26
   75-inch diameter, 79
   79-inch diameter, 78, 79, 97
   80-inch diameter, 24, 25, 26, 51, 52, 78
   84-inch diameter, 118
   revolutions per minute, 52
   slipping, 97, 100
Du Barry, 118
Dunderberg, NY, 118
Dynamometer car tests, 80
Economic unity, 19, 21
Edson, William D., 6, 8
El Capitan, 118
Electric headlight, 98
Electric locomotive horsepower, 96, 100
Electric train lighting, 24
Elida, OH, 25
Elizabeth City, NC, 117
Elkhart, IN, 101
Emergency brake application, 99, 100
Empire State Express, 107
Engine failures, 48
Engineer of Tests, 48
Engineering Societies Library, 8

Englewood, IL, 55, 101
Epilogue, 117
Epitaph, 117
Erie R. R., 51
Exhaust on grades, 54, 99
Expert witness, 49
Exposition Flyer, The, 17, 77, 120
Extended locomotive runs, 49, 79
Factor of adhesion, 97
Farewell to *The Century*, 117
Fast Mail, The, 77
Faure, Elie, 7
Fireman, 52, 55, 97, 98, 119
Firing a K4s Pacific, 52, 55
Firing coal-buring locomotives, 52, 55
Firing oil-burning locomotives, 16, 55, 119
First electric lighted train, 24
First Hudson type locomotive in America, 79
First K4s Pacific type locomotive, 42
First K28 Pacific type locomotive, 34
First power reverse gear, 27
Flat wheels, 99
Flattley, Lt. Col. T. Martin, Jr., 8
Floradora, 117
Foreword, 6
Fort Wayne coaling station, 55
Fort Wayne passenger station, 25, 55, 119
Foster-Rastrick & Co., 18
Four-six-four Hudson, 79, 118
Four-track division, 52, 54, 98
Franklin Oscillating Cam Poppet Valve Gear, 52
Franklin Radial Buffer, 100
Freight trains, 52, 98, 99
Gallitzin, PA, 53, 54
Gallitzin Tunnel, 53, 54
General Electric Co., 96, 100
General Manager, Lines West, Pennsylvania R. R., 55, 56
General Manager, U. S. Military Railway, 6
Golden Arrow, The, Train No. 78, 50, 56

Golden State Limited, The, 101
Goss, Dr. W. F. M., 53
Grand Central Depot, Train Shed, 78
Grand Central Terminal — 17
Departure quay, 96
Gate 27, 96
Main Concourse, 96
51st Street Tower, 97
Grades, 48, 49, 51, 53, 54, 55, 99, 100
Grand Dame, 118
Grate area, 26, 55, 98
Gross ton-miles, 100, 101
Gross ton-miles per train-hour, 99, 100, 101
Haas, Arnold, 8
Hackensack Meadows, NJ, 51
Hankins, Frederick W., 49, 50, 56
Harlem, NY, 97
Harlem River Bridge, 97
Harmon, NY, 17, 96, 97, 98, 99
Harrisburg, PA, 52, 53, 55
Hart, George M., 8
Haubennestel, Lt. Col. John W., 8
Heating surface, 79
Heavy service brake application, 99
Helper engine, 53, 99
High Bridge, NY, 85
High Iron, 118
Highlands, NY, 98
High speed, 52, 100
Hill, Ethel L., 5, 8
Hill, Everett Leforest, Sr., 5, 16
Hill, Howard G., 6, 119
History of American Railroads —
Experimental period, 19
Trunk line formation, 19
Period of combination, 19
HJ Tower, 52
Hoover, Herbert, 117
Horses as motive power, 14
Horsepower output, 52, 100, 101
Horseshoe Curve, PA, 53
Houston, TX, 6, 16
Hudson, NY, 98, 118
Hudson, general design, 79, 80
Hudson River, 97, 98

Hudson River Division, 17, 97, 100
Hudson River R. R., 77
Hudson test results, 80
Hudson test train load, 80
Hudson (4-6-4) wheel arrangement, 8, 11, 79, 97
Hungerford, Edward, 8, 17
Hyde Park, NY, 98
Illustrations, 10, 11
Immigration, 20
Interlocking, 98
Jacobs-Schupert Sectional Firebox, 53
James, William, 14
Japan, 6
Jersey City, NJ, 24
Johnson, Ralph, 8
Johnstown, PA, 54
Jordan, NY, 100
Junction, B&A—NYC, 98
Juniata River, 53
Juniata shops, 25, 26, 51, 54
Kalmbach Publishing Co., 8
Kemble, Miss Frances Ann, 14
Kerl, Sidney, 50, 51
Kiefer, Paul W., 97
Killingworth locomotive, 14
Kittaning Point, PA, 54
Knight, W. B., 8
Kuss, Miss Ann, 8
Lake Shore & Michigan Southern Railway, 17, 24, 77, 78
Lancaster, PA, 53
Larwill, IN, 55
Lasalle Street Depot, Chicago, IL, 78, 101
Lee, Martin H., Locomotive Engineer, 30
Legion of Merit, 6
Library, Engineering Societies, 8
Library, Howard G. Hill Engineering, 16, 117
Library, University of Maryland, 8
Lighty, Mr., Locomotive Engineer, 51, 52, 53
Lingford, Joseph, & Son, Ltd., 8
Lining and surfacing, 16
Linndale, OH, 100, 101
Little Juniata River, 53
Liverpool & Manchester Railway, 14

Liverpool & Manchester Tramroad, 14
Locomotives —
(See list under Illustrations, 10, 11)
American (4-4-0) type, 10, 11, 16, 24, 25, 78
"Arrow", 14
Atlantic (4-4-2) type, 10, 11, 25, 53, 78
Beauty, 7
Belpaire firebox, 50
Boiler pressure, 52, 78, 79, 98, 101
Brick arch, 26
Building, A Century of Locomotive, 8
Cab trip, *The Broadway Limited*, 6, 16, 51, 52
Cab trip, *The Exposition Flyer*, 17
Cab trip, *The Twentieth Century Limited*, 6, 16
Cab trips, 17, 48, 49, 56
Caprotti valve gear, 26, 121
Characteristics, 7, 48
Class symbol, 50
Classification and Diagrams, 8
Compound, 48
Consolidation (2-8-0) type, 24
Counterbalancing, 52, 100
Cylinders, diameter —
22-inch, 78
23½-inch, 78
24-inch, 26
25-inch, 79, 80
25½-inch, 80
26-inch, 26, 79
27-inch, 26, 52
Decapod, (2-10-0) type, 54
Description by Miss Kemble, 14
Design details, 50
Diagrams, Steam and Electric, 8
Diesel-Electric, 26
Drawbar horsepower, 52
Drawbar pull, 52, 79
Driving journal bearings, 48, 49, 50
Driving wheels, diameter —
68-inch, 24, 25
72-inch, 26

172

75-inch, 79, 80
79-inch, 78, 79, 80, 97, 118
80-inch, 24, 25, 26, 51, 52, 78
84-inch, 118
Duplex (4-4-4-4) type, 10, 26
Electric, 8, 10, 11, 48, 51, 55, 96, 100
Experimental, 25, 26
Grate area, 26, 55, 98
Heating surface, 79
Hetton Colliery, 12
Hudson (4-6-4) type, 8, 11, 79, 97, 99, 100, 118, 128
Influence of the, Upon the Unity of Our Country, 16, 17, 19
Killingworth, 14
Limited trains, for, 24, 25, 26, 77, 78, 79, 80
Locomotive runs, 123, 125
Lubrication, 48, 49, 50, 56
Mallet Articulated Compound, (2-8-8-2) type, 10, 48, 49
"Medford", 15, 16
Mikado (2-8-2) type, 6
Mountain (4-8-2) type, 10, 26, 48, 49
New York Central Lines, 8, 10, 11
Niagara (4-8-4) type, 11, 80
Operation, 56
Pacific (4-6-2) type, 10, 11, 25, 26, 48, 49, 50, 51, 52, 55, 56, 78, 96, 101, 121, 122
Pennsylvania R. R., 24, 48
Piston speed, 52
Piston valve chamber, 99
Piston valve cylinders, 26, 121
Poppet valves, 26
Prairie (2-6-2) type, 11, 78
Radial stay firebox, 26
Reverse gear, screw, 26
Revolutions per minute, 52, 100
"Rocket", 13, 14
Saturated, 25
Specifications, 128 to 169, incl.
Speed, 14, 25, 51, 52
Speed record, 25
Speed recorder, 99

Steam, 7, 8, 10, 11
Steam pipes, outside, 26
Stokers, 26, 79, 97, 98, 101
"Stourbridge Lion", 18, 19
Superheated, 25, 26, 121
Superheater, Schmidt Type "A", 26, 79
Switching (0-6-0T) type, 6
Ten-wheel (4-6-0) type, 11, 78
Tests, Texaco D. J. C. "M", 49
Texas (2-10-4) type, 24
Tractive effort, starting, 25, 78, 79, 80
Trailing truck booster, 78
Trailing truck, four-wheel, 79
Trailing truck, KW style, 26
Walschaert valve gear, 26, 50, 121
Weight on driving wheels, 56, 61, 78, 79, 80, 96
Locomotive, The, 8
Log of Performance, 124, 126
Lopshire, W. C., Locomotive Fireman, 119
Lounge cars, 79
Lowell Machine Shops, 16
Lubrication Engineer, 119
Lubrication practice and performance, 119
Lubrication, railroad equipment, 119
Ludwig, E. G., Locomotive Fireman, 119
Mail cars, 77
Main, Charles T., 19
Maintenance expenses, 48
Mallet Articulated Compound Locomotives, 48, 49
Malvern, PA, 53
Manhattan, 25, 56, 96, 119
Manhattan Transfer, NJ, 51
Manual of Railroads, 8
Map, New York Central Lines, 116
Map, Pennsylvania System, 116
Marysville, PA, 53
Master of the Machine, 98
May, Edward L., 8
Mechanical Engineer, 48
Mechanical Engineering, 17
Mechanical motion, 52
Meister, Alfred A., 16

Men and Iron, 8
Mexico, 6, 16
Michigan Central R. R., 78, 79
Middle Division, Pennsylvania R. R., 53, 69
Middletown, PA, 53
Mikados for Middle East war service, 6
Mileage, 20
Montespan, 118
Monument to Class K4s locomotives, 54
Morley, Christofer, 17
Morrisville, PA, 30
Motive Power Development, Pennsylvania R. R., 8
Mott Haven Yard, NY, 97
McCarthy, Jerry, Locomotive Engineer, 25
McClure's Magazine, 17
McCormick, George, 16
Namesake Century, 117
Newark Station, NJ, 51
New Brunswick, NJ, 52
New Hamburg Tunnel, NY, 98
New York Central R. R., 77, 78, 79
New York Central & Hudson River R. R., 17, 24, 78, 79
New York Central and Lake Shore Post Office, 77
New York Central Lines, 6, 8, 17, 80, 96, 118
New York Central Lines —
Development of steam passenger motive power, 8, 77, 80
Early Steam Power, 8
Steam Power, 8
New York Central Train No. 25, 117
New York City, NY, 6, 26, 48, 55, 56, 77, 78, 96, 101
New York Railroad Club Dinner, 1930, 49
New York Tribune, 7, 8
Non-stop runs, 100, 123, 125
Norfolk and Western Railway, 48
Norrell, Thomas, 8
North Philadelphia, PA, 51, 52, 53, 56, 119
North River, 51

North River Tunnel, east portal, 25

North River Tunnel, west portal, 25

North Shore Limited, 78

Observation car, 51, 96, 99, 118

Ohio River, 54

Olive Mount Cutting, England, 14

"On Time" performance, 98, 100

Operator, 100

Orange Blossom Special, The, 118

Organs, pipe, 97

Overheated driving journal bearings, 48

Panic of 1893, 77

Paoli, PA, 53

Parillo, Joseph, Jr., 8

Passaic River Bridge, NJ, 51

Passenger trains, 24, 77

Passenger car-miles, 79

Passenger train-miles, 79

Patton, General George S., Jr., 6

Peekskill, NY, 118

Penn Central Transportation Co., 8, 119

Penn Station, New York City, 25, 63

Penn Station, Main Concourse, 64

Pennsy Power, 8

Pennsylvania Limited, The, 24, 25

Pennsylvania News —
Railroad's account of author's trip, 8, 56, 119

Pennsylvania R. R., 6, 8, 48, 49, 50, 77, 119
Development of Steam Passenger Motive Power, 24, 48

Pennsylvania Special, The, 25, 53

Peters, Mason, 8, 117

Phillips, Loyal, 8, 117

Photographic exhibits, 49

Pipe organs, 97

Pittsburgh, PA, 54

Pittsburgh & Lake Erie R. R., 79

Political unity, 19

Poor, Henry V., 8

Population, 20

Port Arthur, TX, 119

Poughkeepsie, NY, 98

Pounding, 100, 101

Power, John A., 16

Preface, 7

Profile, Lines West, Pennsylvania R. R., 76

Profile, Middle Division, Pennsylvania R. R., 69

Pullman, all room, 56, 78, 80

Pullman equipment car-miles, 79

Pullman, open section, 78, 96

Pullman, streamlined, 78

Pullmans from Boston, 99

Pyrometer, 98, 99

Race Track, Lines West, Pennsylvania R. R., 55

Railroad equipment lubrication, 48

Railroad Magazine, 8

Railroad mileage, 20

Rails and ballast, 52

Railway Age, 8

Railway Gazette, 8

Railway Mission to Japan, 6

Railway Mission to Mexico, 6

Railway Sales Department, 48

Railways and tramways, early English, 14

Rainhill competition, Rainhill, England, 14

Rand McNally & Co., 8

Randall, Dr. Richard R., 8

Rear markers, 99

Records of Recent Construction, 8

References, 8

Relaxation, 53, 55, 96

Rensselaer Yard, NY, 98

Reverse wheel, 99

Rhinecliffe, NY, 98

Riding *The Broadway Limited's* K4s Pacifics, 48

Riding the J-1 Locomotives on *The Century*, 96

Riding qualities, 52, 54, 100, 101, 119

Roanoke, VA, 49

Robert Stephenson & Co., 13, 14

Rochester, NY, 100, 101

Rock Island Lines, 101

Rockville, PA, 53

Rolling mills, 49

Rollinsford Junction, NH, 16

Rule 99, 100

Run of the Twentieth Century, The, 8, 17

Running locomotives, 16, 56, 99

Sander valve, 97, 98, 100

Sanding rails, 97

Scoresby, Captain, 14

Schedule, New York—Chicago —
28 hours 30 minutes, 77
27 hours 12 minutes, 77
26 hours 40 minutes, 24, 77
24 hours, 24
20 hours, 24, 25, 77, 96
18 hours, 25
16 hours, 25

Schuylkill River, PA, 52

Special, 20-hour, 24

Sheedy, J. A., 56

Short flag, 99

Sicily, 6

Signals, 51, 53, 54, 96, 97, 98

Sinclair, T. H., Locomotive Engineer, 119

Six-wheel tank switcher, 6

Slack, 99

Slipping of driving wheels, 97, 98, 100

Slow orders, 97, 98

Smiles, Samuel, 8

Smith, Charles M., 8

Smith, Fred J., 107

Smithsonian Institution, 8

Snow on rails, 100

Social unity, 19, 21

So Long, *"Century"*, 117

Somersworth, NH, 16

Southern Pacific Lines, 16, 48, 55, 119

Speed, average, 14, 25, 51, 52, 53, 54, 55, 56, 77, 97, 98, 99, 100, 101

Speed limit, 96, 97, 98, 99

Speed recorder, 99

Special 3-car mail train, 77
Specifications of Locomotives, 128 to 169, incl.
Spruce Creek Tunnel, 53
Squirt hose, 98
Staatsburg, NY, 98
Starting capacity, 78, 79, 80
125th Street Station, NY, 97
Stationmaster, 52
Staufer, Alvin F., 8
Steam demand, 98
Steam jets, 98
Steam Locomotive, The, 8
Steam Locomotive in America, The, 8
Steam and Electric Locomotive Diagrams, 8
Steam locomotive running, 98, 99
Steam temperatures, 98, 99
Steel mill furnaces, 54
Steel passenger train equipment, 78
Stephenson, George 8
Stephenson, Robert, 8
Stoker, mechanical, 79, 97, 98, 101
Stop on red signal, 54
Storm King, NY, 118
Summary of Performance, 127
Superheat, 98
Superheater, 25, 26
Susquehanna R. R., 51
Susquehanna River Bridge, 53
Syracuse, NY, 99
Table of Contents, 9
Table 1, Log of Performance, Train No. 41, 120
Table 2, Pacific Type Locomotives, Pennsylvania R. R., 121
Table 3, Class K4s Locomotives, Pennsylvania R. R., 122
Table 4, *The Broadway Limited*, Locomotive Mileage, 123
Table 5, *The Broadway Limited*, Log of Performance, 124
Table 6, *The Twentieth Century Limited*, Locomotive Mileage, 125
Table 7, *The Twentieth Century Limited*, Log of Performance, 126

Table 8, Summary of Performance, Trains 29 and 25, 127
Table 9, Class J Hudson Type Locomotives, New York Central Lines, 128
Tangents, 53, 97, 98, 99
Tender capacity, 79
Terminal, West Philadelphia Engine, 33
Testimony, 50
Texas Company, The, 48, 49, 119
Texas & New Orleans R. R., 6, 55
Thermal efficiency, 80
Throttle artist, 98
Throttle, front end, 97
Tivoli, NY, 98
Toledo, OH, 99, 101
Track curvature, 52, 99
Track elevation, 51, 53, 54
Track pans, 54, 98, 99, 100
Track work, 97, 98
Tractive effort, 24, 25, 78, 79, 80
Trailing truck booster, 78, 79
Train, The, 117
Train control, 56
Train delays, 48
Train-heating boiler, 97
Train No. 26, *The Twentieth Century Limited*, 17, 78
Train No. 78, *The Golden Arrow*, 50, 56
Train Tonnage, 25, 80, 99, 101
Train weight, 51, 53
Trains 25 and 26, 117
Trains Magazine, 17, 48
Tramways and railways, early English, 14
Transportation Exhibit, 24
Trenton, NJ, 52
Tribune, New York, 7
Tunnel, Gallitzin, 53, 54
Tunnels, North River, 25, 51
Twentieth Century, The, 78
20th Century, 8, 117
20-hour Special, 24, 25
Twentieth Century Limited, The, 8, 16, 17, 78, 80, 96, 97, 99, 100, 101, 117, 118, 125, 126, 127

Twentieth Century Limited consist, 78, 97
Tyrone, PA, 53
Unbalanced forces, 52, 100
Underground yard, 96, 97
Upper Sandusky, OH, 54, 55, 119
U. S. Army Corps of Engineers, 6
U. S. Army Transportation Corps, 56
U. S. Military Railway, 6
U. S. Post Office Department, 77
U. S. Railroad Administration, 57, 58
University of Maryland Engineering Library, 8
Utica, NY, 99, 101
Vandalia Line, 25
Vanderbilt, Commodore Cornelius, 77
Vanderbilt, William H., 77
Vice President, 96, 101
Wallis, J. T., 26
Walschaert valve gear, 26
Warman, Cy, 17
Warner, Paul T., 8
Warren, J. G. H., 8
Warrior Ridge, PA, 53
Washington Terminal Co., 51
Water, 54, 79
Water level, 98
Water scoop, 98
Wayneport coaling station, 100, 101
Weardale Railway Centenary, 8
Weaver, Clarence L., 8
Weight on driving wheels, 56
Welch, F. C., Locomotive Engineer, 119
Westing, Frederick, 8, 48
Wet rails, 97
"Whiskers" on rails, 54
Whistle, 97
Wilson, G. T., 8
Windy City, 56, 119
World War I, 6, 20
World War II, 6
World's Columbian Exposition, 24, 77
World's Fair Special, The, 77
Zieber, Harold C., 8